Can't Be Broken

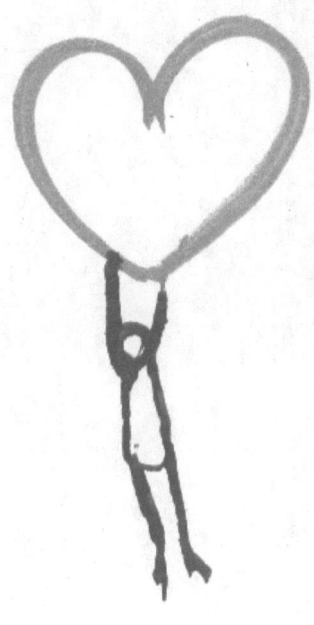

Can't Be Broken

A Memoir

Katie Sexton

Can't Be Broken
First edition, published 2022

By Katie Sexton

Book Layout by Reprospace, LLC
Book Cover Images by unsplash.com/@jannerboy62, ka7REB1AJl4

Copyright ©2022, Katie Sexton

ISBN-13 Paperback: 978-1-952685-49-1

Some names in *Can't Be Broken*, have been changed.

All rights reserved. No part of this book may be reproduced or transmitted in any form or by any means, electronic or mechanical, including photocopying, recording or by any information storage and retrieval system, without written permission from the author, except for the inclusion of brief quotations in a review.

KITSAP PUBLISHING

Published by Kitsap Publishing
P.O. Box 572
Poulsbo, WA 98370
www.KitsapPublishing.com

Dedication

I dedicate this book to my daughter who has shown me
that strength can be found from within
and
my husband, my knight in shining armor.

Acknowledgements

Friends and family have played such an important role in my life, and I want to thank each and every one of those who were there, stood by my side and did not allow me to give up or fall. My parents, Jill and Sean. My sister Erin and her husband Ryan. My loving husband Toby, who is always encouraging me to follow my dreams and is my number one supporter and fan. To my children; Estrella for being the reason to never give up, Robert, my rainbow baby, for showing me a different outlook on life, and Wyatt, my little moose who is such a strong and caring soul. My extended family from another life, the family in Austin from the performing arts community; Tim, Lorne, Jim, Bill, Joe, Robby Jacks (R.I.P), Texas Bill, Dotty, Dave, Eddie, Karen, Nick, Pops, Mysterious Jon, and so many more, I love you all and have always considered you my family. My dear friend Yadira, who, even after being harassed, stalked herself by my monster, and witnessed so much of the horrors unfold, stood by my side and never gave up on our friendship. My aunt Kristi for helping me when I was at a very low point in my life and gave me the chance to change my direction in life, and my cousin Kari, who I have not spoken to in years, but whom I cherished the time we had as friends and roommates. To Dr. Williams, who was not only a dear family friend but also one who provided me with a direction when it came to my monster, thank you, and may you Rest in Peace. To my protectors, my brothers and sisters from another life, and those who I grew up with, I love you all and always will; Big Mike, Jimmy "Mozzy", Joe, Fredo, Eddie, Raul (R.I.P), Phil, Rob, Nate Dog, Jeremy "Joker" (R.I.P), Ruben, Anthony, Elisha, Jess, Desiree, Rachel as well as so many others, and the Down to Earth family. Thank you all!

Prologue

As children, we develop what might be seen as silly fears. We find that we might be scared of the dark, scared of the monsters in books and movies, only to be assured that those fears are just our imaginations taking flight, and do not exist. As we get older, we tend to forget those fears we might have had as children, and when we do think of them, we might laugh at the unfounded fears that we realize were nonsense in many cases. However, from time to time, we might encounter things that make us question reality, such as coming across real-life monsters in our lives. Some may go on in life, not realizing how close we were to those monsters, whether it was in passing or as acquaintances, not thinking about how easily things could be a lot different had situations been a little different. Then there are those times when some of us find that we are not so lucky, and the monsters we encounter fixate their focus on us. They find their way into our lives, and once they are there, create havoc and nightmares that do not seem real at the time. Leaving us questioning everything in our lives, scared to talk to anyone, and thinking that we might be crazy because we have been led to believe monsters are not real and those you hear about are obvious and stick out like a sore thumb, not a person who you once trusted. Only to realize that they are very real, and they do not come in the form of a warty goblin or monster that we once imagined lived under our beds, but come in the form of what might appear to be an average-looking person. Some find ways to get away from their monsters, where we might uproot our entire lives, only to find when do get away, we are left, always looking over our shoulders, with the thought that our monster could be lurking, and waiting for another chance to continue with the plans they have for their victims.

In my case, I have met a few monsters. Some that I was able to get away from without looking back, and some, who to this day, continue to haunt my dreams, even knowing that they can never hurt me, my family, or those I care about ever again. Like many who have dealt with real-life monsters, I have found myself to be suspicious of everyone who comes into my life. I am very cautious about who I let in, and the moment I find the slightest sign of something being off, I detach myself from others and never look back. Because for me, when I second-guessed my choices at one point in life, I quickly realized that my first instincts were spot on and learned to just move on instead of second-guessing things ever again. However, regardless of the personal nightmares I have lived through, I have found that I am stronger than some might have expected, and at the end of the day, I can't be broken.

Curtain Call

As a child, I grew up in a family of actors. My parents were not well-known actors, but they enjoyed the stage. The long weekends of being on stage, late-night rehearsals, and parties, were all part of life on stage that they loved. Their friends were family. They treated me like a niece, and many, I considered extended family, knowing only that they looked after me and cared about me. I always felt safe and had a sense of security knowing that the people surrounding me were part of our family. I can remember the late-night curtain calls, the rush of actresses coming into the dressing room to ready themselves for their next act on the stage, as I would play with my dolls in the corner of the room. I was always in awe of how fast costume changes would occur, where not just the clothes were changed but wigs and makeup, all in just a few minutes.

The dressing rooms smelled of cigarettes that the actresses would quickly light and smoke partially through as they did their changes. This was then mixed with the sweet smells of various drinks that were kept backstage as a quick shot to keep the courage of some going in between acts; along with hairspray, the floral smell mixed with crayons some of the makeup had, body odor, and popcorn from the actresses clothing and wigs as they would shake the popcorn the audiences would throw at the stage, off onto the floor during their changes.

The evenings after a play had ended, would be followed by after-parties. Some at the theater if the bar was available after the closing act, some at the houses of others, and some at my parent's house. Regardless, I found myself waking up after a party, whether we were at home or another house; walking around, stepping over and around people passed out after a night of partying, to get a bowl of cereal or some toast and watch cartoons. I was never curious about the people who lay on the couch behind me or on the floor next to where I would sit. Instead, finding it as another weekend morning filled with cartoons, as I waited for my parents to either emerge to take me home or wake others to clear out our house so they could clean up the messes left.

The parties were part of life, and I did not know different at the time. Whether we spent entire days at bars as my parents went over lines with others, followed by the pre-show dress rehearsals, and ended the evening in the same bar after a successful dinner theater. Or if we left after a show, for my parents to drink, listen to music as I would dance until I passed out, and enjoy their evening with friends, smoking joints and doing lines of coke. For me, it was just another weekend in my childhood. Filled with the smells of alcohol, cigarettes, and marijuana as the essence of my childhood.

The stage was my playground during rehearsals, and dressing rooms were my personal dress-up rooms: places where I could let my imagination take flight as I put on wigs, makeup, too big dresses, and played with my dolls. Other actors would join me in between scenes, assisting with my take on the makeup, and twirl me around. Playing dolls with me and treated me as if I were their own at the time. I felt safe, loved, and surrounded by those who I cared about. However, once my parents added a younger sibling to our family, the life I had known behind the stage, changed. As the years went on the parties were less frequent, and my parents spent more time in offices, working the 9-5 until they found themselves completely depleted.

They were working hard to provide a steadier life for myself and my baby sister. They had purchased an old farm on the outskirts of the city, providing more space for us to roam and play. This new home also provided space to allow my parents to continue to dabble in their passion for acting, but in an extremely limited aspect.

My dad always found ways to create something out of the things he came across, which included turning the inside of the old barn on the property, into a set. This set was a hobby of his for a time, where my dad collected discarded props and supplies, he would come across, in order to transform the inside of the old barn into a spaceship.

My parents continued to seek out acting roles from time to time, but between working full-time jobs, raising two children, and trying to keep afloat when it came to responsibilities, the roles became more sparse as time went on. The life my parents lived, was no longer one that made them happy. They were "working for the man" so to say and finding very little satisfaction in the work they did day in and day out.

The antidote to their mental exhaustion of trying to live the traditional 9-5 life was found when on a vacation; visiting my fiddle-footed grandpa, who was a carnie, biker, truck driver, as well as a cop; and his new wife. This grandpa was my dad's dad. He had been married a few times, traveled a lot, and even lived with us from time to time when I was little, helping out with watching after me at times. I adored this man and enjoyed visits with him. I found that unlike many, I did not see the darker sides of him, and saw the pure innocence of a grandfather, who was unlike my other grandfather, but nonetheless, loved and adored by myself and others.

I can remember the times he had stayed with us, where bringing my grandpa his morning coffee after smelling the lighting of his morning cigarette commenced, was something I looked forward to. I enjoyed riding in his semi-truck when he was working that job, going to the local base for a hot lunch, heading to a fair when the carny life called, or watching my greaser grandpa show up on his bike after an excursion ride that needed to be had to keep his sanity. However, later in life, I learned of the dark side of this man, one I had once seen as one who could do no wrong. Whereas in the older, southern ways one who had a dislike and zero respect for those of color. I did not realize that the ban on watching certain popular shows on television, the avoidance of going in certain checkout lines at the store, or the snickering under his breath as he had picked me up at a friend's house whose parents were a mixed-race couple, were all apparent to others. I was blind to the side that was hidden from me and found it as something I could be grateful for, due to the fact that his life was short-lived, and I had gotten to know the side of him that was the grandpa I adored vs the ugly racist filled side that others knew him well for.

While visiting the small, mountain town, and meeting my grandfather's new wife, we found a town that had a lot of character and even other families. My parents found a small, empty theater, waiting to be revived. The theater was an old opera house, located in the small ghost town where my grandfather lived. It was built as a replica of a nearby famous theater, having similar balcony seats, chandeliers hanging from the high ceilings, a small bar, and a stage that had character; waiting to be brought back to life again. The opera house was next to an old saloon that had been around for over a century and had a history that gave the little theater the history and charm my parents fell in love with. And within a month of finding this little theater, my parents made the choice to leave the mundane life they had been living for a few years, and move our family to another state, to pursue their passion for acting, living their dream of running their own theater, and most importantly, starting over.

As a young girl, I despised the move to another state. A move to a small town, that appeared to not have much going for it. We left everything I had ever known behind, and I had no choice but to go along. Where I had friends both my age and those in the arts community my parents were a part of, but even more, so, my mom's parents, my grandparents whom I adored and enjoyed spending time with on the weekends from time to time. I had been to the small town as a visitor and did not find anything interesting about it, so the idea of making it a home, a home that was a state away from what I had known as my home, was not something that I had approved. However, shortly after moving, I met several kids in the town, finding one, in particular, to change my life and what I knew of life, forever.

This girl I met was unlike other kids I had known. She got my attention by doing tricks on her go-cart in front of the new theater my parents were renovating. Where one afternoon, watching my parents and their new friends paint backdrops and put together props, I found the attention a welcomed distraction. The girl saw my boredom as I had sat on a stoop, drawing in the dirt, and invited me to ride along, which allowed me to not only get away for a bit but also meet other kids in the community. I soon learned that the girl's parents worked at the saloon next door, and she lived just a short walk from its doors. She was the seventh generation to live in the small ghost town, and aside from her family being well known for having been there so long, they were also known for some of the darkness they tried to hide.

The darkness was the turmoil they dealt with daily, where mental illness lay in waiting for opportunities that would put the family as the talk of the town from time to time. Having an uncle take center stage at times, when he would have his episodes over the years, which all in the town knew about, but also knew how to help during those times. Where the family was known for being one that you did not cross, and one who had ties to many of the more affluent families in the area. Leaving many, either stepping lightly around them, or avoiding them altogether. But for me, I found friendship and a view on life that changed me forever.

The girl's name was Monique, and when it came to the ideas she would come up with as ways to keep from getting bored, I admired her creativity. We went from spending a few weeks building a treehouse, one that would be the target of a war of girls vs boys on who would inhabit the treehouse. To find ways to sneak all of the kids in the town out of our bedrooms, as we climbed the walls of the old fort for a night of hide and seek and flashlight tag in the old cemetery. Her ideas of making the best of snow days got every kid involved, as we would hide under bridges, on top of the old fort, waiting to bombard unsuspecting drivers with snowballs as they drove past us.

The ideas were always on the edge of breaking the rules our parents would put into place. Where, as we got a little older, they became more daring, starting with taking cans of gas as we would drive our go-carts to neighboring towns to go swim in the lake 20 miles away, or to even drive our 4-wheelers on the old gold mining trails, to the town below the mountain we lived on, to visit friends. The thing was, both of our families were always busy. My parents were always writing new plays, having rehearsals, making costumes out of clothing found in second-hand stores, creating new sets out of trash, and adding props out of items my parents would come across, and Monique's parents were always either cooking, cleaning, or working in the saloon and restaurant they ran. Leaving us, young pre-teen girls, to do as we pleased without our parents ever finding out.

This freedom to get away with things we did became an addiction, and Monique was hooked. Both of us tried things we saw our parents doing, to see if we would like it as well. When I had begun smoking marijuana I would steal from my dad's stash by age 11, and around the same time, I had tried cigarettes I stole from my grandpa. Always ideas that I went along with, which were ways to see how far we could go. Along with what I would consider petty things compared to what was to come, Monique seemed to always come up with a new adventure.

The new adventures were always ones that were just a little more daring than the last we got away with, and as she began to mature, they became more focused on gaining attention from those of the opposite sex. The thing was, boys our age were still playing with army guys, shooting at us with water guns, and did not have much mind for us, regardless of how skimpy we would dress or how much makeup we would put on. Which, instead, garnered the attention of bar patrons, older men who knew better, but saw two young girls who were unsupervised and starving for attention.

The attention changed rapidly over a year. Where, the first part gained us access to a car after a local patron from the bar gave us, a couple of pre-teen girls, keys to his car to pick up something from his house. When we got the keys, Monique was very aware of how drunk everyone, including our parents, was at the bar, and she also discovered a case of unopened beer in the backseat of the car. So, instead of going on the errand, we were trusted to take, Monique decided to go on a joyride, which ended us flipping the car over a bridge, and me being picked up by a passerby to flee the scene of the crime. The accident was one that I look back on and realize how lucky we were to walk away from.

We drank a couple of the beers from the case we found in the backseat and began to drive on the winding mountain roads. Taking one curve, a little too fast, and being an inexperienced, underage driver, who was inebriated, was a recipe for disaster. The curve was one Monique had not anticipated, and as she began to turn, she got scared and overcorrected the vehicle, which caused the car to hit a rail and flip off the road, over a bridge, and land in the creek bed below. The lady who lived near the accident happened to be a cocktail waitress at the saloon and knew both of us too well. As she and her son came to our aid, another passerby, an older boy who lived nearby, had been on a ride with his girlfriend and pulled over to help. When he saw me, he knew my family, as he had been the one to sell wood for our fireplaces every year and offered to take me home on his way to his house. I got in his truck and sat next to this young man and his girlfriend, in shock at what had happened.

We were sure this would do us in as far as punishment went, but due to the busy lives our parents had, the punishment did not fit the crime. I had to clean the theater for a couple of weeks, and Monique had to do dishes in the restaurant. However, unbeknownst to our parents, this extra time is spent in the bars our parents ran, allowing us to be seen in our skimpy clothing and makeup, by more and more, drunk older men. And the attention we received, was more than our parents had given us, which attracted Monique to the challenge.

Within the first week of our punishments, Monique had befriended a couple of young men who had been riding their bikes in the mountains, stopping in after their rides to quench their thirsts. The men were in their late 20's, were very good-looking, and even more so, had given Monique attention. They claimed that she looked at least 18 and would catcall at us when we would go outside to smoke cigarettes.

The outside breaks were something that made us feel older, stealing packs of cigarettes from the bar, and smoking them, making people think we were older and more mature. But we weren't, we were children, ages 12 and 13, yet these men did not ask or care, and the flirting done between Monique and the men were not hidden. She would show up at the restaurant to do dishes in little dresses, with way too much makeup, and making sure she was seen as much as possible.

After a couple of weeks of daily flirtations, which lead to whispers in our ears, the men invited us to go out drinking with them. They said they would pick us up after 10 pm, which was past our curfews, but with parents working until 3 am most nights, Monique said no one would ever know. And Monique had a plan to make sure no one would ever find out. She had told her parents she would be at my house for the night as we watched movies and played with Barbies with my little sister. She had both bribed and threatened my little sister to keep the secret as well, saying that if parents showed up, to pretend that we were there and cover for us.

When 10 pm came around, I had knots in my stomach. I knew what we were about to do was not a clever idea, but the thrill of it was also pulling me in the direction to do it and see what would happen. We had gotten dressed up, did our hair and our makeup to make us look much older than 12 and 13, and when the time came, we heard the honk of the horn from the corner of the street I lived on, where the men said they would pick us up at. So, we did as planned, and left my little sister alone at the house as we ran to get in the truck with the older men who we had met at the bar.

Upon arriving at the vehicle, we noticed it was a rebuilt, classic truck, and the cab wasn't very big, already had 3 men inside, leaving us to ride on the laps of these older men. I was terrified, but they handed me a beer and insisted I drink up to loosen up and not be such a downer since I had already asked to go home after a few minutes.

After riding for about 20 minutes, the men pulled off to a campground area, started a large fire, and put on some music. They then insisted we drink up since they had brought quite a bit of alcohol to share with us. Within an hour or so of arriving, one of the men began kissing Monique. This act made me extremely uncomfortable, which one of the other men had noticed, and instead of stopping things, he then began to kiss me. Up until this point, I had never been kissed like that, and this was nowhere near the idea of my first real kiss. I had been kissed on the cheek and lips by a couple of boys in the past at school and held hands at the movies. But I had never imagined a grown man would be my first real kiss at the age of 12, and I was terrified, so I just went along with it and followed his lead. And the more I drank, the less stressed I felt about the situation. That was until Monique had gone in the truck and began to have sex with the man she had been making out with. At that moment, I felt sick, which became more of a literal action than a feeling, and once the man was done with Monique, the man who had been kissing me insisted it was time to take us home. When we got back to my house, it was the early morning hours, and my parents had gotten home, so instead of going in through the front door, we had my little sister, who had stayed in my room, pretending that we were there the whole night, open the window so we could sneak back in.

The next morning, Monique had changed a little. She acted differently and began to dress and wear makeup the same way she did that night, every day. She was excited to tell everyone at school that she was no longer a virgin, and that she had an older boyfriend. Even more surprising was the older man. He continued to come around, even go to the bar her parents managed, pursuing a relationship with a 13-year-old girl, right under the noses of our parents, and no one noticed. She got hickeys, which she proudly showed off as a type of trophy, showing everyone that her older boyfriend gave them to her, and her ideas of how to see this man more and more as far as being sneaky, just increased. She was obsessed, and I was along for the ride so to say. Both of our parents enjoyed drinking, both had bars they ran alongside their businesses. My parents: had a theater with a bar and her parents had a restaurant with a saloon, so most nights, they were too drunk to even know if we were home or not. And as time went on, the want or need Monique had to up the antics on what we could get away with, increased.

We had older men come up to the small town we lived in, pick us up, and take us out to party with them. We would make and receive phone calls from these men at a local payphone that was set up at the old laundry mat, across from the RV park, keeping calls from ever going to our houses. Whereat times, we would go out to campgrounds with separate groups of men on the same day. We even found that we could sneak men into my bedroom at night, without anyone ever finding out. Where one evening, after sneaking a group of men into my bedroom, my mom had come home earlier than usual, had come to check on me, talked to me, and never knew that just on the other side of my bedroom door, were 3 grown, older men, in the room of her 12-year-old daughter.

We had found ways to get to the town below the mountain we lived on and would meet up with men in an old park that was in the middle of the town. Having our parents drop us off at a local store or the swimming pool, as we would run off the minute they left, to meet up with the men. The park was more of a large ravine that had once been the main street of the town but had flooded a century prior. Leaving it as one that many did not explore or go near, and allowing us to hide out in the park, under trees, while we drank the alcohol the men would buy us.

People in the small town we lived in were also blind to what was going on. We had babysitting gigs, where one family had trusted us to watch their home and kids for a weekend while they went on a romantic getaway. This trust was something I wanted to keep; however, Monique saw it as an opportunity to play house with her older boyfriend, in a home that was genuinely nice and had a bar filled with various types of alcohol that the owners had collected from around the world. Their children were my sister's age, and when Monique began her game of house, I decided it was best to take the kids to my house, away from the antics Monique was engaging in while their parents were away.

After a night of playing house, I took the kids back to their house, hoping Monique was done, but the antics she had planned had just begun. Where, that next day, Monique invited a group of guys who were part of a local gang, and that evening, I learned exactly what a "gang bang" was as Monique played the willing participant. Allowing each of the guys, to have a turn, having sex with her in the master bedroom of the house. I watched as these boys, some in high school and some in their early 20s, waited outside the room, for their turn, laughing and giving one another a high five on the way out, after they each had sex with Monique. Along with the inappropriate sexual behavior from the 13-year-old Monique, she also allowed her guests to take what they wanted, drink what they wanted, and do as they wanted, which included taking the husband's company vehicle for a joy ride to buy beer in the town below and pick up more people. These actions just made me even more protective of the kids we had been trusted to care for that weekend. When the weekend came to an end, I dreaded the parents of the kids we were watching, coming home, but Monique spent the few hours before their arrival, deep cleaning the house from top to bottom and filling the bottles of alcohol that had been drinking from, with water.

After the weekend was over, and no one found out, I became weary of continuing to hang out with Monique. I did not want to continue with the antics she came up with and wanted to separate from being as close as we were. I began spending time with friends in the town below, as to separate myself, and also have excuses as to why I was not home to hang out or do things with Monique.

I soon learned that my plan of trying to distance myself from Monique was not going to happen. I would come home, after spending a day with other friends, to find Monique hanging out with my baby sister and the little kids who lived nearby. The site was always one that made me sick, and I knew I did not want Monique around my baby sister or any little kids for that matter, knowing what she was capable of. I tried to keep her away from my house, my sister, and even the other little kids in the town, but she always tried to turn things around on me, by making me feel that if anything happened to the kids, it would be my fault for not wanting to continue a friendship with Monique.

These antics continued, until Monique showed up one evening, outside my bedroom window, warning me that she would take my life along with her own, with the hammer she had in her hands if I refused to be her best friend. She gave this warning, threatening to first break my window, then smash in my skull, kill my parents, and herself, if I did not want to be her friend. Which left me feeling as if I did not have a choice and deciding that I believed she would follow through with her threats, as I had seen her follow through with every idea she came up with, regardless of how far-fetched or dangerous they were. So, instead of insisting we not be friends any longer, I gave in. I began to hang out with Monique daily, once again, and followed along, with every plan she came up with, regardless of how dangerous or stupid they were.

By the next year, after continuing to have relationships with a variety of older men, and me being the alibi, I found myself as an alcoholic and a heavy smoker of cigarettes and weed, who was only 13 years old, and had make-out sessions with older men regularly. None who had taken my virginity, but many who had fingered me and played with my still-developing breasts. The men taught me how to give oral sex to please them, and they would return the favor. I was numb to all of it. I had no emotion or feelings towards anything that was going on and I drank regularly, smoked weed behind the old church, smoked cigarettes like a train, and was stealing bottles of hard liquor and packs of cigarettes from my parent's bar. I was drinking, smoking both cigarettes and weed I stole from my dad, at school. Being completely inebriated in front of my parents and teachers without them ever noticing, and spiraling alongside Monique, while our parents were completely clueless about what all was going on.

During this time, I did have boys my age ask me on dates, which I turned down when Monique would point out that they would not know what to do and were too immature for us. My honor roll grades disappeared, and I began fighting at school. Both of my grandpas had succumbed to cancer; one grandpa to lung cancer and the other to esophageal cancer, both of which were caused by their heavy smoking habits, both losing their battles with the diseases that inhabited their bodies within a few months of each other. Which led me to want to numb myself from any feelings, even more so. My parents decided to put me in a private school, in hopes that the environment being a small one, and not one being overrun by preteen thugs, would be better for me. But soon after changing schools, I found even more opportunities to do more. The school I went to was run by hippies, started on a commune originally, and was very laid-back, allowing kids to leave campus for lunches and breaks. It was during this time that I explored more and was introduced to crystal meth for the first time by one of the older men I had dated.

I found the feeling that crystal meth gave me what felt like something of superhuman strength. I could stay up all night, do my schoolwork, I felt euphoric which was better than feeling empty, and I could do it all while still having the energy to party. I also found the ability to lose weight and have the energy I had, without dieting or exercising, allowed me to, regardless of the drugs and men, feel good about myself. Shortly after finding a love for crystal meth at the age of 13, Monique had also become very addicted to the drug. This led her to be even more daring in the things she did, which included robbing a local record store. However, she was sloppy, she bragged about the robbery shortly after it had happened at school and got caught. She ended up being hospitalized instead of being sent to juvenile hall and was diagnosed with bipolar disorder, something that ran in her family.

After about 3 months of Monique being hospitalized, she came back, with more ideas when it came to what we could get away with, which included selling meth, something she had learned about at the mental hospital. Around this time, I had turned 14, and a new kid had moved to the small town we lived in. He was a little older, came from a bigger city, was part of a gang, and had been sent to live with his dad. He had a very hardened look about him; he wore baggy jeans, had tattoos, carried a bandana in his back pocket that was the color the gang he was in supported, and he always had a look of mischief in his eyes, living up to the name he had been given as "Joker". He had experience in selling drugs, and Monique made sure to get his attention and befriend him very quickly. This new friendship not only became a partnership, but Monique also caught the eye of the older, adult brother who was married.

The brother was married to a beautician. He was a biker, and also had a very nice sports car that he liked to show off. He was a very good-looking man, who at the time, had no kids with his wife, and was a newlywed for the most part. He knew Monique's parents, as their dad had grown up with Monique's mom and knew her well. He had a good job, a quaint apartment he and his wife shared, and he treated Monique better than other older men she had dated. Monique fell head over heels for this man, and they began seeing each other quite often. Along with the relationship, the boy had introduced us to the business of selling crystal meth to kids at school and parties. We felt invincible, and we were able to do as much meth as we wanted while selling it. That was until I had taken some to sell on a camping trip I had been on with the private school I had been attending.

The trip went well, I sold all but my personal stash, which I had kept in my compact. On the way back from the trip; the kids I had sold to and I, were exhausted after a few days of taking the meth, and slept in the back of the bus. During this trip back, my compact had fallen out of my pocket, and during the cleanup of the bus, it was discovered. The other students right away recognized it as mine, and when the principal called me into his office, he opened the compact, walked to the bathroom and flushed the contents, then notified my parents. I was suspended.

At the time, my grandma, my mom's mom, had been sick, being diagnosed with cancer just months after my grandpa, her husband, and the love of her life had died from cancer, and my mom went back to the city we had lived in prior, to take care of her. Leaving just myself and my dad at the house while he was working most of the time. Where my mom also took my little sister to stay with her as my mom looked after my grandma. Giving me less supervision, and a 14-year-old girl, to learn that I was able to do as I pleased, coming, and going, with no enforced curfew, and having the house to myself most days. My dad found out I smoked marijuana, and instead of punishing me, he saw the hypocrisy in it all and began smoking with me, giving me the idea that I was invincible and could do no wrong at the time. Which became apparent when I had been caught. So, instead of staying home on suspension from school, my parents had me go back to where we had moved from and stay with my mom to help care for my grandma until the school would let me go back.

During this time, I was a bit lost. The first 2 weeks at my grandma's house were hell. I was coming off the crystal meth I had been hooked on. I found small bottles of alcohol at my grandparent's house, ones my grandpa had collected when he would travel on business trips over a lifetime, which filled several large boxes he had stored away, and in hand, allowed me to dull the body aches and chills I felt during that time. I also found that my parents were not as hard on me as I had expected. They both allowed me to continue smoking cigarettes and marijuana, giving me buds from the stashes they had. My mom even took me to a local head shop that my parent's friends ran and bought me my first pipe and bong. Thinking that by allowing me to smoke weed freely, without having to hide it, they would be helping with the issues I had with crystal meth.

This new way of parenting did allow my parents and me to become closer. Where we could sit back at the end of a long day and smoke a joint, talk more freely, then head to bed after. They treated me differently, almost like an equal, and no longer like a little girl. Which I appreciated and found respect for. I visited with my old friends while there, finding one, in particular, a boy I had known since we were in diapers, to become one I became very close to.

He was a boy who was the son of some very dear friends of my parents. His dad was in the performing arts community my parents were part of, and we understood one another and could relate to a lot of things. We talked about our younger years, children being raised in the arts community of partying and drugs. Finding we both noticed plenty of what our parents did, and both struggled as young teens, experimenting with anything and everything we came across, which also included our sexualities. He was noticeably worried about me; the things I had been involved in, the older men I had dated which made him feel uneasy about where I lived, and the affiliations I had. He voiced that he did not want me to go back, and worried that if I did, worse would happen. Which we both knew, was not something either one of us could prevent when the day came. However, he had me promise to call regularly and to always know that no matter what, he would always be there as a friend to me. I found this rekindling of an old friendship, to be something I embraced and needed. I looked forward to our calls after he got home from school every day, and our weekends to go walking around the suburban streets, looking for trouble that normal teens found.

However, after a couple of months, the school notified my parents that I was allowed to return. Leaving me to go back once again to the life I had tried to forget and feeling such heartache of leaving the safety I found in my grandma's house and my friend who showed me how much he cared by voicing as much, making me promise to always keep in touch. A promise I kept for a couple of years after. Once I got back, Monique informed me that she had recruited a new girl to our operations. She was a girl who lived in the small town we lived in. I had known her as a playmate from time to time, as she lived across from my grandpa. She appeared to be the basic good girl, who looked very innocent and had a reputation as being that. So, seeing her with Monique was quite a shock, and I was happy to welcome her as a friend. See, it was explained to us that by having her on our crew with myself and her both having the look of innocence, we could begin transporting drugs to various areas, without people suspecting us. However, the issue we had was we did not have cars nor were we of the age to drive yet.

With that being our only obstacle, Monique had come up with an idea. Having both myself and Monique convincing our parents to allow us to use vehicles to assist them with errands since they were always so busy, it worked. I had been given the keys at the age of 14, to drive around the small town we lived in, and to assist my dad with getting props, popcorn, and whatever else was needed from our house to the theater. My dad liked the idea that it would help him out and would also give me experience once I was of age to get my license, and Monique's parents thought the same, giving her the keys to their car as well. And within a month of having cars to run "errands" with, we found our parents were again trusting and did not keep tabs on where we went in the cars.

We soon began transporting substantial amounts of crystal meth around the county we lived in. We also drove to pick-up locations near the border of Mexico, getting through checkpoints with no driver's license, just being waved through, seeing two young girls in a car who looked innocent. The time we spent out in the cars became longer and longer, where parents never questioned us or even knew what we were doing. Monique had developed relationships with a few older men, who were also clients, purchasing the crystal meth we sold them. For me, this new clientele was empowering, where prior, I did feel powerless and just went along with what the older men wanted from me, and now, they were paying me for a drug they loved and treated me differently than before.

Around this time, we had also attracted the attention of others in the gang community that resided in the town below the mountain we lived on. These were kids from local families, some of who had moved there from East LA to raise their kids. Many came from families who were associated with some of the more notorious gangs from Phoenix, LA, and Albuquerque, and had a lot more experience in the business we were in. They also found the idea of having a couple of innocent-looking white girls, transporting drugs, and getting through checkpoints without batting an eye, to be genius.

I had known many of the kids from the public school, but now, we were all working together, selling meth to both kids and adults, even a teacher at the local high school was a customer. I felt like I could do anything, and during this time, I made friends with a girl who had an older cousin with whom I had a crush.

The cousin was a young man in his mid-20s, covered in tattoos which included a teardrop tattoo under his left eye, had recently been released from prison, and had a very edgy, cholo look to him that I was very attracted to. He always had his jet-black hair combed just right, not too greasy but just the right amount of product added to keep it in place. This was then followed by the Dickies he wore, which had a perfect crease ironed on the pants legs, and his white wife-beater tank top covered with a button-up flannel shirt that was only buttoned at the top. His care for his appearance also included the other pieces which stood out; a brown handkerchief he had in his front pocket, to show his "Brown Pride" for his culture, family, and his homies. The belt that was too big, yet the excess hung just below his knees as if placed ever so careful, his Nike Cortez shoes which were always so clean as if they had just come out of the box, and the sunglasses that he mostly wore just above his eyebrows, bringing the look and the care put into the look, to be one that I found to be very sexy in a man, and something I admired.

We began to hang out more and more, and he and I eventually started dating. It started with casual flirting, which quickly turned into stolen kisses as he would wait for me in another room or on the back porch of his aunt's house. He would whisper in my ears and sing to me in Spanish, serenading me with the language that flowed off his lips so artfully. Calling me his angel; claiming that my blonde hair, big blue eyes, and dimples, were only something that could only have been sent straight from heaven for him to admire and care for. For me, by this point, the age difference did not phase me, and the man did not ask my age. He knew I was still in school, and his cousin was a senior in high school, so he assumed I was his cousin's age, which I never corrected him on. However, within a month of dating this guy, he became very possessive.

He would wait outside the bar for me when I would help my parents, asking me who I talked to, having gone in the bar to use the bathroom several times, as an excuse to watch me. The possessive behavior increased very quickly, to where, one evening while I was at a fundraiser for my school, he had called the school numerous times, demanding I leave and go home. I had not taken him seriously, until he showed up at my school, grabbed me by the arm, and demanded I get in his car and go with him. I had refused, trying to keep from causing a scene, only to have some of the older kids at the school, come out and yell for me to go back inside. When I got back inside, they pulled me aside, asking if I was okay, and why I was with that man. I did not feel I needed to give them any answers and ignored their concerns.

I continued to date this man until one night, I decided to take the family vehicle my parents had trusted me with and spend the night partying at the river with my boyfriend, Monique, and my boyfriend's cousins. The next morning, when I got home, I found my parents waiting for me. They had not slept the night and took the keys from me. Monique also got in trouble and had to take a bussing job at her parent's restaurant. A trend that others thought to be a solution, as my parents decided that I needed to be kept closer to them and had me get a job at the restaurant Monique's parents ran as well. Due to punishment and the car being taken, I saw the guy I had dated less and less, to where we eventually went our separate ways.

Monique and I found that working at the restaurant just gave us more customers. Those in the back, such as the cooks and dishwashers, were not only interested in what we sold but also in us. They were all older men and knew our families, some had families of their own, but also knew that our families were clueless, and even with our dads in another room, they whistled at us, grabbed our bottoms when we would walk by, and sneak kisses in the walk-in freezer from time to time. This led to Monique hooking up with a couple of different guys on staff and setting up a bed in one of the balconies in the opera house my parents had, to have sex with different men she came across. Always having me as the lookout; pretending to use the restroom downstairs when someone would come in and give a warning by flushing the toilet twice.

Other kids in the small town noticed even when the adults did not, and they wanted to hang out with us and join in on the adventures we were part of. This curiosity led to me hosting regular, staged, sleepovers at my house, knowing my parents were rarely home. Until one night, the gig of sneaking out was up.

Some of the local girls had opted to stay the night at my house, as we had made plans to meet up and introduce the girls to some of the older men we had met. The plan seemed to be one that worked before, but on this night, things had changed. My mom had been feeling sick, she did the play that night and came home early instead of hanging out at the bar. So, we decided to have my sister hang out in my room, play music, gave her instructions on how to act, and even bring us food when we were gone.

All seemed to go well. We had left without a hitch, getting everyone in the cars of the men who were waiting for us, as we drove out to the mountains to find a campsite to park at with everyone. We had plenty of fun; drinking, dancing, doing drugs, and every one of the girls we brought, had an older man to make out with. The night seemed to go very well, all of us giggling as we shared stories of what we each did on the way home. We were dropped off at our usual spot, just down the street from my house. All of us were drunk, laughing as we scurried to get to my house, some of us wobbly, tripping over our own feet, and ready to call it a night. However, we had gotten careless, thinking we were invisible. Since we had done the same thing we had done before, where when we had initially snuck out, we climbed out my bedroom window, leaving it cracked open just a bit, and went out partying. By the end of our night, as we came back, the neighborhood dogs went nuts, barking at us, as we were a group of young girls who were not very quiet and all very drunk. When we got to my bedroom window, we noticed it had been locked, and instead of trying to get the window open, we decided to go in the back door. However, when we got to the back door, it was also locked, so I had the idea that we could crawl in through the doggie door, which seemed to work. That was until we got inside and looked up, to find my mom, standing there, watching as we came in through the doggie door, one at a time. This was promptly followed by my mom making phone calls to all of the parents whose daughters had stayed the night with us that evening. This ordeal led to me being forced to work more, and also ended the sleepovers I hosted.

A month or so later, Monique got her driver's license. Her family also gifted her a vehicle. She had the vehicle customized with a sound system and the tires she wanted. Giving us a vehicle that had more of the "gangster" persona that we had been living in. This was a game-changer. Monique was now 15, could legally drive, and had decided to drop out of school soon after, finding that selling drugs was easier and more profitable as far as she could tell. We had met more people who were able to assist us in growing our business, we had also become pretty popular at parties where kids would wait for us to show up and purchase what we had. We expanded our selling to cocaine, weed, mushrooms, acid, ecstasy, crystal meth, and GHB. And we worked at the restaurant, then partied after work, keeping our parents in the dark as to having no clue to what all we did.

By the next summer, after a year that is pretty much a blur to me due to all of the drugs we did and the days blending, I was able to get my driver's license as well and my parents gave me the old family car, the same car they had let me drive previously. I learned that if I told my parents I was staying somewhere or even that I was camping, they let me do as I pleased for days at a time. With a car, I was able to go out of town, drive out of state to conduct business, and be home at the times I said I would after said camping trips or weekend sleepovers I claimed to be at.

I had crossed state lines many times and experienced a taste of life in East L.A., where most girls my age would never think of venturing to a big city so far away, but due to those I knew who also knew my family, I was welcomed and treated like family. I had gotten cocky and felt invincible. I had gotten to the point where I believed I could get away with anything and decided to go on a big run down to the border. During this run, I did get careless.

The town below where we lived and had to drive through to get home had a curfew for minors, and I had decided that while I did a pickup, I would also do shopping, leaving my time to get back past the curfew time. I had driven in the town before, well past curfew times, and never got in trouble, but I also stuck to the sideroads. However, on my way back into town, I had told some friends I would stop by a party they were at, and when I got there, they were ready to go home, so I offered to take them home before I went to unload my car and go home myself. This plan did not seem to be a bad one, but instead of taking the backroads like I usually did, I decided it was a shorter distance to just drive through town. This decision turned out to be a bad one, and just as I was fixing to turn towards one of my friend's houses to drop them off, a cop pulled up behind us and pulled us over.

The initial stop was due to me changing lanes without a turn signal; however, the officer was very aware that we were all minors and put several of us in handcuffs then had us all sit on the curb while he made a call. As he walked around my car, I knew he could smell the marijuana I had in the trunk. It was potent, and even though it had been double bagged and even packed with a few other drugs, the smell was obvious. Within minutes, we had other cops show up, and state and county vehicles arrived, which included a K9 unit. They began searching my car, to find it loaded with drugs along with some alcohol. My friends were upset that this was happening, and I could not hear, my heart was pounding too hard for me to hear anything else. That was until I saw a familiar car. It was my grandpa's partner from the force. He did not look at me, instead, he went up to the group of officers and they all stood around talking, then one by one, the cops got back in their cars and left. My grandpa's partner went to his car for a few minutes as the officer who had initially pulled us over, took the handcuffs off of all of us and said he was giving us a warning, and did not want to see us out after curfew ever again. The officer handed me a ticket for a curfew violation and one that was unclear but had been scribbled on and did have some of the information on the traffic violation as well as information on the drugs which had been confiscated, however that particular ticket was not signed like the curfew ticket had been. He did not give anyone else any tickets, just warned them that he did not want to see them out past curfew again.

Confused and scared, we all stood there in shock, looking at one another, trying to figure out what was going on. A few minutes after being let out of the cuffs, my grandpa's partner walked over to inform me he has talked to my dad and expected me to take my friends home and then head home myself. He said he told my dad everything and would let my dad take it from there, then both officers left as we got back in my car that had been stripped of all drugs, and drove off in silence.

When I finally got home, I did not know what to expect. I mean, we had gotten pulled over, a huge scene had taken place when drugs were found in my car, all drugs were confiscated, and we were let go. Given a curfew violation and another ticket that did not seem right when it came to the drug charges. So, as I walked in the door, I braced myself, ready to take anything my parents had to say or do to me, I was sure this was it. But I walked in, and the house was silent. Everyone appeared to be in bed, and my parents called me to their room. They asked me what happened, and I told them, they then asked for my keys and told me to go to bed.

The next morning, I dreaded getting up, knowing that I was surely going to be shipped off somewhere or have to prepare to go to juvenile hall since I had a car that had a trunk filled with drugs that had all been confiscated by police. But, when I got up, I was not told anything. I was asked to go to the theater later in the morning to sweep and mop, clean the restrooms and go to work that night, then work at the theater after I got off work at the restaurant, and I was not allowed to go out that night after work. I did not question the punishment, I had expected more to be added on, but that was it. By the following weekend, I was driving again, running errands in the town below the mountain we lived on for my parents, then allowed to go out with a curfew set.

I respected the curfew this time around. I was preparing for the court date that was on my ticket, sure that I was heading to juvenile hall for quite some time and that these days leading up to court, were my last days of freedom. But again, I was wrong.

When the day for court came, I went alone. I walked in to check in with the lady in the front who had the dockets on her desk, and when I told her my name, she had no record of it. She asked me what I had to go to court for and I said a traffic and curfew violation since that is what the tickets said I had been pulled over for initially. She could not find any record of this ticket and asked me for my copy, which I claimed to have lost as well. She said since there was no copy sent to the courts and no paperwork unless I heard back from them, there was nothing else to do. There was still the matter of the curfew violation, which I opted to attend "teen court" for.

On the day I went to teen court, I was sure that the clerk was going to find my missing ticket and I was going to be sent away for it. But again, I was mistaken. I went into a small courtroom that consisted of a judge, then a jury of my peers who were other teens. I pled guilty to the curfew violation and was given community service. As I walked out of the courthouse, I held my breath, waiting for someone to stop me, arrest me, and take me away, but it never happened. The ticket I had, I burned, since it was the only piece of evidence linking me to the incident that night, and it was never brought up again in my house.

Look Here, Miss Thang

Following my day in court, and feeling like I had dodged a bullet, I began to hang out with other friends more and more. I experimented with mushrooms and acid more, where I had even told my parents when I would go on a trip, and they did not object to me doing hallucinogens. Instead, they found that when I told them, I had opened a new line of trust with them, and we respected one another on that.

When my 16th birthday neared, I had plans to drop acid with a group of close friends from the school I went to. We had all become very close, learning that there was so much more to the teenage life to be had than I had lived being friends with Monique. On the night of my birthday, the group of friends and myself decided to have a sleepover at one of the girl's houses, whose parents would be gone for the night. The idea was that we would order pizza that my parents had paid for, drop acid at the time we had told my parents we would drink some beer that one of my friends' boyfriends had bought us, and lock ourselves in the house to enjoy the trip.

This plan seemed to go well at first. My parents did decide to check in on us but found it funny to mess with us, knowing what time we took the acid and what time we would begin to start our trips that night. The antics of my parents were strange, as they drove up to the house and all yelled happy birthday from the car making faces, but we found it funny and continued with our plans. As the evening went on, my friend, Brandy's boyfriend had shown up with some of his homies to check on us and bring us some weed to smoke. The boyfriend was an older man, a leader of one of the local gangs, and due to his reputation, had been given the nickname, "Cucuy". He was not only well known in the gang community but had also been friends with my dad.

Cucuy and his friends all wished me a happy birthday, gave me my own bottle of Mad Dog 20/20 as well as some Boone's Farm, a large bag of weed, and told us to call if we needed anything but to enjoy our night. Which was followed by another group of teen guys we had been friends with, showing up to try to scare us. As this initiated, we had been on our acid trips for a few hours, finding we were deep into the trips that were all individual as we each had a different angle, we had a focus on. However, when the boys began to tap on the various windows of the house, we ran outside to chase them off, which led us to run out of the locked gate and into the town. Leaving us running around the town for a few hours, in different directions, as we continued to trip on acid, and eventually met back up in the early morning hours at the friend's house. Finding the night to be one we all enjoyed and would not soon forget.

This new friendship was one I welcomed. I went on camping trips with the girls and the boyfriends, even though some were older men. I was not expected to hook up with anyone and was also not pressured to drink or do drugs, but I did as I pleased and found the visions of what I had done just months prior, in the years prior, haunted me regardless of how hard I tried to forget.

As the months went by, and another summer neared, I had anticipated all of the camping trips I had been planning to go on with friends, and this year, I planned on going on most of the camping trips. I did still talk to Monique, but I was no longer doing runs for anyone. I felt that the close call when I had gotten lucky with the mishap of supposed missing or non-existent paperwork, was too close, and I was not going to test my luck.

Instead, I had gotten into cocaine and found the numbing feeling as well as the energy to be a bit more subtle. It also did not have some of the effects meth had as far as how it made me feel when I came down off of it, and the way it made me look. Where I did not get the blisters that my parents had thought to be zits, any more and I did not look like a walking skeleton anymore. I also continued to work at the restaurant, which gave me the money I needed to pay for the new habit I had picked up.

By summer, Monique had continued to work on selling the various drugs she came across and we planned a few camping trips together. One trip was one she was insistent I go on and had invited others who I knew well but did not expect to be there. When the day came and we went to set up our campsite, I was surprised to see my Brandy's boyfriend along with several other of his homies show up. Brandy was a friend who was one from the school I attended, and her boyfriend, Cucuy, showed up without my friend at our campsite. We had gone on camping trips together in the past, but Brandy and her boyfriend were always together, and I never saw him out at parties when she was out of town until he showed up at our campsite. I saw him as a friend as he was also friends with my dad and had done some deals with my dad in the past when it came to weed. So, I did not feel uneasy or anything awkward with him and his friends being there.

As the day turned to night, I noticed the guys setting up their tents and one who set up a sleeping bag in the back of his car. We all sat around the campfire, smoking, drinking, and Cucuy had cooked us all dinner, something he always did when we had camped with him before. After we all ate, one of the guys went to his car and brought out some bottles of tequila, and began passing them around. I noticed Monique get up to talk to Cucuy, both looking at me as they spoke and they seemed to make a deal of sorts, but I did not pay much attention to what all was going on. Shortly after, Monique and Cucuy had completed their deal, they both came and sat on either side of me. The song by Biggie Smalls came on, the one called "I'm Fucking You Tonight" as they both sat on either side of me, Cucuy singing the song to me in a very strange way. They insisted I drink and kept giving me alcohol and drugs.

Come nighttime, when people were heading to their tents, I decided I was done. I was extremely drunk and ready to pass out, which I did in my tent. That was until I woke up to Cucuy on top of me. He told me to be quiet and to relax. I was petrified; I woke up to this man, a man who knew my parents, my friend's boyfriend, a man many feared, raping me. I did not scream, I did not move, I was scared to breathe, I just wanted him to finish and leave. But he did not leave after he finished, he instead, laid down in my tent and went to sleep as I lie there in shock at what had happened.

I was a virgin. I had been with older men, but never let them have intercourse with me. I did not want to have sex as Monique did. She would have sex with anyone who would have sex with her, and I had imagined my first time would be having sex with someone I cared about. I did not sleep that night, I could hear Cucuy snoring next to me, but I was too scared to leave or do anything until morning came.

When morning came, I packed up my tent and left without saying anything to anyone, I wanted to forget what had happened to me. I thought I could, but later that day, Cucuy showed up at my house. I heard him in the kitchen talking to my dad, laughing with my dad, and smoking a joint with him. I wanted to leave but he had parked his truck behind my car, blocking me in. I went and sat in my room, waiting to hear him leave, and when he did, I went out to my car to leave. As I started my car, he had turned his truck around, pulled up, and went to my window. He told me that no one is to ever know what happened the night before, and if it ever got out, he would come after me and my family. So, I agreed to keep silent and never speak of it. I wanted to forget and never look back at what had happened. That was until a few weeks later when I was late for my period.

I had not monitored my period per se, but I knew that I always had my period around the same time my friends did, so when their time came and went, and another week passed where I still did not get my period, I knew I had to take a test. The day that this reality set in, I was sick with the thought of everything that transpired. I thought I could make it all go away by never speaking of the rape or looking back at it again, but this made it more real than ever.

After the rape, I had been spending more time with friends I saw as protectors. They were family to me. The day I knew I needed to take a pregnancy test; I went to my friend's house. He was an exceptionally good friend of my family and someone I trusted. He had a nickname of "Shotgun Jay" and was very protective of me and a couple of the other girls I was friends with. He, his brother, and his cousins were like family, more of a family to me than my own. I knew some of the cousins from the small town I lived in, and also from the public school when I had attended it. They watched out for me, and we did not keep secrets from one another. I knew I could trust Jay with my secret, and he was also one to give advice when needed; I had told him and one of my other friends what was going on and Jay went to get me the tests. I can remember sitting there. My friend's holding my hands as we waited to see the results, and when it came up positive, I found myself falling to my knees crying. I immediately knew I wanted to get an abortion but did not know where to go or how to go about getting one done. My friends understood, and even though their own beliefs did not support my choice, they supported me once I told them how it happened.

As I was talking to my friends, and crying as Jay held me, assuring me it would be okay, Monique walked in. She overheard the conversation and poked fun at me for being so stupid as to get pregnant. It was then, that I told her what happened, but as I told her, she did not seem surprised. I also asked her to keep the secret to herself, which I should have known was not going to happen. I mean, she was able to keep the secret, for as far as I know, for at least a full day, but come the weekend, when we went out to some parties, she told everyone we talked to that I was pregnant and getting an abortion.

A week had passed, when I saw Cucuy, the man who had raped me. I saw him at my school, picking up his girlfriend, Brandy, and he looked at me with a very stern look. I knew that if it were to get out what happened and how it happened, he would get in a lot of trouble because I was only 16 and he was an adult who raped a minor and got her pregnant. I also knew he was one to not cross, and the threat he made to me, and my family was one I knew he would follow through with.

Only a few people knew the story, and I had hoped it would stay that way, and that after a month or so, people would forget, and the rumors would end. But it did not happen soon enough. Later that day, Brandy offered to smoke me out after school. I accepted her invitation but did not realize it was her wanting to confront me about the situation.

The town was small, and the rumors had made their way to Brandy about her boyfriend, so she asked me to be honest with her, which I was, to a point. When she asked me if I had sex with her boyfriend, I froze in terror, knowing what he had told me if anyone ever found out. But I could not lie to her, so I told her I had sex with her boyfriend and that was it.

However, even though I told her, and she had heard similar accounts from others, she told me I was lying and that I was not pregnant with his baby either. I wanted to yell at her and tell her that I did not have sex with him and that he had raped me, but I could not do it. I was too ashamed of it all. I felt like I somehow allowed this to happen, I did not stop him, it was my fault, and being pregnant was my burden to bear. I also knew, that if people kept on talking, he was going to come after me and my family. I had seen his force before, I also heard the stories about him, I knew he was not one to cross, and I needed to get the abortion right away to make it all go away.

I found a clinic near the border of Mexico that would perform the abortion, and I needed someone to drive me there. The appointment date was a little over a month out, but finding someone to take me, became a lot harder than I had expected. I had asked Monique, but she had to work the day I had set the appointment up for and said that if she asked for the day off, she would have to tell her mom why, so I asked another friend. My other friend was understanding but she decided to talk to her mom about it, who then insisted I needed to tell my parents. I did not want them to know, I just wanted it to be over, but I had no one else I felt I could reach out to who could take me due to schedules and the distance of the drive which was also over state lines, so I knew I had to suck it up and tell them. I had a little over a month before the appointment day, so I hesitated and tried to avoid my parents as much as possible.

The time leading up to my appointment seemed to go way too slow. I had morning sickness that caused me to have to pull over in the mornings before school and hide my being sick from my parents. This included heading on a cross-country road trip, to meet with family, at my mom's family mausoleum, where we were taking the urns of my grandparents to their final resting place. The trip was one where I had considered sneaking away to a clinic that offered abortions at one of the stops we had, but I could not be sure I could get away for long enough. I had to share rooms with my sister and my parents, all while I had horrible morning sickness, trying to be quiet in the restrooms when I got sick, and when it was questioned, coming up with excuses of car sickness. I found McDonald's French Fries were the only thing I wanted, doused in ketchup, and the craving was one my parents did not see anything off with, regardless of me buying 2 large fries every time we stopped. However, an odd thing that worked in my favor; my little sister had been on a mission to collect every Beanie Baby that was offered in Happy Meals at the time, which driving cross country allowed us to both get our cravings for McDonald's in. Along with my strong need for McDonald's fries, I had to visit with family who I had not seen in many years and keep a straight face on during our time, hoping no one noticed and try to hide everything I had been through from. Keeping the trip for me, one that was very odd and one I was happy to be done with once we got back.

When I got back from the trip with my family, I learned that two friends also became pregnant, both choosing to keep their babies. And even more surprising to me; I had also met a guy. The guy I met was named Romeo, and he was not only handsome, intelligent, a couple of years older than me, and incredibly sweet, but he was my grandpa's partner's son.

Romeo had the look of the cholo I had a thing for, along with a sweet disposition, that was apparent in his smile, mannerisms, and his speech. He drove a sports car, worked a full-time job, and had goals for after graduation. He spoke with intelligence in his speech, something that was different from other guys his age. He did not go out as often as others, was more focused on his grades and work, and unlike other boys his age, he had an almost poetic nature about not only his mannerisms and smile but also in the way he spoke to me.

When we met, I was not interested in dating anyone, nor did I know his connection to my family until much later. The night was one that I honestly had wanted to stay home instead of going out. I had been sick with morning sickness for most of the day and was exhausted, but Monique convinced me to go with her. Of course, when Romeo showed interest in me, Monique had to tell him all about my situation. Which had been a common occurrence anytime we went anywhere; she told everyone we came across and met up with, my condition and her version of my story. So, when I met Romeo, I expected him to walk away from me and find another girl to talk to, but he didn't.

Romeo was against the plan I had, and had offered to be my boyfriend, meet my parents, and take responsibility for the baby. For me, all I could think was that we were both too young. We were both in high school, and had our entire lives ahead of us, besides, this was not his responsibility, and I did not feel that it would be right to put such a responsibility to take on for this kind boy I had just met. However, Romeo persisted over the following weeks. He called me, came to my house, took me out, and was insistent on allowing him to be there for me, but I could not do it. I could not be the one to force this kind boy to put his goals on hold for my mistake. I could not go further with a relationship, keeping a hope that his boy would stick around when it was all said and done, nor make him feel he was obligated or stuck if he felt different at any point, so I broke off the relationship.

After ending the short-lived relationship I had with Romeo, I felt alone. I had people who were there for me, supporting me in my decision, but regardless, I refused to answer people about who the father was and how it happened. I was carrying a secret with me that was slowly destroying me.

I had another guy friend, who had stepped up at one point, not allowing others to tare me down and even allowing them to say what they would about him. Many had thought he was responsible for the pregnancy, and he did not tell people differently. His name was Joseph, and even though he was a good friend, was there for me, I just couldn't allow him to be seen differently, or talked about, so I distanced myself from him as well as other close friends I had.

There were the rumors, many of which Monique had started, most were true, but I never admitted to anyone who was responsible, nor did I tell anyone outside of a few friends I could confide such information in, that I had been raped. This then led to even more rumors; where there were stories of me having slept with numerous men and did not know who had gotten me pregnant, or that I had been so drunk, I do not remember how it happened. Finding the rumors to be dangerous in ways, where guys our age, began to treat me the same way the older men had. Like an object that had no feelings, no morals, and I had become labeled as a slut. I got looks anytime I went out, heard the whispers as I walked by people, and just wanted to disappear. Leaving my close friends, those I considered family, always stepping in, stepping up to stand up for me.

Even bar patrons had heard the rumors, and at one point, while one had been at my parent's house visiting with my dad, he made it his mission to pursue hitting on me when my dad left the room. The man had shown up to the small mountain town as a drifter of sorts and had found work by helping my parents out at their theater and with their house. The day, in particular, I had gotten out of the shower, put on my clothes, and was sitting on the couch watching television. The man came in, sat next to me, and then sniffed me, rubbing his nose on my neck, telling me that I smelled really good. I got up, feeling uncomfortable, and went to change, knowing my friend Joseph would be coming to pick me up soon. I took my time getting ready and had hoped the man would leave, but he did not. My friend Joseph had shown up just as the man began to grab me by the arm, stepping in to get the man away from me. But this, the attention I was receiving, made me sick, I wanted to die at times, and even with the support and protection over me that so many showed, I felt so alone. Leading me to want to proceed with the plans I had to terminate the pregnancy even more so, but I still had to face the issue of telling my parents.

I waited to tell them until a couple of days before my appointment. I kept trying to will myself to have a miscarriage. I tried everything I could think of. I did drugs, any I could get my hands on, I drank a lot, I was reckless, hoping I would just have a miscarriage and be able to move on, but I did not miscarry. The day I knew I had to tell them was a day that has forever been imprinted on my heart.

My parents were hippy types; they partied when I was younger, and they liked to smoke weed and drink. They were more liberal than most, but my dad, was not as liberal as my mom, and even though he did not practice, he was a minister as well. Telling my mom was not as bad as I had thought it would be she was surprised that I had a plan and an appointment already set. She even respected my wish to not tell her who did it or how it happened. However, we both knew telling my dad would be a different story.

We asked my dad to sit down, which he began to do, then as he looked at our faces, knowing something bad was about to occur, he refused, he wanted me to just say what I had to say. He was holding a large book in his hands at the time, and when I said I was pregnant, he slammed the book to the floor and began to cry. I broke his heart. I broke my dad's heart, and I felt his disappointment and heartbreak. I failed him.

He demanded I tell him who got me pregnant, and I told him I would not but that I was getting an abortion so we could put this past us. When I said "abortion" my dad gave me a look like I had ripped his heart out of his chest, and then went to straight disappointment in his demeanor. He questioned how I could allow it to happen, how I did not use protection, how he did not even know I had dated anyone seriously enough, and how this was the one thing that would change how he saw me forever.

The day that I went to get my abortion, I was beyond scared, nervous, feeling sick, and just wanted to fast forward past it all. But at the same time, I questioned my choice. I wondered if I was doing the right thing. I went back and forth in my head about how I could keep the baby, and that it was not possible, that the baby would most likely look like the man who raped me and people would realize the rumor I had tried to put to rest, was true. That if that occurred, I was not only putting myself and my family in danger but a baby as well. I thought about adoption, but what if my rapist decided to make a claim, what would happen to me and the baby?

The 3-hour drive felt like an eternity, and during that drive, I had so much conflict and uncertainty. I took time to slow down and think about things, something I had not done since it all happened. Before that drive, I had either partied, done drugs, drank, or slept. I did not allow myself to think about anything that had happened, nor question my choices. Until then, but even then, I realized I had to follow through, that the choice was one that I could not allow myself to second guess or back out of. I was sure of the decision but unsure of the reality I was living in, having the surreal idea that none of it was really happening, that something like this, could not really be happening to me.

Once we arrived at the facility, we were greeted at the entrance by angry protestors. People holding signs with so much hate on them. Some had demeaning phrases, some had photos of dead babies, and they yelled at us, calling my mom and me murderers, sluts, whores, and said we were damned to hell for going in the building and wished horrible things upon us. While looking at the signs, hearing the words these people said, I wanted to ask them if they thought the same about men who raped underage girls, who threatened the life of their victims they raped and impregnated, and if that would change their views. But I held my tongue, in shock at how much hate these people had for me, a person they knew nothing about. A teenage girl who was scared to death, who had been violated, threatened, and who was making a very adult decision when it came to her body. I began shaking, feeling as if I was in a dream world, wanting to disappear, and not be seen by anyone. My mom grabbed me and shielded me close, walking me in, shielding me from the protestors, and whispered for me to not pay attention to them, to just keep walking.

When we walked in, we went to the front desk, and I checked in. I sat in the waiting room for a short time. Looking around at the other girls and women sitting there, some looking back at me with a look of sadness in their eyes as if they too were scared. Some were there for the same procedure I was there for; some were there for the free medical care and birth control the clinic offered. But regardless, as I skimmed the room, I wondered if any of them were there for the same reasons. I wondered if they too had been raped and were there due to feeling as if there was no other option available to them. Gave me a sense of belonging, belonging to a group that I had imagined, felt the same as I did, and had similar reasons as I did. As I sat there, skimming the room we were all in, a nurse came out, walked me to a room to discuss the procedure, ask me some questions, then brought in some machines. She had me verify the pregnancy by first giving a urine sample which only took a few minutes to get a result from, then proceeded to do an ultrasound. It was at that time, that I had to focus on something else, anything else, I could not look at the screen, and refused to allow myself to acknowledge what was going on. Within about 30 minutes, a couple of other people came in, one a doctor and one an assistant to the nurse. They then explained what was going to happen and asked if I was ready. I wasn't but I shook my head, yes, feeling that this had to happen.

As they began, I did not know what to expect, what exactly would happen, even after they had told me, there was no preparing myself mentally for what I was doing. I can remember the pain when the machine was inserted inside of me, the slight tug I could feel inside my womb, and a feeling of extreme sadness, the feeling of loss that overcame me at that moment. I had not expected such, but it was overwhelming, and at that moment, I turned my head towards the machine that was performing the procedure, to see the blood, and tissues being sucked out of my body, knowing a baby was in that mass of tissue, making me feel an emptiness I had never felt before. However, it went fast, and within a few minutes, I was done, moved to a recovery room, then given instructions to follow for the next couple of weeks.

The recovery room I was placed in was filled with beds, along with a few other girls, all of us trying not to make eye contact, but at the same time, glancing at one another from time to time, knowing we all had felt something similar in the moments prior. That sense of belonging, to a group who possibly understood me more than anyone else in the world had at the time, was a comfort for that brief moment. That was until the nurse came in to prepare me for discharge. It was at this time, I felt even dirtier than I had prior. Aside from completing the abortion, I was notified by the nurse just before discharging, that the doctor noticed an infection and said I had contracted an STD and gave me a prescription.

I was already in shock from the procedure, and all that led up to it, but to also learn that when I had my virginity stolen from me and impregnated, I was also infected with disease, all by the same person in just the matter of a few minutes that it took him to do what he did to me. I was left with the feeling that the abortion was not something I could leave behind me anytime soon if at all, and that regardless, he would never feel or even understand what I felt as a result of his actions.

Then to learn, while I was in shock at how the procedure affected me, that I had been infected by this man. I felt sick to learn he had done more than I had known, but some relief in knowing the medications I was given would clear up the disease he had given me.

When I got home, I did not want to leave my room, nor see or talk to anyone. I felt so low, I did not want to be around others, but I also did not want to be at home, knowing that my dad knew I had had sex, got pregnant, and had an abortion. However, just after the abortion, was Halloween, and a good friend of mine was having a party at her house.

During my brief time of recovery, I had friends come by to try to cheer me up and beg me to get up and go with them. They came by the house to smoke weed with me, keep me company, and try to console me when I had my moments of inconsolable grief come over me. A couple of friends insisted I allow them to do my hair and makeup, showing me that I was too beautiful to lock myself up in a room and grieve. As this insistence and refusal to give up on me continued over a few days, my mom saw the need for me to get out and be a teen, and move on from the situation I had been in. And with that, my mom encouraged me to dress up, have fun, and enjoy myself, so I did.

When I arrived at the party, I felt like all eyes were on me, but as the night continued it seemed to get less tense. That was until Brandy showed up with him, her boyfriend, the man who raped me, the man who got me pregnant, the man who made me physically sick to look at, Cucuy.

I wanted to leave when I saw him and was preparing to do so with my friends until Brandy came up to me and began singing the words to the song that was playing. It was the song by Tupac, "Wonda Why They Call U Bitch". Everyone at the party stopped talking and watched as she sang the song to me in my face, as I watched her boyfriend, Cucuy, standing behind her with his arms crossed, a smug look on his face, surrounded by his homies and the other cholas from his group. I was frozen, I knew if I said something Brandy and I were going to box, and Cucuy would most likely kill me after his homegirls each had a chance to jump me, and they stood there waiting for me to do something, anything. But I did nothing. I took it. I was too tired from the days that led up to the party of grieving that they knew nothing about. I felt different in the way I saw things after the abortion, where life was not the same, and I viewed things from a different perspective in a way. So instead of fighting like many had expected me to do, I took her singing right in my face, a song about a slut. I took in the looks, from everyone; some were in shock, some judging me, and some were sad for me. But I took it, and once she finished, I walked past her, and through Cucuy's group, all making me push through them to get by and out the door, but I took it and did not say a word.

The following months just got worse with the threats, harassment, and torture. I went to school with Brandy, an exceedingly small private school with a total of 40 students. I went to the same parties, hung out with a lot of the same friends, and her boyfriend, Cucuy, began showing up at my house as well. Offering to help my dad, since my parents were building onto their house. Finding mornings as I would wake up, this man, smoking weed, laughing and drinking coffee with my dad. Staying most days, offering to assist my dad with various boards being put up for the framing, and going over the blueprints my dad had created. Showing up at the saloon that was attached to the restaurant I worked at with his homies, which made me feel as if I could never escape this man.

Brandy also found ways to make my life as hard as she could, by harassing me with degrading names, getting others who I had once considered friends to join her in the harassment. Where within a few weeks, she had most of the school joining her. Leaving me to feel alone, wanting to die at times when I wanted to be left alone; only to be made fun of, degraded, and gawked at. Which in hand, led to others in the small town who went to the high school, picking up on the rumors and siding with Brandy as well. Seeing me as the slut who had sex with Brandy's boyfriend and was nothing more than a hood rat: a girl who would have sex with anyone and had supposedly seduced a grown man during who had gotten drunk on a camping trip, a man who was the boyfriend of a former friend, and then got pregnant by another, or at least that seemed to be the rumor at the time.

As time went on, things just continued to intensify when two of Cucuy's homeboys' got jobs as dishwashers where I worked, giving him even more excuses to watch and harass me. The homies hit on me every chance they got. They whistled at me, slapped me on the bottom when I would walk by them and would joke about what they would do when they had their turns with me. I tried to ignore them on the nights I worked, avoiding the kitchen area as much as possible, and focusing on my job.

Then I noticed something, something I had not noticed before. It was the close friendship that seemed very apparent, as I noticed that Monique seemed to be very good friends with all of them. She got his homeboys jobs at her parent's restaurant and bar. She seemed to be very friendly with Cucuy when he came to the bar, and the more I thought about it the more I began to question her, since she was the one to tell people about my pregnancy and who got me pregnant. She was the one who invited them to our campout, the one who insisted I keep drinking that night, pushing drugs and alcohol on me, and the one who appeared to have some sort of arrangement with him, the man who raped me, Cucuy.

I did question things, and when I did, things went south extremely fast.

Shots Fired

During the holiday break, we looked forward to seeing our friends who had left for college and partying with them during that time. One friend, in particular, a friend I will always consider a dear friend; had such an amazing attitude about him. His name was Jason. He played basketball, was on a sports scholarship, and had such big dreams about his future. He was the type, who, when he walked into a room, his energy drew others towards him, and he always seemed to be dancing or singing. He did not have the cholo look about him like most in our group did. Instead, he always wore nice designer tops, jackets, jeans, and basketball shoes, and always had a different baseball cap on. However, it was his smile and his demeanor that was contagious. Drawing women to him in droves, as he just knew how to say the right words to the girls who would come to see him, and knew how to treat each one as if they were the most important one in his life, knowing, that there were several girls he enjoyed seeing and spending time with, yet me watching in awe of his smoothness and how he treated each of the girls he dated.

Jason would come home on breaks, and my dear friends were his cousins, so I saw him often and considered him family as I did the rest of our close group. The times always seemed to go by fast, but we enjoyed the time we all had together. Until that year, as things were continuing to intensify at work, at school, and found I was in a very dark place.

Jason was always incredibly happy, and we had all spent an afternoon together, catching up, and having an enjoyable time. Something that not only everyone else needed, but that I needed most of all. That evening we decided we would all go to some parties around town together, so Jason could meet up with others he had not seen yet during his visit. We did as we had done every weekend and started the evening with a "cruise" downtown to see everyone and get info on where the parties were.

Cruising was a way to see everyone, get the information on where the parties were going to be, and typically started as it began to get dark out on Friday and Saturday nights. The cruise route consisted of a stretch from a local drive-in burger joint, that then took us around a large park where many would hang out to flag down their friends, taking the parade of cars downtown and back up around as we would turn around at the end of the strip, to go back in the circle again and again, until we were ready to all head out to the local party spots. All cars, going very slow as we would talk to those we saw pass by, show off the vehicles, sound systems, and a way for every kid in town to connect.

As we were cruising, we had found a few friends we had pulled over to discuss party plans with. We had pulled over at a local burger spot to meet up and flag others down at.

We all got out of our cars, were talking, listening as the music bumped in our trunks, and came up with a plan for our evening. As we were doing this, a car pulled in, and a 40 oz glass bottle was thrown in our direction. This caused some heated words to be exchanged and guns were pulled. Another guy, who was not part of either group, meeting with his friends just off to the side, pulled out his gun and shot it to get everyone to leave, which prompted everyone to run to their cars. We all jumped in the nearest car and took off to a gas station that was a spot we knew everyone would go to after that. However, as we were leaving, I noticed Monique had pulled up next to the guys who had started the confrontation, then saw a familiar face in the back of the car, it was him, Cucuy.

By the time we got to the gas station and were preparing to leave, Monique showed up. She said she got stuck trying to leave but still wanted to go to the party we were going to. Monique then suggested we take the backstreets to avoid seeing those guys who threw the bottle at us again, and before I could question why she was talking to them afterward, we were all heading out, following Monique down some backroads. As we began turning down several streets, which were even more out of the way than the route we should have taken on the backroads, I began to get nervous. Then, as we turned down another street that had no lights on porches and was pitch black, I saw the car that had thrown the bottle at us, stop and block the street. I looked behind us and saw another car blocking the street behind us as well, and when I turned my head back, I saw the sparks ricocheting off the street. I heard the gunshots, and ducked down, screaming, and sure that they were going to kill us all. It only went on for a few seconds, but those few seconds seemed like an eternity and were the few seconds that changed so many lives forever.

When we heard the cars which had blocked us in and shot their guns at us speed off, I took a second to check myself to see if I had gotten shot. It was at that moment that I heard a scream like no other. Jason had been shot. He was sitting in the passenger seat, blood coming down his face, and a bullet in his forehead, but he was still alive. An older gentleman came running from his house, yelling that he called 911. When he got to the vehicles, he ran right to the seat Jason was in, then yelled for us to go, and rush him to the hospital. He said he would tell the police what he heard and saw but we needed to get Jason to the hospital.

The drive was not far, but it seemed to take forever for us to get there, even as we sped through lights and stop signs. When we got to the hospital, several of the guys got out and carried Jason into the ER. We all got out of our vehicles and ran in after them. One of Jason's cousins called Jason's mom. Then the police showed up.

As the police began questioning us, they had us leave the emergency room and talk to them in the parking lot, and as I was being questioned, all I could think about was Jason, and that is when his mom arrived at the hospital. Jason's brothers were running in with her, and the sound she let out as she was told he had been shot in the head, is one that haunts me to this day. It was the sound of a mother, hearing news no mother, no parent ever wants to hear. Within minutes from that, we saw the hospital's helicopter show up, as they rushed Jason inside. He had a team rushing him to the helicopter, as he lay there unresponsive, prepping him to be transported to a facility in another city.

Shortly after, I was put in the back of a cop car, along with a few others also being taken down to the police station. Where our parents were called, notified of the incident, and notified that we were witnesses and needed to be questioned.

While waiting to be called in for questioning, Monique seemed nonchalant. She was writing on the chalkboard in the room. Drawing pictures of dead pigs, and acting as if it were just another day, acting like she was annoyed that we were even there, less than an hour after our friend was shot.

As we waited, we had an officer ask if we could identify the people who shot at us, which we could, since we knew who had done it, being a small town, the car they were in was also unique. So, we went with the officer to a gas station and made an identification.

When we got back to the station, we were then separated and taken into different rooms for questioning. During the time I was being questioned, I was asked if I could identify the people who it did, stating they had pulled them over again and needed me to identify the people. I agreed to go again but found it odd that we had just identified the men not but an hour prior. So I went with the officer and saw the same car that threw the bottle, the same guys in the front, minus Cucuy who had been in the back of the car when we were at the burger restaurant, the same car that blocked us in and shotguns at us, and I once again made an identification.

After making a second identification, I was taken back to the police station, where I was then asked about guns that someone told them we had with us, as well as some baseball bats. I did not know anything about any guns, and the baseball bats were my friend's due to her younger brother keeping them in there for baseball practice.

Shortly after making the statement, another officer came into the room I was in and asked me if I could identify the men who shot Jason. I found this odd but said yes, and as we walked out, Monique was also being taken to make an identification.

Again, I saw the same car, the same driver, however, the men in the passenger seat and backseat were not the same, which I pointed out. I told the officer that the other men who were in the car before were not the same men they had this time. The officer said OKAY and drove me back to the station. I sat in a room by myself for about an hour before someone came in.

When the detective came into the room this time, he sat down and told me that they were unable to make an arrest because this last identification did not add up and upon searching the car, they found no weapons in the car. I explained that the guys they pulled over and had us identify the first two times were the guys who shot at us and shot Jason. The detective then agreed, then said that regardless, the men claimed they had all been in the car together all night and had been at a party when the shooting happened, and upon searching the car the third time the men had been pulled over, there were no guns.

That is when I lost it. I laughed at the detective and called him an idiot and asked if he thought we were that stupid. For the fact that they pulled over the same men, in the same very distinctive car, which had shot at us, TWICE, and never searched them or the car, then let them go both times they were positively identified. Then the third time, I pointed out that they had plenty of time to drop off the men who shot the guns, and even ditch the guns. The detective had nothing to say to me about the observations I gave and said I was free to go, that they would be in touch if they needed anything else from me.

After that night, I chose to isolate myself more. I started doing more cocaine, this time smoking it, and I just quit paying attention to the world around me. I felt like I had somehow caused it all. I was sure Monique had something to do with it, and that we had been set up, I was the target. I kept going back to seeing Monique talking to the man who had raped me; (the man who had threatened mine and my family's lives, harassed me), just before we followed her and got shot at.

Then as time went by, rumors began to surface about how I was the target, and Monique began hanging out with the man who raped me and his crew more and more after that. She was hanging out with the men we had identified as the ones who shot Jason, and she did not show any shame, instead, she joined in on the harassment towards me even more. Joking to me that I should go to a party with them and making jokes about how I should watch my back. Then things just got worse when Jay, who was with us that night, who did have a record, was arrested because of the claim of having guns with us and him being a felon, not allowed to be around guns. The arrest was heartbreaking. We were all waiting to see if Jason would survive or even wake up, and a man, one I saw as a big brother, someone who was always looking out for all of us crazy teens, got arrested before the men who shot Jason did.

To everyone's relief and even surprise, after 6 months in a coma, Jason woke up. He still had the bullet lodged in his brain, and we were all notified that he will never be the same again. He had atrophied, leaving him having to relearn how to do everything again, such as eating, sitting up, and the possibility of ever walking, being very slim. With the news of Jason waking up, the trial for the shooting had been set.

On the day of the trial, we all showed up to testify but were not allowed in the courtroom. We were told we would have to wait outside and that they did not need to hear from us in the courtroom. When the trial ended, we watched as several people from the gang that the men were all a part of, came out, shaking hands, as if they were proud of the outcome. We were then told that two minors from their gang had pled guilty and that is why our testimonies were not needed. The thing was; when they told us who had confessed, we all knew they had the wrong guys. The teens that confessed were not even there that night, not until that third time the car had been pulled over. It was a small town. We knew those guys, and also knew the men who shot at us, and we knew that regardless of what we said, the trial was over and there was nothing we could do. We were told that the shooting was considered an act of gang violence, the men who pled guilty said they shot the wrong person, that they had been mistaken on who was in the vehicles, and they said that they knew us as another gang in the area. My friends and I, people who were more of a family to me than my own, were considered a gang and had no say so in anything that occurred in the trial. That the final verdict on the shooting was the negligent discharge of a firearm and a case of mistaken identity. Even though they targeted us since we were not allowed to testify, or that they had convicted the wrong guys.

After that was over, I lost all hope and faith in everything. I did not care anymore. I began smoking crack cocaine rocks, dated several different drug dealers, using them to get my next high. I dated many guys, anyone who wanted to hook up, for the most part, not having a care for who they were or what I did with them, but always telling them after I would hook up with them that it was our secret. I did this with men who were in relationships, guys who I knew well, and even guys I would meet with for a one-night stand. I found the secret that I would create with these guys, which gave me a thrill, was better than feeling nothing. It was not so much the sex or even individual guys that I found the attraction to, instead, the attraction was the fact that I could do things in secret, where no one, not even Monique would know, and no one would say anything because, with many of the guys, I kept their secrets as well. Whether the secrets were due to having a girlfriend or wife, or if their secrets were some of the things we did sexually-that others would not do with them. I was able to be a player of sorts, and play games with these guys, by not only meeting with them in secret but also showing no care for them when we would be at parties or other places in the view of others. Which seemed to be not only a thrill for me but also enticed many of the guys I dated to want me even more.

I became reckless. I was numb to feelings. I did not care for myself as a person, nor anyone I had dated. I wanted to feel something, anything, but I felt empty. I partied every day of the week. I would go to school and work, then spend my entire paychecks on crack. My grades were barely passing, and during my graduation, I was doing speedballs in the bathroom before walking to get my diploma.

I had gotten dressed up and had family come in from out of town to watch me graduate, but I did not care. I was more focused on getting high and drunk during the ceremonies, and while walking on the stage to be congratulated for finishing high school and being given my diploma, I felt as if it was all a dream. As if I was not there, and I could not wait to get off the stage to run to the bathroom to do another line before heading out with my friends who had also shown up to show their support during the ceremony.

On the night of my graduation, my friends threw a big party for me. I was gifted many gifts which included drugs, and lots of alcohol, and I blacked out at some point. I do not remember much of the night, just the next morning where I had somehow changed my clothes, hitched a ride with a utility worker, and ended up at my house.

This blackout should have scared me, but it did not, and instead of slowing down, I just got worse. Which, from that night on for the next couple of years, I did a lot of different types of drugs, heavily. I had become a crackhead, where I even did sexual favors for drugs. I smoked crack rocks and was spiraling, but I did not care. I felt empty, alone, and betrayed by way too many people, which led me to have very little trust or even care for many I met.

I had met others in the crack world, a world I never imagined I would see as part of my life. There were people with no teeth, people I would smoke rocks with who had serious hallucinations, children they neglected who were locked in rooms for hours at a time while we did drugs. I did not speak up for the children in those cases, I instead, played a participant in enabling the behavior with their parents.

I watched people pass out after shooting up meth and heroin in their veins. I walked into houses where families had once thrived, finding piles of feces on the floors, no food in the filthy bug-infested kitchens, as parents lay out on the couches, high, and completely oblivious to the children in the other room. I had sex with men just to have sex, to try to feel, something I never thought I would ever have, but finding the sex had no satisfaction nor meaning. I had also watched people hallucinate, seeing shadows that no one else saw, and having extreme paranoia over nonexistent narks that they claimed were always watching them. I found the paranoia some had, was controlling their lives, to where on one occasion, I had to strip down naked in front of a lady who was insistent I had been wearing a wire. The delusion was one where she claimed she saw me talking to a nark who supposedly hid in her carport where I had parked. But even after seeing the delusions of others, and thinking of them as insane, I got to a point where I saw the demons I had heard about. I had always thought of these figures as mythological or metaphorical, but seeing them, changed my perception of the life I was living.

I saw shadow monsters, which at the time, were very real, and others claimed to see the same things I was seeing at the same time, making these demons even scarier on the thought that I was not the only one seeing them. Where, to this day, I still have the clear memory of seeing a demon in the backseat of my car as I was driving home after several days of smoking crack and doing meth. I can remember the look in the eyes of this demon, which was not a transparent figure, instead, a very solid, very real demon creature that I saw when I had looked in my review mirror, sitting in the backseat of my car, looking right back at me. I can remember the look in its eyes, the way it nodded its head in agreeance with my actions, and the feeling I got as if I was on the verge of hitting a point of no return.

By age 19, I had hit rock bottom. I totaled 2 cars, one of which I had gotten lucky with due to not only wearing a seatbelt at the time but also for running late and not having my little sister as the passenger of the car. Where the passenger side had been completely smashed in, and I walked away with a couple of scrapes. Finding that even though I was lucky to have survived, the drugs I was on, gave me the sense of being invincible and that I could continue the path I was on with no consequences.

As the time continued to go on, I cashed in most of the savings bonds my grandparents had given me to pay for college. I stole money from my parents, their business, and my little sister, all to continue to support my crack rock habit since my paychecks and tips were not enough. I was working 3 jobs at the time yet found that I never had enough money to continue to remain high for days on end. I needed help but did not know who I could talk to, who I could trust. I was paranoid and addicted, and I felt worthless.

Jay and my other friends tried numerous times to help me, insisting at times that I stay with them, so they could keep me from getting high, but I let them down each time we tried this approach. Being sober would remind me of all that I had been through. The older men, the rape, abortion, the shooting, and the feelings of hopelessness when I would think back on these times in my fleeting time on Earth, finding myself suicidal when I would get sober. Running away from my friends, people who would do anything for me, to get high and numb myself all over again, spiraling faster each time I went back to the drugs as a way to forget.

During this time, Jay had met an amazing woman, one who was his match in life, and I did not want to ruin that by being the charity case, he and his family cared so much about, but who let them down time and time again. I wanted my friends, those I considered family, to find the happiness they deserved, and not worry about what would happen to me, a crackhead whore. A charity case that was hopeless and deemed to be lost.

I was hating myself more every day. Whereat one point, I would visit with Jason regularly, hoping that I would get past the issues I had. I wanted to find a magical fix for him. Hoping to go one day and see him walking, dancing, and singing as he used to do. I wanted to get rid of the demons that chased me, but even with Jason, I found myself stooping even lower, taking advantage of such a dear and amazing man. For nothing more than my selfish reasons of needing money to get high. Which, after the fact, that I would visit each time, and he would give me money, I felt like I could not get any lower.

I found that when I was sober, I would evaluate everything, thinking about more than I wanted to think about. I would see things that I wanted to ignore, and I would learn more about everything that had led up to the life I was living. Finding that over the past couple of years leading up to my spiraling, I learned the story behind the night I was raped. I learned that I was sold to the man who raped me. Monique had sold me for drugs, knowing I was a virgin. She then set me up to be killed after she had spread the rumors about my pregnancy and told everyone who had been responsible and what my plan had been. It was all a game to her, I was a pawn in that game she was playing, and my life meant nothing to her other than her amusement.

The feeling of betrayal along with everything else I felt, left me feeling like I wanted to die. I felt like my life was not worth continuing, my best friend, or at least the person I had once considered my best friend, had betrayed me to the point of nearly having me killed. Led to living the life I was living, and being seen as a crack whore to many who knew. The song that my friend had sung to me a few years prior, seemed to be coming to fruition. I was not a whore then, but I had become one, and I despised myself. I sold my body in exchange for drugs, and I was numb, inside, and out.

I slept with both men and women, used them, and threw them out. I did not have any attachments, nor did I care to have any. I tried to feel something, thinking that I would find that one sex partner who would make me feel again, but it did not happen. I felt sadness when I was sober. I regretted everything that had transpired, so much, including the abortion I had. The due date I had been given haunted me every year, knowing that maybe things would have been different, better, and maybe I should have taken Romeo up on his offer when I had the chance. Maybe I would have lived a happy life with him, maybe he would have kept his word, and if that was so, then I was an even more horrible person for killing my baby. I felt like I had been selfish, that even though I had friends who had also become teen parents, maybe my life would have been better than theirs had become. Which was a feeling that would overcome me when I would run into Romeo, a hard-working young man, who always gave me a look of disappointment when we would see one another.

Romeo did try to reconcile with me a few years after we had initially gone our separate ways, but when he found me and tried to talk to me, he saw that I was lost. He voiced his concern about what I had allowed myself to become and tried to reason with me on why I needed to stop and come back to reality. We both knew that if my friends who were closest to me could not help me, there was very little he could do. I could see the disappointment he had any time I saw him after that. He cared about me, even after the years had passed, but I let him down, as I did to so many others.

However, my view of him became skewed when one night while partying at a friend's house and doing meth, Romeo showed up at the house with Monique. He was surprised to see me there, but I knew Monique had taken him there on purpose, to show him what I did. Romeo did not go to parties and was very focused on his goals, so seeing him at a party with drugs was not something I had ever imagined I would see him at. The look of sadness, disappointment, and betrayal he gave me when he saw me that night was a look that I would never forget. He grabbed a bottle of alcohol and drank it very fast, all while watching me, holding back the tears I could see welling up in his eyes. He left with Monique not long showing up, and within a few hours, Monique returned to the party without Romeo and covered in hickies. I knew she had brought him there to make me see him with her. I knew that she had taken advantage of him, as I had seen her do to other guys she would get drunk and have sex with. In fact, Romeo was not the first guy she did this with, for me to see. Monique had slept with a few other guys I had dated, even on the same nights I had hooked up with the guys. Where she made sure I knew, which for me I never understood at the time, but can see it was all part of the attention issues she had which were part of her bipolar. So, when she came back covered in hickeys, I asked her who gave those to her. Both of us knew Romeo was not like the other guys and that even though he and I did not pursue a relationship, we cared about one another. But, instead of saying that Romeo had given her the hickies, she laughed and said, "Billy Bob" had given them to her. I chose to try to avoid Monique as much as possible after that night. Knowing everything she had done to me and continued to do, regardless of me putting distance between myself and her. I knew that there was no way to completely avoid her. She worked at the restaurant I worked at, and even when I changed my shifts to avoid sharing a shift with Monique, she would always find ways to walk through the restaurant, making sure I saw her.

These realizations just fueled the need for me to want to continue to do drugs, as many as I could get my hands on, and not care who I hurt or even if I was hurting myself in the process. I felt I had gotten to the point of no return, and no matter how much I did, there were not enough drugs in the world which could make me forget. That was until my family took a long hard look at everything.

It took an intervention of sorts to snap me back into reality. Once my parents had realized I had stolen money, they confronted me about it. I confessed, feeling a relief of sorts in doing so. I told them that I was hooked on crack rocks and that I did not know how to stop. I explained how much I did, how I felt I needed the crack all of the time, and could never feel completely satisfied, feeling I always needed more. I showed my parents the crack pipes I had hidden in my drawers, along with rocks I had there, that I smoked in my room, in their house.

The look on their faces was that of shock. They had done drugs themselves but had never dealt with the ramifications of how far drugs can take someone nor the fact that the person who was bringing this realization to their reality, was their own daughter. They saw the look of desperation I had when I told them about my habits, and the need they had to step in. They then gave me two choices, one was to just leave, find a way to reclaim my life and be disowned if I continued to do drugs, and the other was to move to Texas with an aunt, get clean, go to nursing school, and make something of my life. Wherewith either of the choices meant I had to get clean or be disowned, and if I left for Texas, I was never to come back or I would be disowned.

I was not given much time to consider the choices, as my parents knew that if I was given too much time to think about things, that time would allow me to continue on the self-destructive path I was on. Finding that they had to give me just days to think about the options I had been given, and upon making a choice, acting upon the choice with haste. With this in mind, I made a choice that I felt was the best one for everyone. I knew that I needed to get clean and that if I wanted to move on, I needed to leave the town I had grown to love, people I cared about, those who cared about me, and do the right thing.

I talked to my friends, Jay, and his soon-to-be wife, his brother, cousins, and those I saw as my family, about the options I was given. They told me that they knew that this was not an easy decision but that they also knew plenty of people who had been sucked into the life I had been living and did not have options. I was told about relatives they had, ones who had been disowned due to their drug habits, ones who were lost causes, and they let me know that I was not a lost cause. They also made me make promises to them and told me that they had faith in me. Letting me know that I was stronger than I believed myself to be and that I had an option that was a once-in-a-lifetime opportunity, that if I did not take, they would have to side with my parents on not allowing me to come back.

With that, I took the option of moving to Texas, knowing that if I failed and came back, my family would not welcome me and the town I had lived in would suck me back into the abyss I had fallen in. Knowing how easy it was to get drugs, and how easy it was to have the drugs take over my life. Finding that my friends, regardless of how much they wanted me to stay and had offered to help me over the years to get clean, said that they knew this was the best choice for me. Leaving us all in tears when the time came to say goodbye, but me, being forced to promise that I would get clean, claim my life back, and even more so, regardless of if I or anyone else felt the need for it, I was to never move back because we all knew that it would be too easy for me to fall back into old habits.

After moving to Texas, I took the first few weeks to get clean. It was not easy, in fact, it was a lot harder than I had ever imagined it to be, but my aunt was a nurse and knew exactly how to assist me in detoxing. With her knowledge in the medical field, having worked in the ER for many years as she assisted others in similar situations like my own, she gave me the tools needed to get past the want and physical need I had for the drugs while being monitored closely. The time seemed to stand still, but at the same time, allowed me to reflect. Creating a time in my life I knew I never wanted to have to relive, after feeling the pain and exhausting fight my body and mind had against one another as I slowly got rid of the toxins from the drugs, I had been on for years. I can remember the cravings that were intense during that time, all while my body ached, I sweated both day and night, was very restless, and at times during the detox, considered a way out. My mind and body were against one another constantly. Finding that the detox was not only of the chemicals I had consumed for many years but of the past that I tried to forget about by dulling my thoughts with the drugs. The process of journaling during the time I detoxed allowed me to finally write down things I had tried to forget and face the past, recognizing that it was part of me regardless of how much I wanted to leave it behind. As the days continued, I followed the plan in place, where I had come up with an agreement with my aunt on the steps I would follow to a "T", and not give myself a chance to regress. Which meant, that as soon as I was doing better, I had to find work and enroll at the local school in the nursing program.

This busy life I jumped into, kept me from wanting to go backward. I set goals I was excited for. I had made new friends, gotten a job at the local psychiatric hospital, and found I could dream of a future I did not think I could ever have.

I kept in touch with Jay and visited during holidays, and breaks, as well as during the local Music Festival that we all enjoyed going to each year. Jay and his new wife welcomed a baby girl, and I was fortunate enough to be sober, and enjoy watching my friends live their lives without having to worry about me. I found that aside from getting sober, I had found freedom. I was freed from the grasp the drugs once had on me, and I had no want or need to go back to the life I had lived just a short time prior. I wanted to forget that life, and focus on my future, but that is all easier said than done, especially when it comes to the idea of forgetting.

On visits back to the small town, I had run into Romeo, who I was happy for when I heard he had married. I was happy to see him doing well, yet there was always a part of me that wondered "What if?"

Regardless of having the feelings of questioning what could have been, I chose to continue to move forward with my life. I had goals, ones I was working towards achieving, and even though I had dated, I did not feel when it came to love for another person in the relationship perspective. I had come to the reality in thinking that this small inconvenience, was just something I could not change, and even though I did not enjoy the prolonged company of others I saw romantically, I could enjoy the pleasures I felt when having sex, which was better than feeling nothing at all.

I was sober, I was living, and I was no longer seen as the crack whore in the new town I had made my home. Instead, I was seen as a young, responsible, adult, who was there to finish school, work, and build a future for herself, and I was okay with that.

Change of Plans

The first couple of years after moving to Texas, I was focused on completing nursing school, working, and most of all, enjoying life to the fullest. I had made many new friends, all with similar ambitions when it came to school and work, where we could support one another in our goals and dreams for our futures. I found that I could balance my work and school life, with a social life, where dancing at the local clubs on the weekend, allowed me to get out and release any tension and have fun without the need to add drugs to the mix.

In the summer of 2003, I found myself not only enjoying my 21st year of life, but with a surprise, I had not anticipated. I had people assume that I knew, or had planned on such, but I didn't. At the time, I was enjoying being a young adult, without a whole lot to worry about other than taking care of myself and my dog. I had left a lot of my past behind me. I was in my second year of nursing school, with plans to travel and work in various parts of the country for a few years after I completed the nursing program.

I had just turned 21 and enjoyed going out with my friends in a town that was not my hometown, but one that I called home. The life of work and school during the week and clubbing on the weekends was one I enjoyed. Finding the familiar smell of the nightclubs my friends and I had frequented were smells that many my age also looked forward to. Where the nightlife had familiar smells which consisted of the mixture of various colognes and perfumes which club-goers doused themselves in, before arriving at the clubs, only to add more layers to the scents they wore as they frequented the restrooms in between songs, with a side of hairspray and nail polish scents coming from the restrooms.

This was mixed with the smells of cigarettes and cigars that filled the air, giving the clubs a haze that hovered over the dance floors, followed by the sweet smells of the alcohol we indulged in, and the faint smell of body odor which would intensify as the nights went on.

I found that when I turned 21, I not only got to enjoy the shots that came around in the vials the waitresses carried on trays but even more so, where I went from the big black "X" that was drawn on my hands at the beginning of the night, to being able to get the blacklight stamps placed, allowing me to enjoy all the clubs had to offer. During this time, I had dated casually, and I enjoyed having someone to go to dinner with, meet up at the clubs with, or head to the movies with but did not want the relationship label, put on the situation. I still had the issues of not feeling any attachments and was even seen as a player to some. Finding I did not feel when it came to men, and I had accepted this as a part of me. I enjoyed sex and using them to get what I wanted, on my terms, without drugs being a driving force. I had different guys I dated regularly, played arm candy for when they needed a date at an event or party, who in exchange, paid me in shopping sprees, and pampering. And for a brief time, this ideal way of enjoying my life worked for me.

I had the freedom to do what I wanted. Where I could go out all night and not have to worry about a curfew or having a partner worry that I was flirting too much. I could be with my friends, where we were all young and full of energy that we would let out on the dance floor come the weekend or on lady's night. I liked being able to spend my money on shopping, or the next adventure my friends would come up with, whether it was planned or spur of the moment. I was enjoying being young, being able to party when I wanted, being sober when it came to drugs, and enjoying my life to the fullest.

I had met and made many friends in both the school and at the hospital, I worked at. I had many admirers and found one particular acquaintance, named Eduardo, who was one I had called a good friend, knowing that he felt different than I did at the time. He was one I could call up and go watch a movie with, or head to the Chinese buffet with and eat in front of without feeling like I was being judged.

For the time in the two years from when we met, that I saw Eduardo as a friend, he seemed to listen when I talked, to where I felt that he was someone I could share secrets with about my past that I had not shared with many, as he did with me. Sharing of the rape I had endured in my teen years, where my virginity had been forcefully taken, sold in exchange for drugs by a childhood friend who had set the rape up, which ended in a pregnancy I had terminated. Leaving me scared for the most part, on having trust issues, not wanting to have a committed relationship with anyone, and the guilt I carried of the entire event.

The secrets I held in, were ones I had not told many friends or even my family, about how after that rape, the man who had done it, threatened me. Cucuy was the boyfriend of a friend of mine and had a lot of sway in the area I lived in. To where those threats became a reality when, to silence me, and my attacker tried to get rid of me. But found that instead of hitting his target, he accidentally shot one of my close friends in the head, leaving this friend paralyzed for the rest of his life with a bullet still lodged in his brain.

I shared how after the series of unfortunate events and once the truth began to come out, I was soon followed by a strong line of protection being put on me by my close friends, who swore to not let another man hurt me. Which also led me to feel guilt, doing drugs to try to forget. And my friends, trying so hard keep anything from happening to me and to ensure that the man who had put a target on me, would not come near me ever again. Which all lead me to my choice to move from my hometown as an ultimatum and start my adult life, in a new place, and leave my past behind. Where I was away from the drama of my teen years and where I felt I could move forward.

This past had me feeling safe with the idea of not having any serious relationships. Where having a relationship in which I did not see the other person often, was what I wanted. And during the time we were just friends, Eduardo knew my views when it came to relationships. He also knew I was casually dating another man who traveled a lot for work, and that I and the man I was seeing, had a no-strings-attached kind of relationship. Which at the time, was the ideal relationship for me, but Eduardo was persistent in asking me out often and always asking if I would ever consider being more than a friend.

I had met Eduardo at the hospital I worked at while he was finishing up a contract he had with the hospital security and became friends of sorts during the time he was there. He seemed to always be waiting by the coffee cart, knowing what time I would take my breaks, offering to join me while we talked and I drank coffee. After his contract was up, he had asked if we could remain friends outside of work, and I did not see anything wrong with the idea, so I agreed to be friends. The thing was, he was very vocal in how he wanted more than just friendship with me.

We would talk on the phone, go to the movies, or hit up a buffet, where he would also share things with me about his childhood. About never knowing his father, with the idea that his dad wanted nothing to do with him. Being raised by his stepdad and having his stepdad's family be very close to him, like they were his family by blood, knowing that they weren't but how he wished they had been. He shared with me about how he had a girlfriend when he was in his early 20s, where the relationship did not last long but how he heard that she had had his baby. For Eduardo to later find that she seemed to have disappeared and he had no way of finding where she was or how to get in contact with her. And how it haunted him, the idea that he had a baby out there whom he might never have the chance to know, and not by his own choice. Finding the cycle seemed to have continued, a cycle he wished he could break.

Eduardo was persistent in wanting to spend time with me, regardless of the boundaries I put in place. He claimed to be okay with those boundaries, where I was clear on just wanting to be friends. I saw him as someone I enjoyed going to the movies or having dinner with, but I was not interested in anything more with him. Which seemed to work for me for those 2 years that we were friends.

See when it came to Eduardo, he was not my "type" so to say. His mannerisms and the way he dressed were not in line with those I had been attracted to in the past. He wore slacks, dress shirts, or a polo, and always had nice white shoes or dress shoes on. He was quieter than most guys I knew when we would go out to eat or were in public for anything but seemed to always know my every move. He was somewhat of a strange character which was something he was aware of when it came to how people perceived him. He claimed that he was always passed over for other guys because girls like me never went for the nice guy he claimed he was. Always telling me, that when I was ready to turn down the idea of being more than friends, he was there. And to give him a chance because he wanted to show me that even with the idea that "nice guys always finish last", he could make me very happy, and I would not regret giving him the chance.

Time and time again, I turned down his proposition of having a "real" relationship as he put it. This was not due to his lack of trying either. Eduardo was one who appeared to be the romantic type. He showed this side to me time and time again by showing up with a rose when we would meet up for a movie, buying me gifts as we would walk around the mall after eating, or waiting on a movie to start. Finding jewelry to give me, saying how he knew that it was meant for me to wear. Or buying my favorite candies as we would walk past the candy stand. Always seeking ways to woo me so to say, which would lead me time and time again, having to remind him of how we were friends and how I wanted it to remain that way. That was until 2 weeks after my 21st birthday when I found that the guy I had been dating casually, was once again canceling our plans on going out on the town to celebrate my birthday because of work. This boyfriend was a casual boyfriend, where we did not question one another on what we did when we were not together. I knew he was a wealthy, good-looking, young man, who most likely had other girlfriends in the other places he traveled to often. When he was in town, I was his arm candy who he took to parties, to the clubs, or to events where he said he enjoyed having a pretty face by his side. During the time I had dated him, I had not had any other romantic relationships with other men, not because I wanted to remain faithful, but because I enjoyed having the freedom of having a guy, I could have a relationship with when he was in town, then the freedom to live my life when he was not in town. Without having to answer to what I was doing or feeling like I was being weighed down, and where the emotional aspect was never a question for either of us.

In the months leading up to my 21st birthday, the boyfriend had promised me that he was going to treat me like a princess and celebrate with me. The thing was, he was always traveling and many times, plans would change, or he would have last-minute changes due to work. So, when he had rescheduled the first time or even the second time, I was not bothered by it. It was not until the third time I had decided I was done with that type of relationship. Where I was excited, dreaming about what we would do and where we would go, only to be let down 3 different times.

The second time he had to reschedule, he sent me money to get my hair done at the salon, pick up a new dress, and buy myself a couple of gifts I wanted. Which I did, and as I prepared for his arrival, he called to say that he had to be in New York the next morning and we could celebrate the following week when he had a few days off. But after the third time of rescheduling the plans we had to celebrate my birthday, I realized I was done with that relationship and thought I wanted more. So, I called up Eduardo and took him up on his proposition of going on a real date with him and giving "a nice guy" as he described himself, a chance.

The night we went out, we had gone to a nice restaurant, which was perfect since I had gotten my hair done earlier that day. After dinner, we went to a biker bar to play some pool, where Eduardo told the bartender I was celebrating my 21st birthday. The bartender announced this occasion to all the patrons at the bar, and before I knew it, everyone there was buying me drinks, so much so that, I lost track of most of the evening. I do not think I had ever drunk so much and was sure of it by the next day after feeling the aftereffects of such a binge. When I woke up the next morning at the friend's house, in Eduardo's bed, I realized that I did not want to pursue a romantic relationship with him and left his house as quietly as I could.

I felt bad for sneaking out like a thief in the night, doing the walk of shame, but even after that night, I still did not have romantic feelings for him. He had called later that day to check on me, and I informed him I had gotten to know my toilet very well for most of the day. After the call, I figured that was that, but I was mistaken when he showed up with some juice and soup. Offering to help me with the hangover I was dealing with. He stayed the entire day, caring for me, which was a nice gesture, but not what I wanted.

I had given Eduardo signs, which I hoped he noticed, showing him, I was not interested in pursuing a romantic relationship. Pulling away when he would try to touch me or show any affection towards me. Trying to come up with excuses on my plans during my free time. Only to find that he seemed to be like a lost puppy, constantly following me around after that night, which seemed kind of cute at first until it got creepy. It was like he knew everything about my routines; what time I got home from work, the time I took to go from class to my house, how long I had been home, even on days I would get home early which should have been a huge red flag for me, and he felt he had to call several times a day to ensure I was alone and not talking to anyone.

I did try to ignore the creepiness I felt from Eduardo and expected that he would eventually move on, knowing that he could not go everywhere I went, especially when I went to visit my hometown. See, I had plans that I followed each year, to head back to my hometown for a music festival that took place there. The festival was a kind of celebration that was a tradition in my hometown, and a time my friends from my hometown and I would look forward to. Eduardo was aware of this since I had gone to the festival in the years prior, and somehow invited himself along, offering to drive the 8 hours. Saying that he had nothing else to do and that the music festival sounded like a lot of fun. I felt perplexed by the situation, knowing I would get questions from my family and friends but decided I would introduce him as a friend and nothing else. So, I went along with the plans Eduardo had suggested as he invited himself. Where I knew that the drive was something I did not look forward to and thought it might be fun to bring a new face to enjoy the weekend of fun that was ahead.

When we arrived at my family home, my parents were confused about the fact that I was bringing a man with me, to which I let them know Eduardo was just a friend who wanted to go to the music festival. So, they greeted and treated him as such during the time. I found that to be the easy part, knowing the hard part would be introducing this man as just a "friend" to my friends, people I grew up with, whom I considered like family as they did with me.

The test was proven to be a trying one too. As we drove up to meet up at my friend Jay's house, finding all my old friends were waiting for me to show up, so we could all go to the festival, they all went from talking and laughing to complete silence. This group of friends was my protective ones. They were surprised to see this man with me and to see that Eduardo was not the typical man I would be seen with.

I had dated the "bad boy" types in the past, and Eduardo dressed nicely, showing up with a button-up shirt and dress pants. Eduardo wore jewelry as well, which included a nice watch, a bracelet, and some rings. The rings held meaning for Eduardo, but I never cared to ask what that meaning was, and the rings were something that stood out to others, especially my close friends who were caught off guard by this man. I had not mentioned I was seeing anyone to any of my friends, so they were confused on why I would bring a man with me out of the blue without mentioning him before. One friend decided to make things less tense in the air by introducing himself to Eduardo, which seemed to go well, and others followed suit. As we went to the festival, many watched Eduardo carefully as he followed me, gave others looks, and appeared to be possessive over me when others would come to greet me and give me hugs. This was something that everyone noticed.

After the first day of the festival was coming to an end and we headed to one of my friend's houses to relax before calling it a night, my friends pulled me aside to speak to them in the kitchen, away from Eduardo's ears. They told me they did not like Eduardo, there was something that was not right about him, and warned me to be careful. They did not want to go into detail, but nonetheless warned me that he was not someone to be hanging out with,

This was something they had never done before. I had dated guys in high school and the couple of years that followed when I still lived with my parents, whom they had met, and never once did they show any concern over any relationship I had had until then. They always greeted anyone I dated or was friends with outside our group and treated them with respect and friendship. As we went to leave, they gave me hugs, letting me know that if I needed anything, anything at all, they were just a phone call away. They made me promise to call if I needed them and also promise to ditch Eduardo as soon as I got back home, saying he had something about him that seemed to scare them for my sake.

I knew that they were looking out for me, and I also knew that they intimidated Eduardo as they were not ones to hide the way they felt about those who they could see right through. During the festival, they had said things as we walked around, cracked jokes in both Spanish and English, amongst themselves but geared towards Eduardo. The guys in the group had the look of bikers and Cholos, ones who had the looks of what they had seen and been through on their faces. They were also very protective of me and saw me like a sister since I had grown up with many in the group. And as we left to drive back up to my parents, Eduardo let me know that he did not approve of my friends. Scolding me, saying that a girl like me should not be associated with people like that, and that "he" was ready to drive back home the next day, cutting the trip short knowing I had no choice since I had ridden down to my hometown with him.

Once we arrived back after the trip was cut short due to Eduardo's uneasy feelings he had from my friends, he began showing up to the places I was at unexpectedly like at the school I went to, at the hospital I worked at, and made it clear that did not like me talking to anyone. He hated the ideas I had about my future which did not include him in the long run, and where I did not see myself settling down for quite some time, if ever. Where he would tell me often that things can change, and maybe I would change my mind.

After only a month, to where I had decided things had gone on long enough, Eduardo asked me to marry him. I of course turned him down which did not upset him like I thought it would but only made him more persistent in wanting to spend every moment with me, which I tried to avoid. I talked to my friends about him, who assured me I was doing the right thing by distancing myself from him. They too told me how he would give them creepy looks when they were around, saying that he would answer my phone if I was in the other room as if he had the right to, and seemed to always be right there next to me, watching everyone else and giving warning looks to anyone who dared to look in my direction.

After the first proposal for marriage, Eduardo seemed to get more and more clingy. Which led me to put the brakes on the relationship and try to let him down as best I could. He seemed to understand but insisted I go with him to an event we had planned on going to with his family, which required us to go out of town for a few days together. He said that after we got back, we could go our separate ways, but that he had already told everyone I was coming. Making me feel as if I was obligated to go. Looking back, I know I was very naïve, deep down I knew better, but at the time, I had a tough time saying no. So, I agreed to go, only on the grounds that when we got back, he would back off and quit smothering me. But what I did not know, was that he had other plans in mind.

The plans to go to this event were ones he had let me know about just two weeks prior, but where I agreed to go with him to. It was for a long, 4-day weekend that was ahead, where his family gathered at the farm his grandparents owned. Eduardo would talk about how much I would enjoy it, that it was a lot of partying and really good home-cooked food all day and night. Which did sound like fun to me, a lot more fun than going to my cousins for a cookout of hotdogs on the grill that weekend.

On the day that we were to leave, I was packing my bags, ensuring I had everything I needed, which included my pack of birth control which I kept in my makeup case along with my multivitamins and Tylenol. As I went to grab my toiletries, Eduardo decided to go ahead and zip up my bags and take them to his truck, hurrying me along as I ensured my bedroom was closed and the house was locked up. I had a neighbor who had agreed to house sit and dog sit that weekend, and as Eduardo hurried me along, I went to let my neighbor know where the dog food was for my dog. Telling her that my dog would use the doggy door and gave her the key to check on my dog and my house. Little did I know this hurried action was all to divert me from double-checking my bags and my house before leaving.

It was not until we arrived at Eduardo's grandparent's farm, and I was unpacking my bags that I realized my birth control was gone. Eduardo assured me I would be okay for a few days, and to not worry about it but to enjoy myself, which I was hesitant about, but eventually saw as an easy thing to do around his family.

Those days out there on the farm went by fast. His family liked to party all day and late into the night, which turned out to be a lot of fun for me, or so I thought. As I would drink throughout the day with the others, Eduardo seemed to ensure I always had a full cup, and by night, would take advantage of my drunken condition. He did so in an exceptionally smooth fashion, rubbing my feet, helping me out of my clothes, and making his way into the bed, to where he would get on top of me while I was preparing to out from being drunk and have sex with me. I was a willing participant, as I loved sex, and did not think much about having sex with a person I had plans to ditch in just a few days. During the time out on the farm, I along with others from Eduardo's own family, noticed that he was oddly, completely sober, the entire time, continuing to ensure I always had plenty to drink.

As the time went on and I got to talking and laughing with Eduardo's family, I noticed that his family seemed to be a lot different in a lot of ways than he was. They were very friendly, easy to talk to, and more laid back than he was, which I found to be interesting. Many of them reminded me of my friends from back home, making the conversations easy.

Along with the fun I had with them, I also got a lot of questions over the weekend about our relationship, which I tried to walk around with the answers by diverting them as best I could. Among some of the questions, I also heard remarks from others at the party on the farm who said that they thought Eduardo was gay since he never brought a girl around before. Especially since he was in his late 20s and never seemed to have an interest in girls that they knew of, and because he always kept to himself in a very odd manner.

They also remarked that he had a style that was a lot different from others in the family, was very particular about everything, but had never talked about women. That was until he had met me, and they said that Eduardo talked about me quite often. They went on and remarked on his strange ways, how he is a perfectionist and after seeing his family compared to him, I did not see how he fit in with the group. I did not think much about the comments the family had made about him at the time, but later on, I did find that maybe there was something to those that I should have paid a little more attention to.

When the long weekend of partying was coming to an end and it was time to go back, I had not changed my mind about wanting to slow things down a bit if not for good, and found I was even more so wanting the change in our relationship status when I got back home. Because when we walked in, I was in shock at what I saw when I found my birth control had been thrown around in my hallway and smashed into the carpet.

I say that because, like many women, I knew where I kept my birth control. Eduardo tried to suggest that my dog must have gotten a hold of it. Going on to explain that I must have left them on the bed by mistake and my dog jumped up and got into them, but I was not believing his theory and knew that there was no way that my dog could have gotten it. He was an older dog I had adopted when I first moved to the area, he was an exceedingly small dog and had noticeably short legs. Even if I had left it on my bed as Eduardo had suggested, I knew that he could not jump on my bed without help due to his little legs and his age, and my bedroom door was still closed from when I closed it before I left. Leaving me with a very uneasy feeling, knowing deep down that this guy, for some reason, had purposely taken the pack of birth control out of my bag and destroyed the pack and pills, claiming that the blame had to be on my dog.

After that, I had decided to call it quits with any sort of relationship with this guy, and decided it was best if I moved on at the time. I found myself not wanting to date anyone after that, due to not only the things that had gone on in the relationship in just a little over a month but for the fact that I felt as if he was still following me. And the feeling of being followed became a reality again when I would see Eduardo's car drive by my house, knowing my house was on the other side of the town from where he lived. I would see him sitting at the end of my street, driving outside the hospital I worked and school I attended, and then there were the odd phone calls. Where I would get phone calls with no one answering on the other line, just the sound of heavy breathing, and no way to trace the calls due to them being blocked by the caller. I chose to ignore it all, not let it bother me, get a roommate, and focus on school and work, which worked for a noticeably brief time.

That is until I felt sick. I was convinced I had a UTI and went to my doctor. I had this idea of having a UTI because just before having the burning, I had been peeling peppers that I had taken out of the freezer for cooking with. I did not think about washing my hands before using the restroom and was sure I had a UTI, which caused the burning issues and the need to use the bathroom. I was in denial that it could be anything else, insuring myself over and over, that I had been on birth control for years, and only missed a few days of taking the pills. But all that denial and trying to reassure myself went out the door when my doctor was the one who broke the news to me by saying I did not have a UTI, and I was pregnant. When she told me, I just froze, and it did not sink in until the nurse handed me papers showing the test was positive and I was indeed pregnant. And at that moment, I felt as if all the walls were closing in on me, knowing my life would never be the same again.

After I left the doctor's office, I can remember sitting in my driveway crying, not being able to control the emotion that came out of me. I was first shocked for the most part on the way home, just going over and over again in my mind, that it had to be wrong, thinking it was not happening. Feeling like I was in a bad dream that resembled one of those sad chick flick movies and was sure I would wake up. But once I put my car in park in my driveway, an entire series of emotions came over me. From the crying, where I felt bad for myself, to being mad at myself for allowing it to happen, to then being more upset than I had ever been at any person I had dated, knowing that Eduardo had done this to me on purpose. That he knew exactly what he was doing when he destroyed my birth control pills just a few weeks prior.

I waited a few days. I had not told anyone I was pregnant, that was until my roommate came out and asked me. She did so by pointing out that the entire time she had been there, regardless of it being just a few weeks, I had yet to have a period, knowing that us being best friends we cycled at the same time as we had done for the past two years. Pointing out that I was moodier than she remembered me ever being and she heard me as I cried myself to sleep the past few nights. It was at this time that I felt like I could no longer hold in everything I had to say, and I felt like I could tell her everything. From the friendship that should have not gone any further to the stalking, and this, to where I felt like Eduardo had won, he had trapped me.

My roommate was a girl I had met when I first moved to town a few years prior, a girl who was one of my best friends. And after telling her everything, she told me that she and my other friends would be there for me and support me with any decision I made. I knew she meant that if I decided to terminate the pregnancy, they would be there for me, which would seem like a solution to the situation I was facing. But I could not bring myself to do it. I had terminated a prior pregnancy after a rape, to where I felt a lot of guilt for it, even knowing deep down that the choice at the time was the right one. I did not have it in me to do it again, regardless of how I felt about being pro-choice, I just could not abort the child I was carrying. Which is a choice I am glad I made for the sake of the child, but the choice of telling Eduardo I was pregnant, was one I should have gone against.

See, I was brought up to own up to your wrongdoings, regardless of what it is you have done, you own it. Where anytime I did something, whether it had a good or bad outcome, I could hear my parent's voices saying, "You made your bed, now lie on it".

Which is a moral of sorts that I not only live by but teach my kids to live by as well. So, when I went, against my own best judgment and the advice of everyone else I had told, to tell Eduardo that I was pregnant, I look back and think I should have known and just have let sleeping dogs lie. But that is now the shoulda woulda coulda, that many of us beat ourselves up over when things go awry and are one of the times in my life, that I do wish I could have a do-over on.

It took me a few days to finally make the call to meet up with Eduardo, but when I did, at the time, I found the support he offered was what I thought I needed. I had been a mess for days before meeting up with him. I had gone back and forth on whether or not to tell him, to include him. But I remembered the story he told me of a former girlfriend who had his baby who he found out about through friends that he had never been given a chance to be a dad. And the story of his dad not being a part of his life, which he claimed tore him up inside knowing that he had a child out there who he does not even know where to start on how to find. Finding a cycle that was continuing, one he wished he could change with his kid since "he" claimed, given the chance, he would be there for. Leading me to the choice, where the mixture of being too naïve and heartstrings came into play for me. Because no matter how much I would advise myself that it was best he have no part of mine or my unborn child's life, I felt that maybe I was being cold-hearted in some way in not allowing him to be a dad and giving him that chance of breaking the cycle.

We planned to meet up at Eduardo's brother's house, which he had been living at for a few weeks. I showed up looking like a mess because on the way there, I had pulled over at one point and was tempted to turn around but forced myself to do what I thought was the right thing and tell Eduardo I was pregnant. That ride to his house seemed like one I knew I needed to turn back and run away from. I cried for a good 30 minutes on the side of the road, before deciding to go ahead with my plan of meeting with him.

Every turn I made that brought me closer just made me want to run away further from him. And with that last turn that took me to the house, Eduardo was at, I could see him standing on the porch, waiting for me. At the moment I first saw him standing on the porch, I felt a rush of anxiety and fear come over me, making me ill to my stomach, which all came up as soon as I put my car in park and opened the car door. Eduardo came off the porch and without even thinking twice, held my hair back as I got sick then helped me to the house. I felt frozen, I could not talk, I did not want to talk, I did not even want to look at him in the eyes, but I knew, I had made my bed, now it was time to own up to what I thought I needed to do.

When I told Eduardo I had been to the doctor and learned I was pregnant, he seemed to light up, which just made me burst out into tears, and he embraced me, promising that everything would be okay, and he would take care of us. Which at the time, sounded like what I needed to let happen, for the sake of my unborn baby, allowing the baby a chance to have both a mom and dad in its life.

Within minutes of me telling Eduardo the news, he was on the phone, calling his family and friends. Excitedly telling everyone he was going to be a dad. I had to stop him and let him know that I had not told any of my family yet, because I was not ready to face that music just yet. He told me I was being silly and picked up the phone, insisting I call my parents.

When I called them, I asked both my mom and dad to get on the phones at the house, so they could both hear what I had to say. After hearing my dad get on the phone, I began to cry, knowing that I was about to let him down. But I decided to just tell them, and with the gasps heard on the other line followed by silence, I knew my fear was a reality. I heard a loud bang and realized that my dad had dropped his phone, my mom said she had to go but she would call me back later to talk to me. Leaving me feeling sad and having the same feeling I once had of letting my dad down, come over me once again.

Eduardo's excitement did not stop, even after my fear had become a reality when it came to my parent's reaction. He continued to call others to share the news and told everyone we were at his brother's if they wanted to stop by because we were going to be cooking out to celebrate the good news. Within the hour, we had a house filled with people coming to congratulate us on our big news. People came up to me, giving me hugs, talking to my belly, kissing me on the cheeks, and telling me how blessed I was. Eduardo's grandma came to me, telling me of her dream of water that she had told others of just a few days prior, which she translated to life. Where running water is life. Explaining that when she had dreams of water that there was a new life coming into the family and that she believed there was a lot of life coming since the dream of water happened to be a rushing river, not typical to the streams and creeks she had seen in her dreams before. Leaving me not only perplexed by what she had said but also in shock at the number of people who had shown up in such a short amount of time.

This type of celebration was not at all what I had expected nor wanted at the time, and as it all transpired, I felt as though I was in a bad dream. Almost as if I was not even there at all because all I could think about was my parents and what they were talking about. Once everything had finally settled down, Eduardo told me he would follow me to my house and that it was best that I stay with him for the night due to my delicate condition. I was still in a state of shock from what all had happened in a matter of just a few hours, so I just went along with what he suggested. I had thought about him saying my "delicate" condition as if I was going to break. Thinking that I wish I could go back to earlier in the day when I had second-guessed telling him about the pregnancy, knowing deep down that I had just created a storm that for some reason, I felt was just starting to gain momentum.

We decided to stay at my house that night since my roommate was working the night shift at the hospital, and not too happy with the fact that I went against hers and everyone else's advice on either waiting to tell him or not telling him at all. When we got to my house, my dog came to me, knowing I needed the comfort, insisting he lay on my lap and be there for me. I sat there petting him on the head, thinking about how my life was never going to be the same, thinking about how I was going to take care of a baby, even if "he" was going to be helping, how was I going to do this? I had not had the idea of children of my own come to mind until then, and it was only because the idea was forced upon me. As I sat there, staring off, crying in small spurts, contemplating everything that was happening, Eduardo told me he was going to run out for a few minutes but would be back, and for me not to go anywhere. He went and picked up dinner, some movies, and lots of snacks for me, and the entire time all I could do was stare at my phone, waiting for my parents to call back.

The one night turned into a few days, then a week had gone by where I was still not feeling any better and Eduardo, regardless of how many times told him that I wanted to be left alone, was still right by my side. And to make things worse, my parents, whom I talked to nearly daily, had never called back as my mom said she would. After a little over a week of not hearing from them, I decided to call my parents. I knew that they were beyond disappointed and were avoiding discussing things with me. My dad answered the phone and when he did, the moment he heard my voice he went silent and handed the phone to my mom. I could feel the tension and hurt from the action, even with him not saying a word, the avoidance of my presence on the phone said it all.

However, my mom talked to me, at first, she did not have a lot to say other than ask me how I felt, and what my plans for this pregnancy were. I knew she had it in her mind that I would make the choice that she thought was right, and terminate the pregnancy, but I told her that I was doing okay and that I had told the dad of the baby as well. When I told her that, she went silent as she did before. I waited for a few moments then she said, "so you are keeping the baby I take it?"

I told her that I was, and that is when she began to cry, saying I was ruining my life, and how she and my dad knew that is not what I wanted for myself. She then said she had to go but that she was there for me regardless of any choices I make and she and my dad both loved me.

That type of phone etiquette from my dad became the norm for a while there. Every time I called, my dad would not speak a word to me, instead, he would either hand the phone to my mom or sister or hang up if no one was around to take the call.

The pain I felt from letting my dad down was hard on me. I knew his ways, where I was the daughter of a minister, and he raised me to be smart when it came to my life and actions. Where even though he did not want to know, he knew my mom, who is a Liberal and he being a Conservative, had taught me about my body and how to stay safe from unexpected pregnancies. And how he had expected me to make the most of the second chance on life I had been given. Where I was expected to finish school, enjoy life, possibly settle down and marry then have children after marriage at a much later time in my life. I mean shoot, they did not even know I was dating anyone seriously enough to have a baby with them. The dad of the baby was a man they met once, whom I introduced as a "friend" and had said I was not in a committed relationship with. So, to hear from his daughter, whom he had bragged about daily to friends on my accomplishments and goals in life, is pregnant and unwed, was like a dagger to the heart which he pretended was not happening by avoiding me altogether. That was until the guy, my baby daddy so to say, asked me to marry him again.

Eduardo saw the turmoil I was going through with my family, and he knew my dad was upset with the choices I had made, as well as why he was treating me the way he was. And with that, Eduardo finally convinced me to say yes, by pointing out that the only way I could begin to get my father's forgiveness was if I married and he made me an honest woman. Little did I or anyone else know, that the decision to say yes, was one that I would soon regret.

You are mine

The relationship with my baby's dad was anything but a normal, healthy, or ordinary relationship. Eduardo was very needy and clingy. Always needing to know my every move, even when I was in the house with him, and always suspicious of me. I later realized that those signs, were not cute and that in fact, he was scarily controlling.

Shortly after agreeing to marry him, in hopes of repairing my relationship with my dad, he began to treat me like he owned me. It was like saying yes to his proposal turned on a switch in him that I had not seen until then. I had to tell him my every move, which regardless of what I said, he already knew since it felt as if he stalked me constantly. He was everywhere I was, or even when I did not see him following me or lurking, he seemed to know exactly where I was, who I may have talked to and what I might have been doing. It was as if there were eyes following my every move, reporting back to him, and at times, I believed I saw some of those eyes.

It became apparent others were watching me for him when I would see his cousins casually going down an aisle at the store while I would shop or pull up to a pump close to where I was at the gas station. I brought up these incidences and Eduardo would brush it off pointing out that he had a very big family, both his mom's family and his stepdad's family, who lived in the area we lived in, and there was nothing to worry about. It was all just a coincidence because it was true, his family was exceptionally large, and the friends of the family were also included in ones that were at gatherings and parties adding to the vast amount of people that I would see when out. So, seeing them everywhere was not anything to be alarmed over, or so I had told myself.

As the time went on, I had issues with constant morning sickness that was more like all day and night sickness, which made keeping up with school and work a lot harder than I had expected. The issue with the sickness caused me to have to run out of class or miss class altogether when I could not leave the house due to being stuck next to the toilet.

The same could be said for work, where I would show up and spend a lot of time running to the bathroom. Trying every remedy to ease the sickness that others suggested, where I carried a lemon in my purse, so I could scratch the peel and smell the citrus to help ease the waves of nausea, or where ginger ale and ginger tea were my drinks of choice, but regardless, those were only very temporary solutions that did not last long.

I was worried about how my schoolwork was being affected, where I was falling behind on what I worked so hard to get at. Knowing that the nursing program was something I had been accepted into when others were not. I was worried about keeping up with bills, since I was being sent home due to the constant sickness, and not sure how I would keep up with my house and responsibilities at home. With all the worry and sickness, I was making myself miserable and Eduardo's solution to the stress of trying to keep up with everything was for me to quit school and move in with him at his brother's house.

He made points about how with us both working and paying very little rent at his brother's, we could save up for the baby and get our place within no time, then after the baby was born, I could go back to school. How taking school out of the equation, for now, would allow me to relax when I was not working, then have more energy to work with. He also pointed out that even though we were going to be living with his brother where I could not have my dog, which was a big setback for me on the idea, that my roommate, who loved my dog, could care for him and I could go and see him whenever I wanted. And once we got our place, we could get my dog and bring him along with us. The idea seemed logical and though I felt moving in together was moving too fast, I was pregnant, and agreed to marry him, so I went with it, feeling at that point that it was what it was.

After moving into the brother's house, Eduardo's control became even harder to avoid. I felt as if my life was being dictated upon where I had no say in what or how I did things. These things were simple ones but ones that were bothersome such as, I could only wear certain clothes, and even the scrubs I wore to work needed to pass Eduardo's test. To where if the cut was too low showing any hint of cleavage, he insisted I wear an undershirt or change altogether, regardless of the weather being hot out. This also went to the fact that if clothes, even my scrubs for work, showed off my hips or hugged my bottom to where I might look too sexy, I had to change or wear a longer top. I had long hair, and I could only wear my hair up in a bun, no ponytails due to them being too flirty when I walked apparently. My makeup had to be done a certain way saying that with all of this, I will need to set an example for our child and that he also did not want his future wife going out looking like a hussy.

Along with the control over what I wore and how I looked, he constantly watched everything I ate, as if he was judging every bite. I did not always take everything as he dished it out to me, to where times I just ignored his demands or orders towards me, telling him to mind his own business. Or smarting off, to tell him that I could do as I pleased because he did not own me nor was he my daddy, which seemed to be a phrase I used that would get under his skin.

I had never had a man give me orders like that, nor was I one who kept her mouth shut, but with me only being 5 foot 3 and him being a very large 6-foot 4 man with a short fuse on his temper, he intimidated me. Eduardo would yell when things were not his way, get in my face, put me down, and belittle me in front of his friends and family. Many times, I wanted to get up and fight back, but I was pregnant and now without a place of my own, and due to his control over who I talked to, I was also without any friends.

He threatened my old roommate when she tried to stop me from going with him, and I did try to tell him I thought it was best I stay with her after the way he acted. But every time I would second guess being with him, he would bring up the guilt that I had of my dad, letting him down, and us being a family by marrying, was the only way to make things right for everyone. And if that was not enough, I had family in the area, cousins and such, whom I was not close to but who tried to stop things on more than one occasion. Each time either my friends or family tried to stand up to help me, Eduardo would then throw in the race card, saying that because he was Hispanic or Native American, they disapproved and did not like the idea of us. Even when my Hispanic friends stood up for me. Which, now when I look back, I realize that he pulled every type of intimidation or guilt on me to try to make me stay with him and be under his control, and I allowed it as an unwilling participant in the web he was weaving.

At one point Eduardo had told me that I needed to learn how to care for a baby and brought me a tarantula to look after. He knew I had a phobia of spiders after seeing me scream and squirm many times when I would see a spider and tell him that they were one thing that I hated most. Yet, regardless of my phobia or concerns, he got the spider and insisted it be in an aquarium in the room we slept in.

I hated it, I felt as though it was watching me constantly, which just gave me more of the creeps. But I found my solution to the problem when Eduardo's brother's wife informed me that they would be having an exterminator over, and I should not be at the house due to the chemicals. I agreed with her on the fact that the chemicals would be harmful, and I covered the bed with plastic, made sure all drawers were shut, toiletries were put away, but decided instead of covering up the aquarium with the tarantula as Eduardo had instructed I do to keep it safe while they treated the house, I decided that I would leave it open, in hopes that it would accidentally die. I felt like I had a leg up on the game he played with control because when his tarantula died a few days later, I pretended I knew nothing about how that could have happened.

Within a month or so after moving in, I had woken up to what I thought was a miscarriage. It was in the middle of the night, and instead of running to the hospital, I went to my aunt's house. I was only in the first trimester, just a few days away from the second trimester and my aunt was a nurse practitioner. I told her about a large amount of blood I had lost, the bad cramps, and the large clots I saw in the toilet.

After describing everything, she had me call my doctor who explained that due to it being so early in the pregnancy, there was not much to do other than relax and then go see her in the morning. Eduardo drove me to my aunt's house and stayed the night with me, where my aunt had me place several pillows under my legs to help with the bleeding. When the morning came, he drove me to the hospital where my doctor said she would meet me, and instead of going to park and join me, Eduardo left me there. Alone, to deal with whatever came next.

The visit was a dreaded one, I had seen several large clots of blood in the toilet the night before and continued to have horrible cramping that was joined with bleeding, so I was convinced I had had a miscarriage. I had to check-in at the ER, where the triage nurse asked me many questions and then said that my doctor was there waiting for me. And when I went back to see the doctor, they decided to do an ultrasound to see what was going on, that is when they confirmed I had indeed had a miscarriage. In the same sentence, the doctor informed me that there were two sacs in my uterus, one that was empty, appeared smaller than the other sac, and one with a healthy baby still nestled safely inside. As she said this, she turned the screen for me to see, to see this tiny gummy bear-looking thing, bouncing around inside of me. Leaving me in awe of what I was seeing.

The doctor then went on to explain that after getting bloodwork to confirm, she believed that I had been pregnant with twins and lost one of the twins, which can happen as she pointed to the empty sac. Explaining that when it comes to twins in that first trimester, a miscarriage can happen for many reasons, one being that the other embryo had not developed properly.

She went on to do an exam to make sure my cervix was okay and decided that due to the miscarriage of one of the twins, and me just a couple of days from the second trimester, the best thing to do was to put a stitch in just to make sure my cervix remained closed for the remainder of my pregnancy. She called this stitch a Cervical Cerclage and explained it was just a precaution. The setup for the procedure seemed to be simple, and even though the idea sounded scary, it seemed to not take very much time to complete. Once they had completed placing the stitch, the doctor asked if I had someone who could pick me up, because she advised that I stay off my feet for a few days, and warned that I might have some cramping, and spotting for a few days as well. I assured the doctor that I did have someone, that he was just waiting outside for me.

I went to checkout, called, and left Eduardo a message since he did not answer. After grabbing something to drink, I started to the parking lot, and I noticed Eduardo's brother's car with his brother inside waiting outside of the hospital. I went to the car when the brother informed me that Eduardo had asked him to come and pick me up and take me back to the house. I was confused at this, but the brother could not tell me anymore because he said he was confused as well as why Eduardo just left me there.

When we drove up to the brother's house, I noticed there were quite a few people there and that they were having a cookout. Eduardo was there as well, cooking at the grill, and laughing with others who were standing around him. I looked at the brother and asked what was going on, and he explained that they were indeed having a cookout and thought I knew since Eduardo seemed to have arranged it after getting back from dropping me off at the hospital.

I noticed some women there whom I had never seen before. I went to Eduardo and asked him what was going on. Eduardo then asked if I was still pregnant, with no emotion behind the question or any sort of privacy about asking it in front of the people there, and I told him I was but that I needed to talk to him. Eduardo followed me to the bedroom and asked me what was wrong with me. I explained that I had apparently been pregnant with twins and lost one of them but that I had to have a stitch put in place to keep the baby I was still pregnant with, safe. Instead of offering any sort of affection to show compassion, Eduardo scolded me, saying that I lost one of his babies and that somehow it was my fault for being careless. He then ordered me to stay inside.

As he left the room, I stood there, feeling alone, and lost. I could not believe what was happening, the way he was acting, once again changing his mannerisms towards me when others were around. Where he went from being a happy man, excited about becoming a father, insisting I marry him, to not even caring or showing any compassion for the fact that I had lost one of the babies. Instead making me feel as if it was my fault as if I had done something wrong for that to happen. And for me, even though I was unaware I had been pregnant with twins until I lost one, I felt the loss. I was mourning in silence and felt that I had shame in mourning the baby I had lost, that maybe I did somehow cause it to happen. With the shame and heartache, and the feeling of being alone, I did not think of anything else. I did not want others to see my anguish, so I made myself try to forget, numbing my feelings before heading out to sit with, but not try to socialize with, the guests at the house, fearing I might burst into tears.

I did stay inside for most of the party, but as I sat on the couch, I could see a woman standing close to Eduardo. I looked at his brother's wife and asked who that woman was. She shrugged and said she had no idea, that she must have been one of Eduardo's friends. So, I got up and decided I would introduce myself. I did so, thinking, that over the past few months of the relationship we had, I had met all his friends. Ones he worked with, childhood friends, and those who were friends of his family, but had never once seen this woman. She had not been at any other cookouts or gatherings that he and his family had, which were often.

When I walked out to introduce myself, Eduardo stopped me, and then said very loudly for everyone to hear, "What do you think you are doing out here? Do you see any other women out here?"

I looked at him with a look of, "are you serious?" on my face. Then after looking around and seeing a few other women I replied to his ass of a remark. I told him that I did see other women, for one, the woman standing next to him, and a couple of others standing with some of the other guys out there. And I went on to ask who she was, to which he informed me that she was none of my business and that my business was inside with the rest of the wives and girlfriends where I was to stay.

Eduardo then went and handed this woman a beer, turned to me, and again said that I needed to go inside and mind myself there. The brother's wife came out and asked me to come in with her when Eduardo informed her that I needed to go to bed since I was not feeling well. As we walked in, all the women inside stopped talking and stared at me. It was as if they knew. They knew the sadness I was feeling, the confusion I had, and the terror that awaited me as if my fate was set in stone before I had become aware of it, but to where they all knew.

The brother's wife then asked me to walk with her to the room, asking me if I was okay. I told her I was not, and that this was insane, asking why he is acting like that and demanding to know who that woman was. She told me she was sorry; she knew I had been at the doctor's, and her husband had told her what had happened. She said it was best for me and the baby if I just laid down and she would bring me something to drink and a plate once the food was done. Before leaving the room, she turned and said she would also try to find out who that woman is as well.

I spent the rest of the day and night in bed, and once everyone had left, Eduardo came into the room, acting like a fool and with attitude. The first thing he did was try to force me to have sex with him, but once I said that I had a stitch that needed to heal, he stopped. I again asked who that lady was, and he informed me that there was no lady and that I was being stupid. He then grabbed his pants, put them back on, and left. I did not see him until the next day when I was told to not ask questions again and to just keep my opinions to myself.

When the days turned into weeks and I was getting further along in my pregnancy, I noticed that there was no money being saved or put aside for us to move on his part. I brought it up a few times and he would point out that we had our phone bills, car payments, and insurance, so that is why we did not have any money. But I noticed more, where I knew what he made, and saw him buying video games, going to the movies and out to eat regularly, buying himself designer clothing for big and tall men, waiting at Walmart on Monday evenings to be the first to purchase the new movies that were being released. And not one penny being spent of his to buy items for our baby, to help me with my copays on the prenatal care, or help me with anything.

In fact, when it came to the baby or anything that had to do with the baby, he was not supportive at all. He had not been to any appointments or asked for any updates when I did go. That was until it was the appointment to measure the baby and find out the gender. I was surprised that he went, and I was excited to finally find out what I was having, only to be let down once again.

When we went in to do the scan, Eduardo told the tech to not reveal to us what the gender was, that it was to remain a surprise. Which for me, was a shocker since he never once had been to an appointment, showed any interest, nor mentioned that he did not want to know what the baby was. I asked that the tech let me know and said I would not tell him, but he grabbed my arm hard and gave me a stern look, then told the tech that we were going to keep it a surprise.

I felt as if everything was all under his control, and I had no control over anything in my life, which was not just a feeling but a fact. After the appointment he told me what the name of "his" baby would be, I objected to the name, and it seemed that we argued about the name for quite some time. The name he chose was to be Phoenix, a name that I was not keen on, but one I look back and see that it might have been a suitable name knowing what I know now in how things had unfolded. In fact, when it came to the baby's name, all we seemed to do was argue for the most part.

On the days or nights when Eduardo would go out and insist I did not need to know what he was doing, then force himself on me, I felt helpless. I had been violated in so many ways and felt as if I no longer had a voice. "No" was not a word he seemed to recognize, at least when it came to me. I would come up with excuses to keep him from what I now know was raping me, because I did not give him consent. I tried to tell him that I was tired, or that I worried for the baby, but none of that seemed to matter to him. Eduardo was going to do what he wanted to me and when he wanted to me, even if I was fast asleep.

As time went by, and he was not showing any initiative in moving out of his brother's house, or helping with anything baby-related, I knew that I had to do something. I needed to get away, not just to a home where I could raise my baby, but away from him as well, away from the control he had over me. So instead of waiting any longer for Eduardo to show me that he was still wanting to move forward with the baby, a relationship which I was not wanting any longer, or a place to bring the baby home to, I went to my boss and asked for extra shifts at the hospital.

When Eduardo asked me why I was working so much, I went on by telling him that they were shorthanded at my work and needed me to work extra. This extra time I took at work also allowed me to have very little time around Eduardo, which was a relief to me on so many levels. I took any money I had left after paying my bills and saved it away until I was just over halfway through the pregnancy and had enough to get a townhouse and move with.

I gave Eduardo another chance before leaving, I told him 2 weeks before I was initially planning to make the move that he needed to pull his head out of his ass and man up or I was gone. He got incredibly angry at the idea, of not only being told he needed to man up but also being told this by "his woman" as he put it. With that last blow-up, I waited for him to leave for work, packed my things, and stayed with some friends until my townhouse was ready for me to move in.

When I left, I felt liberated and free. I felt all the heaviness in stress and uncertainty leave my thought-filled conscious. In my mind and heart, I was ready to take on the life of being a single mom, I had gone over my finances, got on the list for the childcare I wanted early, continued to put money aside, and I was moving forward without him. That was until a few weeks later, after I had moved into my new place, Eduardo showed up unexpectedly at my townhouse. He said he was just there to talk, saying he could not sleep and that he needed me, that I was his. I told Eduardo we will make custody arrangements when the time came but that I did not want to be with him.

While we talked, I noticed him checking out my little townhome and making remarks on how I did not have a television or real furniture other than my bedroom furniture and some items set up in the nursery. Making fun of the folding chairs I had in the living room area, using milk crates as a table and shelving. Or my computer being out of place in the corner with my desk and chair in an empty dining room. Which I explained was not important, that it was important to be ready for the baby and I did not need anything that I did not already have. He looked at me and snorted, then asked about my dog, and why he was not there with me since I loved him so much. I explained that my dog was at home with my old roommate who had become very attached to him and that he was happy there, so I would let her keep him. He again snorted, looked around my home from the front door, and left.

I had put that confrontation at just that and had anticipated I would not be seeing Eduardo again anytime soon since I showed him that I did not need him nor showed him any emotion that would lead him to second guess my decision. Or at least that is how I had hoped he saw it.

Another week had passed by, and I was continuing to move forward, picking up things here and there for the baby, and getting comfortable living on my own again. Until one morning, when I woke up to a knock at my front door. I walked down the stairs to my door to open it and see a furniture delivery truck outside and a gentleman with a clipboard standing there. He asked me my name and then asked me to sign the delivery form. When I told him he must be mistaken, he once again confirmed my name and said he was there to deliver an order that had been paid for and that was all he knew. He said it would not take but a few minutes and asked me to step aside while they unloaded the truck.

The guys who were helping him, brought in couches, a coffee table with matching side tables, a dining room set, and a new king-sized bedroom suite. As they brought in things and went up and down the stairs, setting up everything, asking me where I wanted it, I just stood there, confused about what was going on, that was until the gentleman handed me a receipt. As the other guys were picking up the pieces of cardboard and plastic that came off everything, I looked at the receipt and I saw whose name was on it. The moment I saw the name I demanded they take everything back and do so right away. The gentleman said he would but that he would need for me to pay the pickup fees, and I could do that by going to their store and make arrangements to have everything picked up.

I continued to argue with this man, and as I did, I looked up to see Eduardo walking up to my townhouse with flowers, candy, a huge stuffed animal, and a smile on his face. I was shocked. The man who had delivered the furniture walked back to his truck then drove off, leaving me with Eduardo kneeling on one knee as he handed me everything in his arms, and pulled out a small box with a ring inside of it. Eduardo then went on with saying that he knew that he has been difficult and realized that he was being selfish in not helping, but had I just waited, he had the money and was planning on getting a place for us to live in.

I told him I was not going to wait, and the baby would come regardless as well, and that the baby needed a home to come to. I explained that his brother and his brother's wife had their own kids, and I was not going to bring a baby home to someone else's home. That is when Eduardo said he agreed, and he was surprised that I was able to move and get my own place but now that I had it, and he had furnished it, we could move forward with plans of being a family. With that being said, I felt dread coming over me, and as that occurred, he placed the ring on my finger and told me words that haunted me for quite some time, "you are mine, and there is nothing you can do to change that because we are forever bonded with the baby you are carrying."

Living a Lie

The days seemed to blend together. I was not feeling like myself I felt as though I was a spectator, watching my life that was not my own from the outside, knowing that I had to find a way out and soon.

After the proposal and the surprise furniture delivery, I found myself being forced into something that I was not wanting. Eduardo moved in, without asking me or discussing the situation with me, or even getting a "yes" to his proposal of marriage. I had woken up the day after the furniture was delivered to my doorbell being rung. When I opened it, Eduardo walked in without asking and had several of his cousins following him with his things in the boxes they were carrying. No questions, just helping themselves to MY house, MY home. I did wonder if Eduardo's cousins knew that I had not invited him to stay or even move in and that I had not even given him an answer to the proposal. All while they assisted him, most likely wondering why I had a look of both anger and confusion on my face and was questioning Eduardo with no response from him.

Within minutes of Eduardo's arrival, he was acting as if he lived there all along, making plans for a cookout later in the week with his family, a housewarming party. Taking his shoes off, unpacked his things, and invited a couple of his cousins to stay and watch a game on the television he had brought with him, without even acknowledging my presence, or seeing the state of shock on my face at what had happened in less than 24 hours. Instead, Eduardo ordered me to the kitchen to get some sweet tea for him and his guests, along with something to snack on, then ordered me to go back upstairs and change out of my pajamas.

To say I was in a state of shock was an understatement. I was confused, angry, upset for not being heard during the whole scene that was unfolding, and felt helpless. A feeling that I was even angrier to feel, knowing that I was the one to get the house, move, and do it all for my unborn baby when he refused. Why would he move in when he was perfectly content living with his brother, and why would a person think it is okay to just move in with someone, without ever being asked to do so.

I had not even a moment to gather my thoughts on everything that was happening, it was like my life was being taken over and I had no say in it. As I went upstairs to change out of my pajamas, I noticed that Eduardo had already put his clothes in the dresser he had delivered. He had his shoes in the closet, there were clothes that were Eduardo's hanging up as well. The bathroom had his toothbrush already unpacked and sitting in the holder as if it had been there all along, all the things that he and his family brought in just less than an hour prior, were unpacked and in their places. I had never seen such an event unfold, nor imagined such a thing before this. I sat on the bed, looking around at everything, realizing that he was taking over, and Eduardo knew that I was scared of him and thought that there was nothing I would do to stop him.

I decided to take a shower to gather my thoughts. As I stood there, watching the water roll off my belly that had my unborn baby inside, I began to think about everything that had happened in less than a year. I thought about the stalking he subjected me to over the past year if not longer. I thought about his selfish behavior, how he was trying to control me again, and how I nearly felt as if I was defeated. Then I thought about my baby, about what he had said about giving the baby the family it deserves, with both parents in the same home. How this was not only right for the baby but also what he had me thinking that my family wanted as well. I weighed out the pros and cons and thought about the things he had said about "me being his" and how we were bonded for life. I went back and forth on what I wanted to do vs what I thought was the right thing to do, knowing that Eduardo had not given me much choice when it came to my life or the life of our baby, and trying to come up with a solution that I could see as a solution.

As I got out of the shower and got dressed, I walked over to the nursery, where I had the crib, bassinet, swing, rocker, and dresser all set up. I sat in the rocker and stared at my bedroom across the hall, and saw my old bedroom furniture sitting, nicely stacked between the two rooms. And that is when I had come to a decision, something I had thought might work for all of us.

I began dragging the bedframe, mattress, and box springs into the nursery. I moved the crib over just slightly to where I could make enough room for my bed. I then set the bed up, went back and dragged my old dresser into the room as well, and went to my bedroom and began taking all my things out of the closet and placing them in the nursery closet. After I got the final pieces of my things from my bedroom, I once again sat in the rocking chair, contemplating the future, and how this could work.

I fell asleep in the rocker, and after about an hour, Eduardo came up the stairs to check on me. He asked me what I was doing and informed me that his cousins had left but would be back later. I told Eduardo that I had made a decision, and for him to please listen to what I had to say. I explained how I never told him he could move in, that I never said I would marry him, or that I even wanted all this furniture or his things at my house. I went on and explained how I moved the furniture to the nursery for me to use, and if he was going to be there, it was just for the baby, and we were not a couple. That we could live as roommates, caring for our child.

After I had told him what I had decided on, Eduardo then laughed and said there was no way in hell that he was going to live here and not have his wife living as his wife under the same roof, that I was just hormonal and acting crazy. He then went on and said that first off, I would not be sleeping in a separate bed from him, that I was his and I was not to defy him. Second, because I was his, I would do and say as he pleased, starting with showing him some respect both in front of guests as well as when it is just the two of us. That I needed to grow up, stop being a foolish girl, and understand I was to do everything that was expected of me as a wife and soon-to-be mother. He went on and said he would soon teach me the lessons I needed to learn, but until then, I was to obey him or else I would have to face consequences, and my ideology was very childish and selfish, not thinking about "our" baby in any of my decisions.

I was once again in a state of shock, thinking how this is even happening? I mean, I never agreed to anything, but in Eduardo's mind and way of thinking, my opinion or thoughts were to be taken with a grain of salt. Leaving me to have to follow along with this plan. But I knew I had rights. Later that evening the cousins showed up with food, we all ate, and after they left, we went to bed. Eduardo warned me to either sleep in the bed with him or else I would regret it later. I did not argue, I lay in the bed, not being able to sleep, but anticipating the morning to come to where I could figure out what to do next.

When morning came, he got up and left for work, leaving me home alone. The moment he left, I got dressed and then walked over to the management office for the townhomes. I asked the manager what I could do to make him leave, and she went to pull my file. She then asked me a few questions, asking me his name and information. As I told her, she seemed to have a look of confusion on her face and handed me my file, showing that he was on my rental agreement, and asked if that was my signature at the bottom of the page next to his. I told her it was, but that I never added him to the rental agreement and that he just moved in the day prior. She then pointed out the date on the paperwork and it showed the day I had indeed signed the paperwork. I tried to tell her he was not there; he was never there with me and that I never agreed to let him live there. She went on and explained that I would have to go through the process of having him evicted, but that it has him marked as my spouse, and I would most likely have to go through the courts which could take time.

I was once again in a state of shock. How could this be happening, how did he do this, what is happening here? Then as I left the office, I passed by the maintenance office, to see some familiar faces, two of which were Eduardo's cousins and one who was a friend that had been at the cookout at his brother's; the day I had told him I was pregnant. I realized at that moment I was right in my feelings thinking I was being followed, Eduardo had eyes on me, he may not have been physically following me, but he had others do his bidding. I went back to the office and tried to talk to the manager again, and she informed me that I would need to go through the courts because my signature was on the papers and there was nothing more she could do for me. Before I left the office, I asked if I could get a copy of the rental agreement, which she did, and I took it back home to read over and over again.

When I got back to my townhome, I called one of my friends and told her everything, which she agreed was insanity and asked me what I was going to do. I did not have an answer, other than I was going to confront Eduardo and demand he leave. She warned me to be careful and asked if I wanted to come and stay with her. I found the invitation tempting, but that was MY house, not Eduardo's and I was not going to give it up to him. She said she understood but wanted me to call if I needed anything.

The day seemed to go by much slower than the past two which seemed to sort of blend together in one messy splatter of drama that was unfolding. That afternoon, I found myself exhausted and went to lie down since I did not sleep well the night before. When I woke up, it was dark out and I could smell food cooking in my kitchen. I knew Eduardo was home, and I knew that I needed to confront him. So, I grabbed the copies of the rental agreement, and walked down the stairs, gathering my courage as I took each step.

I walked to the kitchen, hearing Eduardo singing to the Tejano music he had playing on the radio, and seeing him cook 2 very large steaks, some steamed vegetables, and baked potatoes that he was pulling out of the oven. He looked over to see me standing there, and asked me to go sit at the table, which he had set with a fresh bouquet, candles that were lit, and juice in a glass for me. I told him I needed to speak with him, and he once again directed me to the dining room, saying that he will bring my plate to me.

Within just a couple of minutes, he came out of the kitchen with both mine and his plates filled with food in his hands. He said that I needed to eat more red meat for both me and the baby and that he was going to make sure we were both healthy. Before taking a bite, I pulled out the rental agreement and asked him to please explain why his signature is on there. Eduardo then said that he wanted to see it, so I handed it over. He threw the papers in the air and laughed, saying there is not a thing I could do about it; those papers were legal as far as any court will see it and to just forget about it and move past it. That he needed me to know that I could never escape him, and as long as I listened to him, everything would be okay, but that once I had the baby, anytime I disobeyed him I would have consequences. He then came over to my plate, began cutting my steak, and fed me a bite telling me how good it was and to eat up because his baby was hungry. I grabbed my fork and ate the dinner he had prepared, all while watching him very closely, feeling sickened by everything about him. His look, his mannerisms, his voice, it all made me sick.

After we had finished eating, he went to grab his jacket and keys and told me he had to help his cousin with some things and would be back later. I did not care what it was he had to do, as long as he was not at the house, I felt safe. I read for a little bit, took a shower then went to bed.

A few hours after falling asleep my phone rang. To my surprise, it was my cousin calling me at just past midnight. I looked over and noticed that Eduardo was not home. That is when my cousin went on to ask me if I knew where Eduardo was? I told her that he said he would be at his cousin's helping him with something but that was all I knew. She then went on to describe a man and asked if that was Eduardo's cousin. I said that it sounded like him, and she then laughed. She said that she was at a sex toy store with her boyfriend, and Eduardo was there with his cousin and 2 women, one of which was hanging on to Eduardo as they walked up and down the isles, looking at the videos and various products in the shop together as if they were a couple.

I asked my cousin if she was sure about this, and she said that it was Eduardo. She was sure due to the fact that when Eduardo saw her, he quickly went down another aisle away from her and that her boyfriend pointed out that it was Eduardo as well. I thanked my cousin, for letting me know and I got up, put some slippers on, got in the car, and drove to Eduardo's cousin's house.

When I drove up, Eduardo's truck was not there, in fact, no one was there, so I decided to call him. He did not answer. After trying to call from my cell phone a few times, I decided to look for a payphone and try to call from there, and he answered the call. The moment he realized it was me, he hung up. With that, I decided to drive out to this sex toy store and confront him. On my way there, I passed his truck, and I turned around to follow. I am fairly sure he knew I was following because Eduardo then sped up and I lost him.

I went back to my house and sat at the table, laughing. I could not believe what was happening and wanted him gone. I mean; the whole proposal, the moving in, making himself at home in my house, and telling me what was expected of me, to this in just the matter of a few days? It was all insane. I was feeling that this was the way to get rid of him, that he would surely leave knowing he had been caught, or at least I had hoped he would leave.

Within the hour, Eduardo came back to my house. Angry with me and asking me why I was awake. I then went on to tell him about an interesting phone call from my cousin, and how I went to his cousin's house where he said he was, but no one was there. I told him I tried calling but he did not answer until I called from a payphone to which he hung up on me from. I told Eduardo to pack his shit and get out and never come back.

He then laughed at me and said that he did see my cousin, but she was mistaken. That he was at his cousin's house, and he was going to come home but the cousin asked if he would go with him to the sex toy store. Eduardo explained that it was late, and he did not want to wake me, so he took his cousin to the store and planned on coming home right after. However, when they arrived, the cousin's girlfriend was there and that is the woman who my cousin saw, but she was mistaken because the woman was all over the cousin and not him. He claimed that he tried to say "hi" to my cousin, but my cousin and her boyfriend quickly went out to the parking lot, most likely to call me and make things sound so much worse than they actually were. He swore this was the truth, even had crocodile tears saying that I was his life and that he did not want anyone else, and my cousin is just trying to cause trouble between us because my family cannot stand that he is Hispanic.

He then went up the stairs, as I sat, looking at everything, in disbelief of all that had transpired. Thinking how does any of this make sense? And knowing deep down, that this entire situation was insane and that if I stayed with him, I was living a lie in more than one way.

A week had passed by since that incident at the sex toy shop, and Eduardo went on pretending as if nothing had happened. I still had questions but was working more so I could save money for when the baby came. At the end of the week, Eduardo told me that he wanted to go and see a movie with me and that he wanted to invite his cousin to come along as well. I thought that this was a good idea, allowing us to get out and go on a much-needed date after what all had transpired. So I agreed to go.

When we arrived at the theater, the cousin showed up with his girlfriend. We all walked up to the box office and the guys said that they wanted to see an action movie. The girlfriend and I cringed at the same time, and the cousin suggested we go and see a different movie together that started just after their movie would start, so we agreed and went to see separate movies.

The movie that the cousin's girlfriend and I went to see was not as long of a movie as the one the guys went to see, and we were done about 30 minutes before they were. So, we decided to sit and wait in the lobby for the guys to get out. As we sat there, I felt that I had to just ask this lady about that night the week before, just to ease my mind. We began to talk and when I brought up the adult toy store, she turned red, grabbed the cross that she was wearing on her neck, then told me that she would not dare go to such a place, but she did know who was with Eduardo that night, and she was not supposed to tell me. I insisted she tell me, that I would tell Eduardo that I figured it out. She then went on to explain that she had met this other woman a few times, that Eduardo was seeing her on the side, and that this other woman knew about me. She said her name and told me she worked at the Walmart, the same one Eduardo went to every Monday evening to buy new movies from and where he bought all his video games from. That this Walmart was the one on the other side of town, which is quite a way out of his way, to go to for anything, and that the lady he was seeing was the video store manager there.

After she had told me all of this, we saw the guys coming out of their movie, I thanked her, and we parted ways. I was silent the entire ride home, I had so much I wanted to say to Eduardo but wanted to wait until we got home so I could kick his ass out. When we arrived, Eduardo asked me why I was so quiet, I then told him that he was a sorry piece of shit who needed to pack his things and leave, then walked to the nursery and locked the door behind me. He began banging on the door, demanding I tell him what was going on. I ignored the yelling and began to get ready for bed. He then broke down the door to the nursery, which scared me.

That is when I told him I knew everything, that he was cheating on me, and asked why he would work so hard to try to get me to be with him if he had someone else. Eduardo then said I was crazy, that I need to stop listening to everyone else because they just want to break us up, our family up, because they are all jealous. He told me I was imagining everything, that this girl did not exist. He went on and insisted that there was no one else and that I was not thinking straight due to the hormones. By this time, I was tired, so I told him that I was going to sleep in the nursery that night and we would talk later.

When I got up the next morning, Eduardo had already left for work that day. I kept thinking of everything that had happened, knowing deep down I was right on everything. As I sat there and stewed over everything, I decided to go online and look up some things. That is when I came across sites that had online chatrooms and forums. I saw an online community of women, who were there supporting one another, not even knowing one another in real life, but talking about real-life situations.

There were many questions about pregnancy and even relationships on there, comments that I could relate to and for the first time in months, I felt like I could talk to someone and just put it all out there. When I posted my first comment, I found that within minutes I had responses. So many great comments, giving advice and showing understanding. I had not put it all out there just yet, in fact, I just went on and opened a discussion on miscarriage or what some referred to it as "disappearing twin syndrome". I had responses from those who had similar experiences, all within the first trimester as well. I went on asking about the stitch I had placed on my cervix after losing one of two babies and asked if anyone else had something similar they had experienced, which only a couple of ladies claimed they had.

I then saw discussions on strange cravings, weight gain, mood swings and so much more. I had found the outlet I needed, and a community of women who seemed to understand and could relate to everything I was going through, minus the drama that had unfolded in my relationship. That was until I came across a thread on a chatroom, on birth control failing, and some women doing it on purpose to some who did not know why it happened. I started slowly in joining the conversations in this chatroom, testing the waters. I mean until then, I had never really explored the world of the online communities that were out there. I had heard about forums, had friends who were on some, shoot, even Eduardo was in various chatrooms for gamers and one for movie lovers. As the day went on, I began to share more and more, not going into details just yet, but sharing little tidbits here and there.

By that evening, I felt so good. I had let out so much in just typing what I had questions on, sharing experiences with others as well as offering support to those who shared as well. I found a community that would become more than just online support, but with some, lifetime friends later down the road.

Throughout the next few weeks, during my free time, I spent it writing on various chatrooms, and reading threads I came across that were relevant. Then one day, I had a woman on one of the threads who said she had seen me on other threads ask me if I had Yahoo Messenger. I did but had not used it yet and decided to start using that as well for more personal chats between the ladies I became virtual friends with. The thing was, at the time, I and the baby daddy shared a computer and when I went to open the chat up, I noticed Eduardo had his chat saved on the computer. I left it alone, that was until I got to talking to one of the new friends and told her some of what I had been going through. That is when she said to open the chat and see if there is anything there. So, I did, and within the first few seconds, I found the lady he was seeing but that he denied seeing there.

They had quite a bit of chat on there, in fact, Eduardo was chatting with her earlier that day while he was at work. Their chats were very intimate, and in one I noticed that she had asked about me. Eduardo told her that I was some crazy clingy chick that was pregnant after a one-night stand, and he was only there until I had the baby then he was taking the baby away from me because I was unstable and could not even take care of myself. Eduardo told her numerous times he loved her and that once the baby was born, they would be together and raise MY baby as their own.

He also went on to say that he insisted I sleep in my own bed, that I was a sex-crazed crazy woman and he had to be careful when he slept because I would do stuff to him, but no matter how much Eduardo tried to call it off with me, I just did not get the picture. He claimed that I begged to live with him after he moved out of his brother's and got his own place to prepare for the baby and agreed to live as roommates, but because I was pregnant, he did not want to upset me because I had a temper.

I FELT SICK! I mean what was I reading??? This was insane, and to top it all off, everything Eduardo told her was a lie, so I know that everything he told me was also a lie. I told the online friend by copying and pasting their conversations, and she was in just as much shock as I was. I then called one of my friends to come by to show her, because I needed others to see that I was not crazy as he seemed to be portraying to others. I felt like there was another angle to all of this. All of his crazy antics, the things he did and said, and even more so, I worried about what he could possibly do to me and the baby once I delivered. He was making plans with this woman, the woman he told me did not exist, and I knew I had to protect my baby and myself. Knowing that he was not as predictable as I had once thought he was, and instead, he was very calculated and there was a lot more to this than we were seeing.

The online friend asked to call me, so when my other friend showed up, we put her on speaker and talked. I told both friends everything, from the birth control pills to him moving in after I left, which my friend could agree with since she witnessed a lot of the craziness without knowing all the details. She said that everything made sense in a very twisted way, after I filled in the blanks for her, she saw the big picture and both women were scared for me and my unborn baby. We discussed various scenarios, none of which ended well for me. We had talked about stories and movies that we had read or watched, which had crazy twists and turns, and always seemed to go wrong in some way. Leaving us to all know that this was not a good place for me to be and that I was not safe. They both suggested I call my parents and see about getting far away from there to get away from him, so I did. My friend left and after I hung up the phone with my online friend, I called my parents.

When I told my mom what was going on, she told me that she knows I am stressed, and that pregnancy can cause women to act out of sorts, but that it was all in my head. That apparently Eduardo had been calling to talk to her regularly about me, and how Eduardo was worried about my mental health and the baby. He had voiced concern on many occasions, and when I had moved out into my place, he was scared that I might hurt myself or the baby after it came since I had terminated a previous pregnancy. He told my mom that I was very childish in many ways, but that Eduardo was going to take care of me and the baby and keep her in the loop if any concerns arise. Leaving me in a state of shock to know that he had said all of this, that my mom had never asked me about these concerns until now, and that she believed him, leaving me to feel alone and having the feeling that if I did leave, he would somehow turn it around on me. After that call, I felt perplexed and sick, and I did not know what I would do since my idea of going to my parents' house, was no longer an option.

I went back on the chat and talked to the friend, told her what my mom had said, and she said it was like I had said in our prior conversation when my friend had come over to talk with us, that I am living a horror flick of sorts. I got off the chat and sat there, staring at all the messages between Eduardo and that other woman. Thinking, how can she honestly believe all this crap, and how could anyone believe any of it that he was spewing? I then decided that since I needed to go to the store, I would drive across town to the Walmart that the other lady worked at and confront her. Tell her the truth about everything and ask her to help me leave him. Which, on the drive over, I had come up with a scenario on how things would go, what I would say, and how we would handle the situation after putting the truth out there.

When I arrived at the Walmart, I found it a lot harder than I thought on the drive, to just go in and confront this woman. I delayed the action, I walked around the store for what seemed like an eternity, buying more than I had gone there for, and trying to get the courage to walk into that little video store and talk to this woman. After I had checked out, I walked my cart to the video store, I stood at the door for a few seconds and spotted her talking to a customer. It was the same lady from the cookout months back when I had lost one of the babies. And seeing her, I could feel a lump in my throat, a feeling of anxiety, anger, and being scared all at the same time. I did not want to make a scene, so I walked my cart out to my car and unloaded it, then after I returned the cart, I walked into the store and began pretending like I was looking for a movie. I heard her talking to another customer, then when that person left, I looked up and our eyes locked. She knew I was there, and I knew it was now or never, so I walked to the counter and introduced myself.

She looked at me with a scared look in her eyes and said that she knew who I was but did not know why I was at her store. I explained that we needed to talk, that I came across some things and I know Eduardo had been dishonest with both of us. She asked me to tell her what it is that I came across, and that is when I told her that I had been chatting in some online forums, and Eduardo and I shared a computer. During one of the chats, a friend wanted to chat on messenger, and when I went to open my messenger, his chat log with her came up.

She had a confused look in her eyes, and I continued to explain that I shared their chat with my friends, who had been witnesses to the madness I was going through with him. That I had left him at his brother's house, and how he moved into MY house after I left him, proposed to me numerous times, gave me a ring, and swore that she did not even exist. She then looked at me and asked what I wanted her help with? I told her that I wanted to confront him with her and make him be honest with both of us, and after that, I would have nothing more to do with him, so she could do with him as she pleased. She agreed to a meet-up, and we exchanged numbers before I left the store to make plans.

Cheater Cheater

A week after that confrontation, I received a phone call from a man. The man claimed to be the other woman's husband and he wanted to know if I knew "they", being his wife and Eduardo, were seeing one another. He told me he got my number from a piece of paper that she had left on the counter and when he saw my name, he was fairly sure he knew who I was. I told him that I did know. He went on and told me that he and his wife had 3 kids, had been together since they were in high school and that he loved her dearly. I felt bad for this man on the other line, who was crying and obviously heartbroken, as he must have just found out about the affair behind his back. I let him know that I had been aware of it only just recently as well, but I had my suspicions in the months prior. I told him I was sorry for him, but that I had to deal with my side of this mess, and I wished him luck.

The next day I called the woman up, I told her about her husband calling and she said he had found out about the affair from a friend who had seen Eduardo and her together at a bar. I told her we could meet up with Eduardo the next day. That I would tell him about the new restaurant I wanted to try and once we got a table, she could come and join us, so we could confront Eduardo. She said she liked the idea and agreed to meet up.

When Eduardo and I arrived at the restaurant, I felt ready to have this confrontation and get this whole mess over with once and for all. I was excited to see his lying, cool mannered ass, squirm as the two women in his life, who he lied to, told him that they knew everything. We had been seated right away after arriving, and as our drinks were brought to the table, I saw the woman come in. I looked up and she saw me, then walked to the table. When she got to the table, I told Eduardo, "Oh you would not mind if she joined us for dinner would you?"

The look of utter fear in his eyes at that moment was priceless. He stuttered, got fidgety, and then looked at me and asked what was going on. I told him, "Oh, you know, since you two are planning on taking my baby after it is born, and since we are not together, thought we should talk about everything, and have you answer our questions."

He right away said that he never said any of that, and why would I say we were not together, in the same sentence he had an oops moment, and looked at her, and said, "What I meant was…" The thing was, I had printed out the conversations they had on messenger, and I gave both of them a copy, then asked him to complete what he was saying.

He looked at the papers, then claimed that he did not say any of this, that I was crazy. And I pointed out, "like the crazy you said I was in that chat? Or like the crazy, you keep calling my mom about that I had no idea of until she told me. Letting me know that you called her regularly, concerned about my mental health."

He stared at me, and all I could see were the beads of sweat coming down his forehead. I showed Eduardo the ring he gave me and said that he could keep it, that I would never marry him, and that he needed to get out of my house. I looked up at the other woman and saw the shock in her eyes as they welled up with tears. I let him know that now that I have said what I had to say, and I asked her if she had anything to add. She said she did, then she looked at him and began asking him why? Why did he say this or say that? Why he had asked her to leave her husband and that she had told her husband about the affair a few days ago.

Eduardo then looked at her, looked at me, then told her that she meant nothing to him and got up from the table and walked out of the restaurant. She got up as soon as he walked out, and I decided to pay for the drinks we bought and left. When I got out to the parking lot, Eduardo was waiting for me in the truck, while she was at his rolled-up window screaming at him and crying. I stood back and let her get it all out, then when Eduardo saw me, he backed up the truck and demanded that I got in. I refused and told him I would get a ride, and that he better not be at MY house when I get there. He sped off and the woman then offered me a ride to my house.

We did not talk on the way there, but when she dropped me off, she told me that she was sorry and that I would not have to worry about her being in our lives ever again. I hugged her then got out and walked up to my front door.

To my surprise, Eduardo was not there and had not been there to get his things as of yet. So instead of waiting for him, I decided to start packing his things up and threw each box and bag to the bottom of the stairs as I filled them, feeling better and better with each one I filled up!

A few days had passed by, I had placed Eduardo's things outside the front door with a note saying that he needed to get a moving truck and make arrangements to have the furniture taken out of my house. I had not heard from Eduardo, which was a relief for me. It gave me time to have the locks in the house changed, the door he broke in the nursery fixed, and to once again plan on the arrival of my baby that I would be raising on my own.

I turned back to those online forums, going from the discussions of pregnancy to discussions on being a single mom, on cheating exes, and sharing stories with the other women on there. I enjoyed reading the comments from what I would post, replying to them, also reading other threads, and leaving comments on those discussions as well. I found it as a nice outlet at the end of the day, where I could talk about my concerns when it came to childbirth, my fears behind it all, and not only get advice to help ease those fears from moms who had been there, but also show that other moms were not alone when it came to those fears and concerns as well.

I felt as if things were coming together, and I was getting excited to finally get closer to the B-Day I was anticipating. That was until I got a phone call. It was Eduardo and he wanted to talk to me. I told him he could talk over the phone, but he said that he needed to talk face to face. I told him that his things were outside, and he said he knew this and had already picked up some of the items but wanted to come over to talk. I told him that I did not feel comfortable with him coming to my house, that we could meet somewhere in public, and he agreed.

I told him to meet me at the park that just happened to be across from the hospital I worked at. When Eduardo arrived, he had brought his cousin and one of his nieces along. The cousin and niece went and played at the park as we sat at a table to "talk". He told me he missed me, that he was sorry. He then asked me why I did what I did as if he had no idea why I would have a confrontation and include the other woman in our personal life.

With that, I stood up and explained to Eduardo that if he does not know why then we were done talking, that I could not deal with him trying to turn the tables on me again. Eduardo grabbed my hand, stood up, and embraced me. He then tried kissing me, and dropped to his knees, crying, begging me to forgive him. Saying he would change, that he wanted us to be a family and he never meant for things to get that far with the other woman. That he made a mistake and was sorry.

I looked at this grown man, crying at my feet, begging me to forgive him. I then explained that I did not want to talk to him about anything other than getting his stuff out of my place, and what we will do once the baby comes. He then cried more, begging that I forgive him and give him another chance. He said I could keep the furniture, that the baby needed a nice home to come to. That I was right when it came to having a home for it to come to once it is born, and that I was going to be an amazing mom. I told him I had to go but we would try to talk again another time.

The next morning, I woke up to a knock at my door, it was Eduardo, and he had a box of my favorite donuts and juice in his hands. He handed everything to me, then grabbed the last box on the porch, kissed me on the cheek, and told me to have a good day. That night at work, Eduardo showed up with take-out for dinner. He dropped it at the front desk and left. The bringing of breakfast and dinner to me every day continued into the following week. Where he would just show up with breakfast and juice, leave then do the same at my work, leaving me dinner at the front desk.

I found the suggestion was one that was a little too late, but some of my coworkers who had no idea what all had been going on, said that I was lucky and that "he" was very sweet. The idea of calling him sweet made me sick because I knew different, I knew he was anything but sweet.

Time continued to pass, and I was getting closer and closer to the end of my pregnancy. I had enjoyed being able to finally relax and not have to worry about Eduardo stressing me out. He continued to bring me breakfast every morning and began leaving notes with the food, or messages on my phone, hoping that I had a good day and had sweet dreams.

For the most part, once I got past the all-day sickness I had early on in the pregnancy, I had had a pretty by-the-book pregnancy. Some heartburn and a stuffy nose, but nothing to worry about, other than the extra pounds I had put on which probably had to do with all the donuts I ate, that was until I was at work one day. I had been working extra shifts, taking on as much as I could so that I could put plenty of money aside for when the baby came. I was putting away some patient records when I felt a sharp pain in my lower back. The pain caught me off guard, stopping me in my tracks. It lasted for a few seconds then subsided. I went on about my work thinking it was just a freak pain when it happened again, then a few minutes later it happened again.

My boss, the charge nurse for the unit I was on, had been watching me and had begun timing me as I was in the back putting away files. She then walked over to me and asked me to sit down so she could check my blood pressure since I had turned red in the face and my feet and ankles were very noticeably swollen. She wrote down the blood pressure, squeezed my ankle, handed me a bottle of water then asked me my doctor's name. I told her and she right away went to the phone and called her office. Within a few minutes, the pains continued and one of the security guards came in with a wheelchair to take me across the street to the main hospital to the labor and delivery where my doctor was waiting for me.

As I was headed across the street, my friend, one I had shared a lot of the drama that had occurred, saw me and said she would call my parents for me. I thanked her and told her to tell them that I do not know what is going on just yet but to let them know I was being taken to labor and delivery. When we got off the elevator to L&D, I saw my doctor at the nurse's station, she told the security guard to take me to the room just across the hall and asked the nurse to have me put on a gown and check my vitals again.

At this point, I had not seen the results of my vitals since my charge nurse had written them down and called my doctor right away. So, when I looked up and saw the blood pressure results of 186/102, I knew why I was taken to a room right away. The pains continued to come and go, and as we watched the machine, the nurse left with concern on her face. The doctor came in and looked at the contraction monitor, then asked me when I felt the baby move last. I told her that I was sure it had moved around when I had lunch. She then ordered a stress test to be done right away and had me pee in a cup, asking that they put it as a STAT order and test it for excess protein in the urine.

I had many friends and some family who worked in the main hospital, and that day one of my friends happened to be working on the L&D floor. The doctor asked if she could take me down to the imaging lab and handed her a list of orders that she had written. On the way down my friend explained that they were worried I had preeclampsia and that the baby was not tracking well either, so that I was going to have an ultrasound done and that they were going to put me on a monitor that is designed to track the baby for an extended time, called a stress test.

The tech in the imaging lab who was in charge of the ultrasound was there waiting for me. She helped me on the table and began the ultrasound right away. The moment I heard the heartbeat that was my baby's, I felt a sigh of relief. I then noticed that she was measuring the baby as well, and that is when I saw it. I asked the tech if that was a girl part that I was seeing? She zoomed in and confirmed that yes, it was indeed a baby girl in there. At that moment, I felt so much love and excitement come over me. I mean, I was in love with the baby I was carrying, but now, I finally knew that she was a girl, and I knew even after Eduardo had denied me that right.

After the ultrasound was done, the tech took me to another room and hooked up some leads to me then explained that I would need to try and stay as still as possible for the next couple of hours so that they could monitor the baby. I agreed, I mean, I was still in a state of euphoria finally knowing what I was having and daydreaming of the baby girl I was carrying.

As I lay there watching the machines and excited to run to the store and pick up as many dresses and pink things as I could, Eduardo walked in. The moment I saw him, that euphoria I felt, quickly turned into dread. I asked him what he was doing there, and he said that the nurse called him since I still had him down as the emergency contact. I did not know what to say. I knew I needed to stay calm and allow the test to complete, but I did not want him there, the man who had not shown much concern prior, being there, pretending to be the concerned father.

I told him that I needed to be quiet, due to the testing, and so we sat there in silence until the nurse came in to unhook everything and take the tests to the doctor. A few minutes after the nurse left the room the doctor came in. She explained that the contractions seemed to have stopped, and when they checked my cervix last, I was still at a 0 and the stitch was still in place. She then went on and explained the blood pressure concern along with the swelling and slowed movement of the baby, but said that at this time, she could not be certain if I had preeclampsia, and had a room set up for me to do testing from.

When we got to the room, there was a big orange jug in a tub of ice. The nurse explained that I needed to fill that jug, along with 2 more, with urine, so they could get results that were clearer on if I had preeclampsia. She said that this can take a day or more depending on how fast I can fill up the jugs with urine, but that once they had the pee they would have results pretty quickly. She then looked at Eduardo and said that they were setting up a family room for us, so he might want to run home, grab a few things then stay up at the hospital with me. When she said that, I tried to stop her from saying more, I said that we were not together when he stopped me and said that he would run to my house, pack a bag then come back to care for me, and with that, he left.

I was being over-run, again! He had once again, spoken too fast for me to process what the heck was going on and about 45 minutes later, he showed up with my bag, a pillow, and some movies to watch. Eduardo then said that he talked to my mom and gave her the room number and told her that he would keep her updated. I looked at him and told him he didn't need to stay with me, that I had a friend who would be checking on me later after she got off work. He seemed to not listen to what I said because he then grabbed the menu and asked me what I would like to snack on, and went to fill up my cup with water, encouraging me to drink up and keep drinking so I can fill up all those jugs.

My mom called and asked if I was okay. I told her I was, that I was just tired, and she told me to relax and that Eduardo was there to take care of me, to let him since he was trying hard. She then said that she would check in on me again the next day, but to relax and get some rest. That call made me uneasy but at the same time, I was too tired to argue or protest the issue due to the meds I was given to help lower my blood pressure and help with the severe stuffy nose I had.

Later that day, my friend showed up after she got off work. When she walked in, she was surprised to see Eduardo there. She came to the bed I was in and asked me if I was okay. I told her I was, told her about the blood pressure spiking up, the stress test, then without even thinking twice I felt an urge of excitement and told her, "Oh yeah, guess what?"

She looked at me and sort of smiled asking me what it was I was excited about. That is when I blurted out that I was having a girl!! I explained that they did an ultrasound to make sure the baby was okay and that I noticed a girl part, and the tech confirmed that the baby was a girl!

At this point, I had forgotten that Eduardo was in the room, which was until I looked over and saw the look on his face. He was upset that I had ruined the surprise, but I did not care. He got up and left the room saying he was going to the cafeteria to see what they had for dinner. When Eduardo left the room, I laughed and then told my friend that he did not know and had said that he did not want to know what we were having. She then laughed along with me, as we both giggled saying "oops!"

She asked me if she needed to stay in the room with me and if I was going to be okay with "him" there? I told her that I had still not forgiven him for anything he had done. That I did not even ask him to come up to the hospital but that I had him down as my emergency contact, so my doctor had told him I was there. I explained that he was nothing but a piece of dog poo in my book, nothing but a cheater and a liar. She hugged me and told me that she would come by before her shift in the morning and for me to call her if I needed anything.

Shortly after she left the room, Eduardo came back with a large tray filled with food. The smell was not all that appetizing and just made me sick. The nurse came in a little bit later with my tray, which was a bit more bearable than what Eduardo had got. After eating, I rolled over and went to sleep, avoiding any eye contact or conversation with him.

Throughout the night, I got up to pee quite often, drinking lots of water in between so that I could fill up those jugs quickly. And by morning, I had all, but one jug left to fill, making me feel better that I would be able to go home soon and get away from Eduardo. My friend came by with one of my favorite donuts. She had one for herself as well and as we ate, Eduardo got up and went to get himself something to eat. We laughed when he left and then I told her that I just had one more jug to fill. She told me she had to get to work, but that if I was still here at lunch, she would stop by, otherwise she would come by my house after work.

After lunch, I had finally filled up that last jug. The nurse sent the jugs over to the lab and said that because it was a STAT order, we should have results pretty soon, around the time my doctor does her rounds. She said it was okay to take a shower and get dressed for now, so I took her up on that and enjoyed a nice warm shower.

When I got out of the shower, Eduardo was in the room, on the phone with his mom, telling her everything and that we were having a girl. That kind of shocked me, because he did not seem angry about telling her, in fact, he had some excitement in his voice. After he got off the phone, we did not talk much, other than, can you turn that up, or hand me my water.

Later on, the doctor came in, saying that the tests were negative for preeclampsia, but that she wanted me to relax. Try to stay off my feet and not work, if I did have to work, to do light duty. She also looked at Eduardo and said that I would be needing his help, that she did not want me going up and down the stairs at my house a whole lot, nor carrying anything too heavy. That I needed to try and keep my feet up for both mine and the babies' health.

As we went to pack up to go home, I told Eduardo I would have my friend come by to help me and that he did not need to worry, that I would be okay. He then looked at me and said the doctor told "him" to take care of me, no one else, and he was going to do just that, to make sure both me and our daughter were okay. I did not want to argue, so I agreed, on the grounds that he would leave once I was cleared by the doctor, and that he would be sleeping on the couch. He agreed and with that, we headed out of the hospital and to my house to stay there for me to relax.

After leaving the hospital, we found that we were able to settle into a routine of sorts. I only had a few weeks left until my due date so, during the day I would pick up things here and there. Eduardo would get up in the mornings, make or pick up breakfast then head out for the day. I found the downtime to be nice, but I was getting antsy. I went on the various forums, where there were discussions on bed rest, blood pressure issues, and swelling. All of which seemed to be pretty common issues that many either had or have had.

After taking a few days off, I went back to work, to try and get as many hours as I could before I delivered my baby. The ladies at my work were extremely excited as well and had thrown me a surprise baby shower. I was not expecting that, in fact, I had not even thought about having a shower due to all the drama I had gone through in the months leading up to my due date. So, the surprise was a very pleasant one. And following that surprise, I was treated to even more surprises when some friends from school also got together and invited me over for what I thought was a lunch date, to come into another surprise baby shower. Then within the next couple of days, Eduardo's sister called to invite me to the farm because the family wanted to have a baby shower as well. Giving me one surprise after another, and giving me lots of adorable pink items, handmade items, and more that were all perfect for adding to the nursery and list of supplies I had for my daughter's arrival.

A couple of weeks had passed since my stay at the hospital, and even though I was to slow down and take it easy, I wanted to ensure I had enough money to be able to relax and recover after having my baby. I also did not make any plans for Eduardo to help with anything, because even with the countdown on, Eduardo still, had yet to get one thing for his unborn daughter. Not diapers, blankets, baby care items, or any cute little outfits, nothing. As for me, I had picked up several adorable pink dresses, tights, diaper covers, diapers, and more to add to the lineup of baby items we had. I was getting ready and doing so with the same mindset of doing it all on my own.

After being back to working and being close to my 38-week mark in the pregnancy, I started to feel worn down. I was tired and sore, and I honestly felt pretty crappy. I mean, you hear people talking about that pregnancy glow, but I was not seeing it nor was I feeling it. My head had been hurting, and the swelling was getting worse. The nurses I worked with knew I was to be on light duty, but I could not stand sitting in the corner filling paperwork all day and not doing much of anything else.

I had come home one day, and after taking off my shoes, Eduardo noticed that my feet were extremely swollen and that I looked like I did not feel well. I told him I was only tired and to let me be, that I would soak my feet and go to bed. I then put myself on-call for the night, to try and make some extra money since with the on-call nights I made quite a bit more than I would for a regular shift.

Later that night, I got a call to go in and help with late-night admissions. I left and told Eduardo that I would take the rest of that shift and stay up there for the next shift as well if they could use me. As I walked out the door, I got sick and threw up in my front yard, but I told Eduardo that I was fine and to just go back to bed and that I would be home later the next day.

When I arrived at the hospital for the on-call shift, I found that it was putting stickers on, faxing, and filing paperwork to help the night shift out before the day shift came in. Which was simple work for the most part. I was put in the corner by the filing cabinets, computer, and fax machine, where I did not have to get up for really anything, could log in orders, fax paperwork, and even take calls from the doctors, allowing the night shift crew to continue with the admissions they got.

Then when the day shift crew came on, I was still working. The charge nurse came back to the area I was in to check on me when she said that I looked really bad. I told her I was fine, but I had a horrible headache. Before she had a chance to say anything else, the phone rang and to my surprise, it was my doctor. Apparently, Eduardo had called her, voicing concern over my health and how I was somehow being stubborn. The charge nurse got on the phone and told my doctor what she could see just by looking at me. She then took my blood pressure, and without telling my doctor the results said, "we are taking her across the street now."

I tried telling my boss that I was okay, that I would drink some water and finish my work. She looked at me and said there was no way in hell she was going to allow that to happen, that I needed to get in the wheelchair and go across the street immediately. The urgency must have been a great one, because instead of waiting for someone to transport me, she took me to the labor and delivery floor herself, asking me why I was pushing myself like I was, that she knew I was on strict orders and that my health was more important than anything else at that moment.

When we arrived on the floor, she handed my doctor the results from my blood pressure, the doctor then took over and wheeled me into a room, had a nurse follow her as she gave out orders for blood work, have leads put on and to call Eduardo and let him know they are admitting me.

Within the hour, Eduardo arrived, and the doctor had results on my labs, stating that she was right, I had preeclampsia and they would need to induce me right away. I looked at Eduardo and cried, I told him to call my mom and let her know, which he did before he made calls to his family. As the calls were being made, the doctor asked the nurses to come in, so she could remove the stitch she had placed on my cervix earlier in the pregnancy.

The nurses came in, began to start IVs with saline and Pitocin, and gave me some medicine to help with the headache and blood pressure issues I was having. Once things had calmed down a bit, the phone rang, it was my mom and she said that she and my sister were on their way, that they were going to drive and will hopefully be there before I delivered. The drive was an 8-hour drive at most, and due to the weather conditions getting worse with snow falling, I found the idea of my mom and sister on the road made me worry. Which I was assured was something I did not need to think about at that time.

After an hour, I was able to fall asleep, and after a few hours had passed, I started feeling the pains of labor coming. They were not the strongest contractions, but they were starting and since I was still at a 0 dilated, the nurse who was caring for me said it would be a while before anything happened so that my mom should have plenty of time to get there. With that, even with the pains that were coming and going, I decided to try and sleep some more.

I slept until I was woken up to strong and intense pains in my lower back. They were coming and going regularly every few minutes. I remember thinking that it was insane, I did not expect the pain to be so intense. After an hour of not being able to sleep, or even attempt to stay still, the nurse came in to check me. I was finally starting to dilate and had made it to a 3. She explained that it was good, but that I still had a long way to go, showing me the chart on dilation and where I was, compared to where I needed to be before delivering.

The pain continued through the day, and by that evening, I still had not progressed much. My mom and sister made it to town and came by the hospital just as the doctor came in to check on me. The doctor explained that it can take time and that she would break my waters in the morning if it does not break during the night. She then ordered some Cervidil and told me it should help speed up the process. She also let us know that she had 3 other patients in labor as well, so she would most likely be there all night if anything were to change.

After the doctor left, my mom and sister left to go and check in at the hotel and get something to eat so they could prepare for a big day the next day. I was unable to eat due to the doctor's orders, so ice chips it was. I prepared for a long night, but due to the preeclampsia, I was not allowed to get up and walk, instead, I had to have a catheter put in and had a bedpan as well. They also covered the rails on my bed with towels, to provide a bumper explaining that preeclampsia can bring on seizure activity, which they are not anticipating but to be safe from head injuries they needed to add padding to the bed rails.

Nurses were coming in and out every hour or so, checking vitals, and contractions, and making sure I was doing okay. Then about 3 am the nurse noticed that my contractions had stopped. The doctor came in, and after checking me decided that the Cervidil must have stopped the contractions, so they removed it, and put me back on a drip of Pitocin. She said that she would be back in a few hours to check on me and possibly break my waters.

The contractions started back up just before the doctor came back to check on me. She said I was at a 5 and could get something for the pain at that time if I wanted, which I of course did. She then said that after we got the epidural in, she would come back and break my waters. Which sounded like a plan to me.

Within a few minutes, the team came in the put in the epidural, and after I went to lay back down, the nurse said she would send for the doctor to break my water. I asked Eduardo if he could get me the phone, so I could call my mom to let her know. As I sat up, I felt a gush of water pour out and told him to get the nurse and tell her never mind, the waters broke. I called my mom and told her what happened, and she said that she and my sister would be there with me shortly.

The day continued, and as it did, all of Eduardo's family came up, filling up the hall and waiting area, which was not what I nor my mom had expected. My aunt and cousins also showed up, and when they did, the contractions began to get worse. As this happened, I could hear arguing in the hall outside my room. Eduardo told me he would go see what was going on and be right back. My mom and sister went to the cafeteria to get lunch and had left just before whatever was going on outside my room had started. Eduardo came in and said that I needed to have my family banned from the room. That my aunt had said to one of my cousins that she was going to advise me to not put Eduardo's name on the birth certificate. I told Eduardo that he did not have a say, since we were not married.

The nurses came in due to alarms going off, and turned off the lights, telling everyone to settle down because I was in a very delicate state and could not be stressed out due to the preeclampsia. They explained that the light and noise can cause issues with my blood pressure and the less noise and light the better. As things started to progress, I felt so sick. I told the nurses I had to poop, and they said that meant I had to start pushing. They checked me and said that yes, I was ready to start pushing.

The doctor came in, made some comments about the crowd gathered outside my room, and then said that only a few people could be in the room. I told the doctor that I wanted my sister and mom there and that Eduardo could be there as well. The doctor then ordered everyone else who was in there to step out into the hall.

I had a large family suite, and there was a curtain that divided the room from the delivery room to the family area with the couches and television. Eduardo's mom and sister went to wait on the other side of the curtain, peeking in every so often to see the progress.

As I pushed, Eduardo had a video camera recording the event. The doctor said I needed help holding my legs back since they were numb, and Eduardo handed the camera to my sister to continue with the recording. I had tried to tell her to stand behind Eduardo, but she was a very curious teen who aspired to be in the medical field herself one day, so the birth was an extremely exciting thing for her to witness and record.

The pushing seemed to go on for what seemed like forever. I did not think I was getting anywhere with it, and every time I looked over at my sister, I would have to tell her to back up because she was recording EVERYTHING. I can remember looking out the window, watching the large snowflakes fall as I gathered my strength. The doctor needed to assist with the delivery and grabbed some clamps along with this thing that looked like a plunger, and once she was set up, she told me, "One Last Push!"

With that last, big, assisted push, my world immediately changed forever. I was a mom!!! My princess came out screaming, a noise that melted my heart, and when I held her for that first time, I felt more love than I had ever felt for anyone in my entire life. The numbness to feelings I had, were gone, I fell in love with this tiny baby girl. Everyone else in the room was a blur to me, all I could see what this perfect, baby girl looking right back up at me as we stared into one another's eyes. To my surprise, Eduardo started crying and showed what appeared to be real emotion for the first time since I had met him. Eduardo's mom came in to see her new grandbaby with tears of joy coming down her face, and as I looked around, I could see both my mom and sister crying as they looked at this precious life I had just given birth to. Eduardo's mom scolded me, saying that I made her baby cry, then congratulated me on a job well done. That moment in time was one I will forever cherish, as the moment that I became more than just another person, but this little girl's mom.

After I held my baby for a brief moment, Eduardo went to hold her and show her to my mom, sister, his mom, and sister, and let everyone get a chance to hold her, giving the doctor some space as she assisted with the delivery of the placenta. He then went to the hallway and waiting area to let everyone know that she was here, then handed the camera with the recorded birth on it to his brother for everyone to get a chance at watching.

Due to my preeclampsia, I was put on a drip of morphine and magnesium, which numbed my entire body and my brain for that matter. I was exhausted and then the last thing I could remember clearly was my aunt coming in to notify me that there was a video camera being passed around and that my cousin saw it and told my aunt that it shows all my business and Eduardo's entire family had seen it. I was too tired and now high on morphine to respond. I tried to tell Eduardo to get the camera, but he ended up getting mad and wanted my aunt and cousins out. The rest of that day was all a blur, I remember people coming and going, a few leaving gifts, and wanting to see the baby, but for the most part, I was out of it.

After the delivery and falling asleep, I can vaguely remember Eduardo coming in to wake me and have me sign some papers. I was not in the right state of mind due to the morphine making me feel like I had sand in my eyes, to read or sign anything, but Eduardo said it was important and had me sign it. Shortly after that, he came back with more papers, saying it was just the papers for the baby's birth certificate and for the doctor to give the baby the shots she needed. Not thinking about reading things over, I signed and went back to sleep.

That was until my mom and sister came in to ask me why I had my aunt and cousins removed from the floor? I told them that I did not know, and they said I signed the papers to have them removed. I then told them that Eduardo brought papers in right after I delivered and insisted I signed, even helping me to do so but that I did not remember what they were for. At that moment, I think my mom then believed me on everything, that Eduardo was controlling, and I was not crazy. She kissed me on the head and said she would be back; told me I did a wonderful job and that my baby was perfect and so beautiful.

I slept for most of that afternoon, only waking up a couple of times to wanting to get up and move, but due to the catheter still being in, and me being a fall risk due to the medications they had me on, I could not get up. It was not until later in the evening when the doctor cleared me of being in any danger from the preeclampsia, that I was able to finally get up from that bed that I had been confined to for the past couple of days. When I got up and tried to put my house slippers on, I realized that my feet were larger than ever, and knew that the water weight I had been carrying had all gone to my ankles and feet. Making the walk to the bathroom one that was harder than I expected, to where my legs felt like sandbags, and I felt like I had anvils for feet.

I went back to my bed and rang for the nurse to bring me, my baby. When they brought her in, they asked if I wanted to nurse her, which of course I did, but had no idea how to do it right. The lactation specialist came in, and helped me with that first latch, encouraging me as we began nursing and ensuring me that I was doing just fine. I can remember looking down at my baby, as she nursed away, and her looking up at me, which was one of the greatest feelings I had as a mother, being able to provide nourishment for my baby.

We kept her in the room with me for the remainder of my stay, minus the times they had to have the pediatrician do his checks and tests on her. I then asked the nurse how I went about getting the birth certificate. The nurse looked at me with a confused look on her face and said that my husband had me sign the papers and they were already filed. I then told the nurse that I was not married and that I do not remember signing anything, which she said to wait and came back with my chart showing me copies of the paperwork for the baby's birth certificate. Showing that I had indeed signed it and that it was all filled out, where Eduardo gave the baby his last name without talking to me first.

I thanked the nurse for clarifying that for me and said that I did not remember due to the medications, and she agreed the meds can do that. I then sat there, holding my baby, realizing that Eduardo was the reason why my family was kicked out when all "his" family were allowed to stay and that he knew that I was not planning on giving my baby his last name. I knew at that moment, that I could not allow him to hurt my baby or try to take her from me like he had said he would do, with that other woman. That I needed to protect this little girl who is so innocent in all of this and never asked for any of the crazy mess she was born into.

I looked forward to being discharged and starting my new life as a mother. I also looked forward to being away from Eduardo, knowing we needed to discuss a plan, but also knowing that I would not have to see him every day once I was discharged, or at least that was my plan at the time. However, it was all a lot easier to imagine and think about than it was to actually do, and I learned how hard it can be right away.

People talk about new parent jitters, where many may feel like they do not have a clue, but what they do not always mention is that first day when you are released from the hospital. I mean, the nurses are amazing, they are there helping new parents, showing them how to change those diapers with the delicate umbilical cord hanging on. How to wash the baby, how to care for the umbilical cord site, how to nurse the baby, and so much more.

The nurses become friends for a moment there, as we begin to find our footing in the world of parenthood, there for us to ask any questions and assure us that we are doing okay, but only for a moment, it seems. And on that first day, when you leave the hospital and are home, alone with your new baby, those new parent jitters become a reality. Where you do not have that nurse to assist you or answer any questions you have, and for me, not have a mom right there to help and talk to at any time to answer questions or give me a break after that first week of no sleep commends.

In fact, I realized that there was nothing that could have prepared me for that first week home. The first night, it had continued to snow, to where my car had to be left in the parking lot at the hospital due to it being buried in several feet of snow, and the lights in the house flickered when the wind blew. I was too scared to sleep, not because of the snow but because I sat there, watching her as she breathed, would startle in her sleep, or whimper, preparing for that big cry when she would need to nurse. I was given a journal from the hospital, it was a nursing and diaper change journal, where I could keep track of the feedings, and diaper changes and ensure that she was peeing and pooping enough.

I also had medical equipment to use on my newborn as well. Because when she was just a couple of days old, she became jaundiced, and her bilirubin levels were high. So, the hours before being discharged, I had to be taught how to use the Bili blanket, which was a blanket that we carefully wrapped around her midsection that had UV lighting inside. Helping to give her the light therapy she needed to help bring those bilirubin levels down, which can also be helped with exposure to sunlight in short amounts of time, but since she was born in the winter during a snowstorm, the Bili blanket was what we needed.

I found that regardless of not having my mom's help, surprising enough, Eduardo had stuck around and was helping some. I say some because he did not do much, but take the baby so I could sleep, but only when I asked him to. He did not change diapers, try to bathe her, change her clothes, or do anything unless I asked him to watch her. Other than that, he cooked the meals, but also made messes that he did not clean up and did not help during the night either. After that first week home and feeling like the baby and I were getting into a steady routine when it came to feedings and diaper changes, Eduardo's mom came to visit.

She was an extremely sweet woman and came in to help clean the house by cleaning the kitchen, doing laundry, and even insisting I take a shower while she spent some time bonding and rocking her granddaughter. She also informed me that Eduardo's brother was coming to pick us up, so we could dig my car out of the snow and bring it home, and while we were doing that, she would watch the baby. I appreciated the help she offered, even if it was only for a day, it was a nice mini-break to get back into being more than a mom, but a human again.

When we arrived at the hospital, Eduardo and his brother got out with the shovels his brother had brought along. The two began digging out my car, to find that it was a lot harder to do since the lower layers of snow had turned into ice. After a lot of arduous work, shoveling, and breaking ice, they finally dug my car out. I went into my work where my friend who worked the front desk had heated some water to use on the car, so I could open it up since the doors were frozen shut. We got the car out then I drove back to my house. When I got there, Eduardo's mom was mopping the floors and the baby was sleeping in her bassinet that we brought downstairs for naps. When I walked in, I thanked her for helping out and that is when she asked if she could talk with me.

I said we could talk, and she said good, because the boys were going to run to the store before they came back, and there are some things we needed to talk about. At first, I felt like she was going to say that I needed to marry her son or maybe be mad since I was not wanting him to be there. But instead, she sat me down and said that there are some things about her son that she thinks I should know. About his dad, and how Eduardo has a lot of the same personality traits. She went on and explained that she left Eduardo's dad when he was just a baby. That his dad was very abusive and controlling, and that he was an exceedingly difficult person to have any sort of relationship with. She continued by saying that she had to leave Eduardo's dad in the middle of the night when Eduardo was just a baby and that she saw the same things in her son that his dad had. That his dad was mentally ill and was a very scary person. Like Eduardo, his dad was a noticeably big man and had a very short fuse when it came to his temper and expressed to me that she worried he was just like his dad.

As we were talking, Eduardo and his brother showed up. Their mom quit talking about him and asked me if I was thirsty then walked to the kitchen. I found myself feeling a bit uneasy knowing that for one, his family seemed to be aware of his issues, and for two, that whatever it is he had, it was something that appeared to run in his family.

In the following days, I could not stop thinking about what his mom had said, watching Eduardo and thinking maybe it was true. But as time seemed to continue, Eduardo started to show more and more compassion towards me. It was a strange way of showing it, but it was his way. And after we got through that first week and a half of caring for our baby on our own, I was woken up to flowers, a card, a beautiful cross, and Eduardo on his knees on the side of the bed. Waiting for me to open my eyes. It was Valentine's Day, and even though I knew what day it was, I had not expected anything from anyone that day.

I found myself in a daze of sorts, coming out of sleep and waking to Eduardo in the nursery, kneeling as he watched me sleep. He kissed me on the forehead and then went on to read off the words he had written on a piece of paper. Where he apologized for being difficult during my pregnancy, for not being there for me when he was needed most, and for not stepping up to prove his love to me as he knew I deserved at the very least. He continued and said that he is not a perfect man, but that he was there, and the moment he had laid eyes on his baby girl he knew that with us was exactly where he needed and wanted to be. Exclaiming that there was nothing in this world he wanted more than to have us be a family.

He then put the ring in the box it had originally come in on the nightstand next to the bed, reached over and placed the tray with fresh fruit, chocolate, and coffee he had prepared on my lap, and went to the crib to pick up the baby as she began to fuss. He sat in the rocker, singing a song to her in Spanish, as he gently touched her cheeks and kissed her on the forehead telling her, "Te Amo mi Nina."

As I watched Eduardo with our baby girl, I felt as though there was more to him than I had ever realized, that maybe, just maybe him being there with his baby was what he needed. And him being there with us, was what we all needed.

The days after having my baby seemed to go by so fast. I had a routine down from the nighttime feedings to times I would nap with my baby, the times when Eduardo was home and would take the baby to give me time to clean or take a shower. And once we hit that big 1-month mark, he asked me if I had made a decision on "us."

He knew that I would be going back to work soon and that I did not want him staying at the house, and this time, he did not move his things in or even try to push the matter. The thing was, I had thought about us. Things seemed to go smoothly over the past month, and I was starting to feel something for him. It may have just been because he was the father of my baby and that I felt my heart flutter when I would catch him singing or talking to our daughter or falling asleep on the floor with her. I had wanted to put the past behind us, and start over, and after thinking about it, I told him that I would agree to give "us" another chance and that he could move back in.

When I told him my decision, Eduardo seemed to light up from the inside. He gave me a huge kiss then went to his brother's house, where all his things were still packed up, and brought them back to my house. He told me that he knew it would take time for me to trust him again, but that we had all the time in the world, and as long as we were together as a family, everything would be okay.

Within that first week of us being a couple again, he asked me if I had considered getting married. I told Eduardo I was not so sure about that idea just yet, and he told me he would ask again later. He seemed like he was respecting my decision on things and was not pressuring me into things.

Another week had passed by, and it was time for me to go back to work, and for our daughter to go to her first day of daycare. I was a nervous mess, but I had expected as much. In fact, I had gone on during the days at home to talk to the ladies on the forums, talking about sore nipples from breastfeeding, the color of the baby's poo and if it was normal, the nighttime feedings, and even the idea of giving my relationship with my daughter's dad a second chance. I found the replies to the relationship part to be pretty 50/50 where some said that he sounded like he was sincere, to those who said to run and never look back. When it came to the discussions on going back to work, I found my first troll joining in to put in their two cents on the matter. Saying that I was abandoning my baby, that childcare places are horrible places for a newborn, and that if I could not afford to stay home with my baby then maybe I should give her up.

I found the troll comments to be hateful and very alarming for me at the time because that was the first time, I had ever had a troll do such a thing, and target me, making me second guess everything and make me think that I was a bad mom. I took it to heart at the time, even with others who came to defend me from this awful person, they told me to ignore the person, that they were wrong and that I do what I feel is the right thing for me and my baby. And the one friend, who I remained online friends with for many years, who came to my aid said that at the end of the day, said, "your choices and decisions when it comes to parenting are the best ones."

I had considered telling Eduardo about this online community I had found but decided not to, I wanted to keep that to myself, as my own outlet that I did not want to share with him.

Then the day came to take my baby to daycare for the first day, I felt a series of fears, anxiety, and sadness come over me. When I dropped her off, I did not want to leave her, I cried in the parking lot but knew that she would be just fine. We had a schedule for our days, where I would drop off the baby in the mornings on my way to work then Eduardo would pick her up when he got off work and I would see them both at the house after I got off. This schedule seemed to work for us, and I felt better knowing that it was working.

That was until my baby was turning 2 months old. I had been working for the past few years at a psychiatric hospital that was just across the parking lot from the main hospital. After having the baby, I was back on the patient floor, working closely with the patients and not doing as much paperwork as I had done during the end of the pregnancy. I loved it. I enjoyed the day-to-day therapies we did with the patients, the one-on-one interactions, and knowing that we were there to help. Now there were dangers, but that can be said with just about any job out there. The thing is, when it came to the dangers, the idea of catching an infection from a patient was the last thing I had thought of happening in a mental hospital. That was until it happened to me.

I had felt sick for a couple of days, which happened to be my days off. On the second day after running a fever, I decided to go to Urgent Care which was across the street from the daycare. I did not want to take the baby to Urgent Care and expose her to the germs there, so I took her to the daycare in the morning and planned on picking her up after I got done being seen by the doctor.

While at the doctor, they noticed sores all over my throat and mouth, but I tested negative for strep and the flu. The doctor said that he would treat me with antibiotics and some cough medicine. I took the prescriptions across the street to have filled then went to pick up my baby from the daycare. When I walked in, the lady at the front desk said that she was not there, that she had already been picked up. I was confused since the only ones who could pick her up were me and her dad. She then showed me the sign-out sheet and showed me Eduardo's signature showing that he had picked her up. I thought it to be strange since for one, he was supposed to be at work and for two, I never told him I was taking her that day, it was a last-minute decision on my part.

I left the daycare, picked up my prescriptions then headed home. When I arrived, Eduardo was not there. So, I decided to call him and ask him what was going on. He answered the phone and explained that he did not feel comfortable with me just leaving the baby there at any time and said she was at his cousin's house.

I found the whole situation to be strange, but I hung up and I drove to the cousin's house and picked up my baby. Shortly after I got home, Eduardo came home and explained that he did not feel comfortable leaving the baby at daycare and explained that he had lots of family in the area who could help. Which would also save us a lot of money, so I agreed, and we decided to begin taking the baby to his family when we had to work.

Later that day I noticed the baby was not nursing well. Then later that night I noticed she had not wet a diaper which meant she was not getting any milk. So, I pumped and noticed that I had plenty of milk. I decided to put the milk in a bottle, but she still would not eat. I woke Eduardo up to tell him since the baby was crying but would not eat and he ran to the store to pick up a can of formula to see if she would drink a bottle of formula. When he got back, and we prepared the bottle, we were both surprised that she would not eat that either and continued to cry. By this time, we only had another 2 hours before the pediatrician's office would open so we waited. We called the after-hours number and they set up an appointment for us to be the first ones seen that morning.

When we got to the doctor's office, we were seen right away but told that the baby had a cold and that she would be fine. This diagnosis did not seem right, in fact, they had not checked her, and did not seem to care that she had not eaten since the early afternoon the day before nor had a wet diaper since then either. As we went to get in the car, we decided to drive across the street to the pediatrician's office where one of Eduardo's friends worked at. This friend also happened to be the one that we made the God Mother of our daughter.

We walked in and she was surprised to see us. We took the baby out of her carrier and showed her, told her about me being sick and about how the baby was not eating and had no wet diapers and that her doctor had said it was just a cold. The doctor at the office overheard us, came over and asked to see our baby. He walked her into a room with us following, did an exam then told our friend to call the hospital and have the baby admitted right away.

My heart sank, he carried the baby out of the room and was trying to comfort her as she continued to cry. She had been crying for hours and was so worn out, that she was going hoarse. He placed her in the carrier, grabbed his keys, told our friend to hold calls until he got back then told us to load her in the car and he would meet us at the hospital.

When we arrived, we saw the doctor waiting by the elevators. We went up to the children's wing with the doctor and as we got to the floor, a nurse came to get the baby, and he grabbed the chart she had put together and then ordered labs STAT. Within minutes we were in a room, the baby was being cared for, having blood draws, and being taken to another room to get an IV to push fluids done. As they did this the staff went on to explain that she needed fluids because she was extremely dehydrated. I was a mess. All I could do was cry; I was scared for my baby but also so mad at the pediatrician we had for not even checking our baby properly.

The nurses on the floor were truly kind and offered us drinks and snacks while we waited for the results. When the results arrived, the doctor came in and said he was confused, that she was testing negative for everything. He then looked at me and asked me if I was sick as well, and when I said I was, he asked me if I would do some blood work, which I agreed to without any hesitation. He went on as they drew blood and asked me a series of questions, one of which asked me if I had been exposed to anything at work. That is when it occurred to me that I may have, that I had a patient who had a horrible self-inflicted wound that had festered, and it was contagious but only to those with an open wound. I went on and said that I did not have any open wounds, that I wore proper protective clothing, and doubted I had been exposed. He then asked me if I was breastfeeding, to which I replied I was.

The doctor left the room, and I could hear him on the phone calling the lab, asking them to check for a few different things. Within the hour, he came in and said that he has answers and that both myself and the baby needed to be put on IVs right away. He explained that my nipples were an open wound, and somehow the infection from the patient infected me and I infected the baby. I felt relief in knowing we had a diagnosis, but guilt in the fact that I unknowingly, made my baby sick. As the day went on, several of the bosses from my work came by, they had heard what happened and offered support for us while we were in the hospital. We had lots of Eduardo's family come in bringing flowers, stuffed animals, and cards. Then later in the day, when Eduardo left to get a shower and pack some bags, my aunt showed up. She said that she had asked to be notified when Eduardo left and that she needed to talk to me.

I was so happy to see her since I had not seen her since the day I had my baby. She went over to look at the baby and told me she was gorgeous, and she was proud of me. She then sat down in a chair next to the bed I was in and told me that she was moving. That she had some things for me at her house, but she wanted to offer me to take over the payments on her house. I told her I would love to, that I would need to talk to Eduardo, but let her know I wanted the house. That is when she stopped me and told me that she had talked to my parents already, and there was one stipulation on this proposition. Where, for me to have the house, I had to leave Eduardo, that he was not to be at the house, but that this was a chance for me and the baby to get on our feet and for me to work towards having my own home. She said she would be taking the next couple of months to go through things in the house, and pack things. Assuring me I had time to come to a decision, but to not wait too long, because if she did not hear from me in the next few weeks, she would put the house on the market. I began to cry and told her I did not realize the papers he had me sign were to have her, and my cousins removed that day. She told me that she knew, and she knew that he used that moment to make his move. She warned me that she had an awfully bad feeling about him, saying he was bad news and I needed to leave him. She then hugged me and kiss on the forehead, kissed the baby, and left, reminding me to let her know soon.

I was in shock, I mean, did she just offer for me to take over the payments on her house? My aunt's house was an older house but was a large house. It had several bedrooms, 3 living areas, a full-sized finished basement, and 3 yards. She had lived there for many years and had lots of updates done including the kitchen she had remodeled the year before. So, the idea was exciting but at the same time, that meant I would have to leave Eduardo for the last time. I look back at this choice and think that I should have just done it, but that is another shoulda woulda coulda time in my life that I always think about.

After several days in the hospital, the baby and I were finally cleared, and she was back to nursing like a champ again. I had told Eduardo my aunt was offering her house to me, but I did not tell him that she had been to see us in the hospital or had seen the baby. He of course told me that she was only putting that stipulation on because he was Hispanic and that she did not like him because she was a racist. Now when I think about it, she might have been, but she had never voiced her concerns about race towards him or even brought it up to me. She would only say that she did not like him, that he had a look about him that was one she recognized, and it was nothing but trouble.

When we got home and unpacked the car from all the many stuffed toys, balloons, flowers, and gift baskets we were given, I noticed one basket that I had overlooked before. I could not remember seeing the person who brought it in, and I had not even read the card that was attached until then. I opened the card and when I read it, I realized the card was for Eduardo, and the other woman, the one who worked at the Walmart, had brought that basket to mine and my baby's room at the hospital. I was livid, I handed Eduardo the card and the basket she had put together with football-themed clothes and toys for the baby along with a baseball cap for him in there.

I then told him that I would take my aunt up on her offer and to please thank that other woman for helping me make the decision. Eduardo had a confused look on his face, and when he read the card, he stood up and told me that I was not going anywhere with his baby. I took the baby upstairs to put her down since she was sleeping, and when I walked back down the stairs, Eduardo was waiting for me. And that is when it happened when he slapped me so hard that I fell to the floor. He then picked me up and slapped me again, kneeling over me, telling me that I was not going anywhere, and it is time I showed him some respect. He said that he was tired of trying to prove anything to me and that I was going to accept things for what they were, and to never question him ever again.

I laid there on the floor, covering my head, scared to feel the brunt of another blow from him. I had never felt such pain that had been inflicted by someone I cared about, that was physical pain, that was intentional. I was in shock, I did not know what to do, I was too scared to move, and just laid there and cried. He then came over and demanded that I get up, to which he then walked me to the couch, grabbed a wet washcloth, and cleaned up my face, asking me if I understood him, and to stop crying, go upstairs and fix my makeup.

I went upstairs, but I did not want to go back down there with Eduardo, I was scared of going back down the stairs, so I just laid in the bed in the nursery and fell asleep. When the baby woke up, I got up to nurse her and change her. I ended up doing that for the rest of the day, not leaving the room, that was until it was nighttime. It was getting late, and I had hoped he passed out on the couch, so I went to wash up and get ready for bed.

When I got out of the shower, he was waiting there for me, he then grabbed my arm, pulled me to the bedroom, and told me that I was his and I was to do my "wife" duties. I told him I did not want to get on the bed and that I needed to get dressed, and that is when he grabbed my towel, closed the bedroom door, and pushed me on the bed. I tried to get up, begging him to let me get dressed. That is when he forced himself on me and raped me. Telling me to be quiet or else I would wake the baby, but that I was to be a good wife to him and please him whenever he wanted.

While he did this, I felt numb, like I was not there, thinking about my baby, and wishing that I would somehow get away at that moment, float away, far away from him. But I did not in a physical form, instead, I just pretended to not be there.

This type of action became something that went on frequently, and as time went on, he told me he was going to put another baby in my belly, and that I would be giving him lots of babies in fact because I was his, as he continued to remind me. The rapes became a normal thing for me, occurring so often to where I did not try to fight him off anymore, instead once he was done, I would get dressed and sleep in the nursery, hoping I was safe from him and keeping my baby safe from him. But I was wrong. He had no care or mind for raping me in front of the baby, even though she was sleeping in her crib, I could see her as he forced himself on me regularly.

As the time went on, and I was not getting pregnant right away like he had expected me to, he insisted that I do certain things to try and increase my chances of getting pregnant. I tried telling him that breastfeeding can cause me to not get pregnant, thinking maybe he would back off, but instead of him backing off, he insisted I stop breastfeeding. That he would leave me alone once I was pregnant again, so it was in both of our best interests.

I was once again alone and scared. I went to the online forums but did not see where I could share such, I was ashamed that I allowed this to happen. I felt gross, I felt ugly and worthless. I became depressed. I was able to care for my baby and felt joy in that aspect of my life, but I hated myself. I found some threads on postpartum depression or the baby blues as some put it, and I told Eduardo I wanted to go see a doctor. He agreed and told me that I needed to fix my mind, so I could have more babies for him.

When I got to the doctor's office, they first said that I was due for a pap smear, which I was scared of having done, knowing that they would surely see signs of rape. But the doctor did not say anything, instead, she asked me if I wanted to start taking some antidepressants to help me. I told her I did, then she asked if I needed birth control. I sat there and thought about it, knowing I did not want to bring any more innocent children into that house, then said that yes, I did but asked if she could give me a shot instead of the pills, I would prefer that. So before leaving, I was given a birth control shot by the nurse in the office. Knowing that I had to figure out how to leave and do so before it got any worse.

Living with a Monster

The time seemed to slow down, and I honestly just felt numb. I was numb to feelings, to the nightly rapes, to everything. It seemed like I could not concentrate, nor find the motivation to make the plans I needed to make to leave. So once again, I turned to those online forums, where I read threads on the baby blues and the medications that the women there had taken. I then read one comment where a woman said that even though the medications got rid of her thoughts of worthlessness and hating herself, she felt like a zombie with no feelings at all. That is when I decided to stop taking the antidepressant medications and try to find a way out.

After a few days of not taking the medications, I began to feel like I had a clear head again. And I noticed things that I did not notice while I was on medications. I realized that it was too late to take my aunt up on her offer because, during the time I was on medications, we did go to her house. She had left me a garage door opener to her house, allowing me to pick up a few things she wanted me to have, but by then, she was already moved, and her house was sold right away.

I decided to call her and thank her since I had not done that yet, and when I called her, she was noticeably disturbed. She began to yell at me, telling me how dare I allow Eduardo in her house and to steal from her. I was in shock; I did not steal from her, nor did I let him go to her house and steal either. She then went on and said that a neighbor had seen Eduardo and another man in a truck, pull up to her house then load the truck up with lots of really nice items that she had in the house. Stealing items from her house that were new such as clothing, some furniture that was her daughter's, a television, and more.

I swore to her that I knew nothing about it, and told her I would find out, but that I was so sorry it had happened. When I hung up, I realized he had used my car several times, and my car had the garage door opener to my aunt's house in it before I gave it to my cousin. That he must have taken it and stolen the items mentioned from my aunt.

Later that day when Eduardo got home, I confronted him. Telling him a neighbor saw him do it and he stole, that the stuff was not given to him. Eduardo then got in my face, grabbed me by the throat, and threw me against the railing to the stairs. After I fell, he walked over and kicked me in my side, and told me to never accuse him of bullshit things that my crazy aunt must have made up. And that he had never permitted me to call my aunt, then kicked me again, saying I was forbidden to talk to her ever again. He then demanded I get up and go upstairs. I couldn't, I was still trying to catch my breath from when he kicked me, that is when he picked me up by my hair, bent me over the couch, and raped me while I cried and could hear the baby crying upstairs. When he got done, he slapped my bottom ridiculously hard, pulled up his pants, and told me that my fine ass needed to get in that kitchen, get his supper ready then get upstairs to take care of his baby. He then pulled me up by the hair again and bit me hard on my neck, leaving a large mark for all to see. Saying I was his, and him leaving his mark on me would show everyone that I was his. And until I married him, he would make sure I was marked as his.

He kept to his word, leaving hickeys on me that were visible and hard to cover up with just makeup. He would leave a new mark each time he raped me, marking what was his as he would say. That is when I began wearing undershirts to work regularly, and turtlenecks, hoping to cover the shame that was under the clothing.

A few months had passed, and Eduardo called me at work and asked me to meet him at an address. When I got there, he was there with the baby and seemed to be overly excited for me to be there. We walked into this house, it was empty, yet open for us to walk into. He then went on to explain that a person he knew owned the house, and wanted to sell it to us, that I could use my school money to put a down payment since I was not going back to school anytime soon.

I looked at Eduardo, with an angry look, because we had not discussed me not going back to school, nor had I mentioned any money I had for school. That is when he pulled out an envelope that was delivered to me in the mail and had information on the account I had. Showing me, it had the money in it that was left to me by my grandparents to pay for schooling, the remaining amount of money that I had not spent when I was hooked on crack. He pointed out that he could see that I paid off my car a while back from the statement and that I had access to that money anytime I wanted it. He told me if we got married, he could control the finances but until then, I needed to think about our family and our future, and the house was part of that future.

As we walked around the house, I noticed that it needed to be painted, one of the rooms needed to be remodeled, and the flooring throughout needed to be updated. I just saw a mess, to where he saw, what could be our home. Eduardo went on and said that he already had plans for redoing the things which needed work, and his cousins would be glad to help as well, which would save us money. He then said to head back to my house, and he would be there right after, so we could make plans to move.

I had not agreed to anything, but he seemed to be just making plans without talking to me, asking me if that is what I wanted. When he got back to my townhouse, I had just gotten done giving the baby a bottle and took her upstairs to bed. When I came back down, he grabbed me, but not in a forceful way this time. Instead, he began to caress me, rubbing my breasts, and removing my clothes, while I stood there frozen and scared of his touch, thinking "he" was going to strike me or hurt me as he had done numerous times over the past few months. As he did this, he began kissing me and sucking on my breasts. He then picked me up and carried me to the couch where he pulled off my pants, then went down and began to carefully lick my clit. I did not want to be there, I pretended I was not, and closed my eyes, hating the fact that I was enjoying the feelings he was giving me, pleasuring me, and trying to make me have an orgasm. He then inserted himself inside of me and instead of the forceful act of raping me, he slowly made love to me. I kept my eyes closed, imagining it was someone else, because I did want to be loved on and caressed like that, but not by him. But I was enjoying it, and I felt that I had to take that pleasure as I could get it because I felt trapped, thinking this was what I would have to live it, and mine as well make the best of it.

When he got done, he got up without his clothes on, walked to the kitchen, and fixed us two plates of food. He brought me my plate and fed me each bite, as he kneeled between my legs. Once the food was done, he got up, and washed off the plates, leaving me there speechless as to what had just happened. He then came in, picked me up, carried me to my old room, the one he was using, and laid me on the bed. Instead of raping me like I thought he was about to do, he grabbed some lotion and began to massage me. Giving me more pleasure once again in his touch, which I was torn over throughout this. For one, he made me cringe. I was scared to move, but at the same time, the touch, the touch that was like that of a lover that was gentle to my skin which he had abused so many times before, was one I craved, leaving me feeling good but bad about feeling good.

The next day, as we got up, Eduardo insisted we go to the bank and apply for a loan to purchase the home, using my school money to put as a down payment on the house. When I began to second guess the choice we were about to make, he got in my face, choked me then stuck his hand down my pants. Where one hand was squeezing my neck, holding onto my life as I gasped for air, and the other was gently caressing my clitoris. He then whispered that it was not a choice for me to make, because he had already chosen for us. Quietly demanding that I was to get in the car, and when we got to the bank, we were going to do exactly as he said, and we were going to move into our own house and be a family. Hopefully having more babies to add to our family soon.

I was living a life that was not my own. I was watching my life from the outside, screaming to get away, to run, to only be scared to death of this man, knowing that if I left and got caught, he would hurt me and possibly hurt my baby or take her from me. Knowing that I was stuck and alone. Where the family I did have that was still nearby were not close family, the only close family I had was gone and wanted nothing to do with me. That the friends I had, did not like the fact Eduardo was there, and that we were living as a happy couple, as he threatened me to portray to everyone. Where I was being forced to act a certain way around others, giving off this fake persona of being happy and in love.

As we drove to the bank, he grabbed my hand, saying that as long as I remained a loyal, loving wife, he too will be a loving husband, and will be sure to please me as he pleasured himself. I looked at him with a look of fear, the type you might imagine having if you looked over to see that serial killer from the horror movie you had nightmares about, sitting next to you in a car, holding your hand, pretending to be loving when you know that it is all a lie. Everything about this person is a lie, and regardless of how he portrays himself to others, you know the truth of the monster that is inside.

When we arrived, he quickly went to open my door, helping me out, grabbing the baby carrier with the baby sleeping inside, then walking me up the stairs, holding my hand to only let go to open the doors for me as we walked into the bank. We were greeted as we walked in, and then went to a room with a man who had paperwork with my information on it on his desk. This man introduced himself to me and explained that they had already started the paperwork and just needed my signature and my ID. Eduardo grabbed my hand and kissed it, then said, "this is it, baby, we are going to be homeowners."

As the guy went to make copies of my ID, I looked on the desk to see that he had copies of my birth certificate, my social security card, and information from the bank where I had my school money, needing a signature for a transfer. I knew Eduardo had been there, that he had filled out all the paperwork, taken my information without discussing anything first, that when he showed me that house, he had already decided, and regardless of what I would have said, he was going to get his way.

The guy at the bank returned and had lots of paperwork for me to sign, where I could see that Eduardo had already signed everything previously. As this man handed me paperwork, he let me know what each form was for, saying the amount for the mortgage we were getting, what our payments would be, the duration, and the information on the account that Eduardo had opened as a joint account to which we were going to transfer the remainder of my money to. And I signed it all, not by choice, but by force. The force of knowing what he was capable of doing to me, and the force of the fear of what he would do to my baby if he would take her from me if I did not do what he said.

The process of getting that house seemed pretty simple compared to what I had expected, but it was also a for sale by owner sale, which made it easier. And once we had signed all the papers, the friend who had owned the house, met up with us just a couple of weeks later to give us the keys to the house.

Within a week of getting the keys, we had moved out of my townhome and had moved into the new house. We only lived out of one room for that first week. Where during the day, Eduardo's cousins came, ripping up and replacing flooring, fixing insulation, painting, and putting in new doors throughout. I was surprised how quickly they got things done, to whereby the end of that first week, I was able to move furniture to the rooms and begin unpacking everything.

The thing was, regardless of how nice it was turning out, I hated that house. I hated every inch of the house, even the nursery I painted and decorated during the remodeling process for my daughter. I hated the yard, the trees, the garden, the driveway, the porch, I hated being there. Memories were made, when we celebrated my daughter's first birthday in that house, where she took her first steps, but at the same time, I wished to be far away from that place. I had found ways though, where I would claim to fall asleep in the nursery or needed to comfort the baby for any reason I would come up with. Giving me time to sleep, where I did not feel like I was a sex object that was used any time of day or night, even at the times when I was sleeping, or when I would quietly beg him not to. The nursery, even though it was just one room over, was my own personal escape for the most part.

I say that because it had a door that would lock easily when it closed all the way, and on those nights where he would find me out of bed not there to pleasure himself with, he would come to the nursery. I learned about the locking door by accident the first time but used the excuse that I did not mean to close it, to keep him from getting angry or violent towards me. Pretending to not hear him when he would knock on the door at night, hoping he would just go back to bed and leave me alone.

On the nights when Eduardo would go out with friends, I found myself looking forward to the night alone with my daughter, hoping that he would stay out and that I would not wake up to him on top of me. And that way of living became the norm for me. I felt as if he succeeded, he broke me, and I allowed him to do what he pleased. I did not question him or even talk to him much.

After being in the new home for a few months, Eduardo came in one morning, asking me to get dressed up and be ready to leave. I did as he said because I did not feel I had any choice. When I came out, he said to get in the car, we had something to do that day. As we drove downtown, I had not a clue what he was up to. That was until we arrived at the courthouse, and he pulled out some paperwork that said, "Declaration and Registration of Informal Marriage" on the top then asked me to go inside with him. I told him that I wanted to wait, but he said that we were just moving forward with our plans of getting married and that later on, we would have a big wedding, but we needed to get this done first. We then walked into the courthouse, where we walked to the clerk's office and waited in line to turn in the paperwork. When we handed in the paperwork, the lady at the desk asked for our IDs and birth certificates, the filing fee, read off an oath, had us sign the papers, and handed us a copy of everything after she stamped all the copies she made.

When we left, I felt sick to my stomach, I did not want to go through with this and felt so helpless in all areas of my life at the time.

I felt defeated, that was until about a week after we had signed those papers that I felt were sealing my fate. I was at work, and I received a call while I was on my break on my cell phone. To my surprise, it was that other woman on the other line, the one that worked at Walmart. She told me that I needed to leave Eduardo, so they could be together. I told her that I was unaware they were together. She went on and told me she was with him earlier that day and not only described what he was wearing but also the outfit my baby was wearing. I knew she had at least seen him because I was the one who dressed my baby that morning before work. She then continued and said that she had been at my house with him, then went on to prove it by describing not only the nursery and some of the things in the master bedroom but went on to say how it looked like a different house from when she saw it before. I hung up on her not wanting to listen anymore.

Then my phone rang again and again, I decided to let it be and go back to work. Shortly after I got back from my break, the phone at the nurse's station rang, my boss had been on the unit with me that night and answered. She was confused about me getting a personal call on the nurse's station phone but thought it could be urgent or something to do with my baby. It was not, it was her again. Leaving me shocked to question how she got the number to the unit I was working on and got through to the nurse's station, I later found that Eduardo had the number and had her call me at that number.

When I answered I was not expecting her to be on the other line. My stomach dropped, and I asked her what she wanted. She said she wanted him, so I told her that she could have him and hung up. She called back, then went on to tell me how sweet his kisses were and how they would also be taking my house and my baby from me, to raise her kids and my baby together as a family, and that I needed to just back off and let it all happen. I stopped her and said that there was no way in hell she was getting my baby or my house, that they can both go to hell and be together there. I hung up again, then when she called back on my work phone a third time, my boss answered and told her to quit calling and harassing me.

An hour later I went to take a smoke break when my phone rang again. It was her. She continued to go on about her relationship with Eduardo and told me that they would be taking my baby since they have proof that I was unstable, and I just needed to understand now that this would be happening soon. She then hung up before I had a chance to say anything more.

That is when I made a choice that I would regret later on but could not stop myself from doing. I called her back. She did not answer, so I left some messages. I say some because, at the time, cell phone messages could only last so long, and well, I had a lot to say to this woman. I called her many horrific names, explained that the reason his kisses were so sweet was because he had been licking my pussy last, and I threatened her. I had to call back several times to complete saying everything I had to say, which included many vial threats towards her, promising that if she even put a finger on my baby that she would soon regret it.

I could not believe what had just happened. I was once again in shock as to what was happening in my life, thinking that this sort of thing does not happen to people. I tried calling Eduardo to talk to him about what had happened but after all the calls I had made, my phone had died, and I needed to get back to work. My boss was sitting there, asking me what took so long, and I told her what I did. She laughed and said had it been her, she might have said a lot more. We laughed about it and went about the shift.

When I got home, I confronted him, only to be slapped and punched in the gut. He told me to never come at him acting crazy like I am going to do something to him. That I was brave thinking I could get away with that, then he pulled off his belt. He grabbed me by the hair, ripped off my scrub bottoms, and whipped me with his belt several times. Talking so calmly, saying that he can do and say as he pleased because he is the man of this house, and I am there to please him, give him babies, and take care of him and those babies.

I screamed the whole time, begging for him to stop, which eventually woke the baby. As she began to cry, he let me go to her before she came out on her own, then he sat on the couch playing a video game as if nothing had happened. A few minutes later we heard a knock at the door. It was the police. They said that they had complaints of a woman screaming and a domestic disturbance. He tried telling the police that it was nothing, claiming we had a little argument, but the officers asked to speak with me. He walked into the nursery to get me, and had a look on his face, warning me to not say a word.

I was at a point where I did not care anymore and told the police that we were fighting. I showed them my face which was still red from where he had slapped me. The officer looked at it, then another cop pulled up. They talked with Eduardo then came back to the house and said that it appears that things have settled down, so they were going to go, but to try to keep it down if we get to arguing. I was floored! They did nothing, even after showing them my face and showing the welts on my bottom from the belt.

I watched as they drove off, and once they were out of sight he laughed and said that he let them know that I was mentally ill, showing them an old bottle, I had from the prescription I had taken. He told them that I had outbursts and that the marks on my face and bottom were self-inflicted. He then sat back down and played more of the video game. I went to be with my baby in her room, away from him, trying to figure out how and what was happening.

After the baby went to sleep, he called me into the bedroom. There he had me take off all my clothes and stand naked, in front of him, as he inspected me, holding the belt he had used to hit me with earlier, in his hand and lightly rubbing it on my skin, making the hairs stand up. Humiliating me as he walked around me, looking me over very carefully. He then grabbed my hair and threw me towards the bed and raped me. Telling me the whole time that bitches need to be shown their place, that just like a female dog, I needed to be broken in and that I was his, and that I was not to ever forget that.

Then as he finished, he told me that he got a phone call last month, saying I needed to go in and get another shot. He said that when he asked what shot I needed; the lady told him a birth control shot. He laughed again and said that I was a slut, I was his slut now and that hopefully soon I would have another baby for him since I would not be getting another shot anytime soon. He said had I just obeyed him, things would be so much easier, and he would treat me better, but until then, this is it. And that when it came to things he did outside of the house, with whomever he pleased, it was none of my concern. Informing me that if he wanted a whole slew of "sanchas" he would. That it was his right to have me as his wife to have his babies and that it was his right as a man to have a woman on the side if he wanted.

After having him admit to having a side chick, the one who worked at Walmart, I felt even dirtier than ever. Knowing that he was having sex with me and this other woman and that I had to accept it for what it was. The thing was when I mentioned this other woman to others, which by that point the only people I saw were his friends and family, he would deny it. Telling everyone I was crazy, and that I was constantly imagining things that were not happening. I tried to talk to the God Mother, telling her about the other woman, and some of the abuse, thinking, hoping she would somehow help me. She seemed to listen but when she confronted him, she believed everything he told her. Because anytime someone would question him, he would show them that I was on psychiatric medications, even though I had quit taking them over a year prior. Claiming that he had a challenging time having to deal with my delusions and that I was violent towards him and would also harm myself to try to get him in trouble.

Leaving me to the realization that he would go to any length, to somehow give off a false persona of being a family man, caring for me. Forcing me and possibly this other woman, to be participants in his fantasy. Where I was sure others knew of the other woman, and I knew it was all to prove to his friends and family that he was some sort of badass, and not the strange guy they once all thought was gay due to the fact, he had never had a woman around. Who now had a woman at home who was there and "his" to do with as he pleased, along with a woman on the side?

I felt like every time there was a beating or when he raped me, or even when the other woman would come up, I was falling deeper and deeper into the rabbit hole Eduardo had dug for me. It was getting so bad that I almost believed that maybe I was going crazy too, since everyone around me was convinced, including my mom, and no matter what proof I had, he had something else to counteract my evidence. I was living in a nightmare that I could not wake up from. I had no one to go to, no one that could help me.

I then decided that I needed to take legal action and went to talk with a lawyer. I felt I finally had someone who was going to help me, and after meeting with the lawyer I decided that I needed to get back to school as well. So, I went to the college, I applied for grants, scholarships, and loans, knowing that the money I did have was gone. All of it.

When I got back to the house, I wanted to inform Eduardo that I was done with him. That I enrolled back in school for the following spring semester, and until then, we needed to discuss custody of our daughter. And instead of coming at me like I thought he would, he got on the phone and called my mom.

He went on and told her that I was being selfish. That I enrolled back in school and instead of focusing on my mental health or being a mom, I was going to work and go to school full time, neglecting everything else in my life. Listening to him, I was sure that my mom would laugh at him, and disagree with his thinking, but a few minutes later he handed me the phone. My mom said that I was not thinking straight and that it was selfish of me to want to go back to school, and I needed to focus on my family and health first, then later on, maybe look into going back to school.

As I hung up the phone with my mom, I turned around to a slap across my face. I had had it, so I punched him back. Eduardo laughed and instead of an open hand hit to the face, he clenched his fist and went to swing at me, only to miss when I ducked, and he hit the wall. That is when I kicked him in the testicles, not once, but twice, using as much force as I could, feeling so much glory in the act of feeling them crunch under my foot. He fell to the floor, not being able to catch his breath, and I knelt to him and told him that I was not going to be his ragdoll that he can throw around anymore, and I was leaving him.

When he finally got up, he tried to get in my face, and that is when I warned him that I may not have any friends nearby who would come to my assistance but that as he knew, I had friends, ones who I can call who would gladly take care of him for me. I let him know if he tried to stop me, it would be the last thing he did. With that, and the look of confusion on his face, I felt as though I had found my balls that he had taken away from me.

After that, he did not say much to me nor try to have his way with me. I told him he needed to move out, but he refused, making it known that it was his house too. So, I decided that I would once again save up, and move out, because even though all my money was in that house, I hated it and wanted to get far away from it all. I found I was finally able to sleep at night, without the worry of him coming in, and that I could sleep in the nursery, keeping myself and my daughter safe with the locked door at night.

I felt so good about the future and was preparing for the coming months which included going back to school when I realized that I had not had a period. I was furious, knowing that this is not at all what I wanted. But I went to the doctor, and when she confirmed my fear, I was furious. I went to the house to talk to him, to tell him that I was done, and demanded he leaves my house. I did not want to tell him I was pregnant.

When he told me that once again, he was not going anywhere and left for work, I went to the bank. I was going to clear out my account and get a new place to live, I was not going to wait any longer. That was my plan until I got to the bank to find that my account had already been emptied. Both the accounts, in fact, including the joint account we had, were empty.

I walked into the bank to talk with someone because the account I had there where I was saving up money to move from, was one that I was sure he did not know about. But when I asked the lady at the bank when the money had been removed, she looked it up and said the money had been removed earlier that morning, and my ATM card was used. She pulled up the screen to show me, asking me if I had shared my card with my husband or requested a second one as it showed on my account that I had done? I told her I was not married and left. I needed to find out what was going on. So, I decided to drive out to Eduardo's work and confront him about the situation.

When I arrived at his work, I noticed the other woman's car there, and as I walked up to his office, I could see them sitting, sharing lunch together. Other people in the office watched as I walked in, pushing the stroller with my daughter inside of it, stopping to stare to see what I was doing. As he looked up from talking, he told the other woman to leave and that he would call her later. He asked me what I wanted, and I told him that I had gone to the bank, claiming that I needed to pay bills to find our account was empty. I then went on and said that my other account was empty as well and the bank had informed me that he had withdrawn the money earlier that morning.

He looked at me then laughed, saying that I thought I was smart but now that I did not have any money, what was I going to do? When I asked him how I was going to pay the bills, he answered me by suggesting I go and beg for money, maybe go to a church and ask, that he did not have any money.

I was once again floored. I did not want to cry or make a scene since I was sure he had told everyone at his work I was crazy, so I left and went back to the house to try and think about what I could do. When I drove up to the house, I noticed one of his cousins pulling out of the driveway. As I got closer, I noticed the cousin had dropped off a car. I stopped the truck to see his cousin inside. He got out and asked me how I was doing. I told him that I was confused as to why this car was at our house. The cousin explained that earlier that morning, Eduardo had gone to the cousin's car lot and paid for the car in cash, and he was just there to deliver it. That is when I started to cry. The cousin asked me if I was okay and I told him I was not, then broke down and told him about the money, how I was going to leave Eduardo and that no matter how hard I tried to get away, he would find a way to stop me and try to break me.

The cousin seemed to be one that for once in what seemed like forever, believed me. He hugged me and told me Eduardo was a piece of crap. He pulled out his wallet and handed me some of the money he had in it, then said they would take the car back and for me to stop by the lot to pick up the rest of the money. He also stated that if I needed anything, to call him and he would be there to help me. He said I was too good for Eduardo, and he wondered why a woman like me was with someone like Eduardo, in fact, which was a question that many others in the family asked as well. But that he had his suspicions, just could not prove anything.

With that, I felt like I was doing the right thing. I felt like I had someone on my side for once in an awfully long time, and that I knew what I needed to do.

After leaving the house, I followed the cousin to the car lot he owned. He gave me the money Eduardo had taken from my account, then gave me a card with information on it about an apartment complex that a friend of his managed. He told me to let them know he was sending me and that if they needed anything they could call him to verify. Before leaving I thanked him and he told me I needed to take care of myself and my daughter and to be careful.

I left the car lot and went straight to the apartment complex that was on the card. It was a nice complex that was not far from my work. When I got into the office, the lady at the desk asked me my name and then said she was glad I was there, that the cousin had just called her to let her know that I might be stopping by. She went on and asked how soon I was wanting to move, and I explained that the sooner the better, that is when she said that she would have a unit available for me to move into by the end of the week if that worked for me. I right away began to cry, not sad tears, but tears of relief and happiness. I filled out the paperwork and ran to get money orders to secure the apartment. She had me sign a lease and told me by Friday, that she would have the keys ready for me, so I could move in.

I was ecstatic! I mean, I found a way out, one that I was sure was going to work for me. And as I headed back to the house, I thought about how I would leave without him interfering. I decided to take the money I had left and went to a different bank, opened an account, and put the new address as my address on the account, with hopes that Eduardo would not find out. I went up to my work and had Payroll also change the direct deposit to the new account as well.

When I arrived at the house, I took my daughter inside with me, then went to grab some boxes. I went through the house, packing, and placing the boxes I packed in the closet, to keep them hidden until I could remove them on Friday. As the time went by that day, I began dreading Eduardo coming home, having to remain at that house, even if it was a few more days. I felt that any more time there was too long.

As the sun started to go down, Eduardo pulled up to the driveway. I felt scared but at the same time, was going to try to avoid talking to him as much as possible. So, I went to the kitchen to prepare dinner for myself and my daughter.

He walked in, then went straight to the kitchen, demanding that I give him the money. I told him that I did not have any money and that I spent it all. He yelled and told me that he was going to find it, then went and dumped my purse out. After not finding any money in there, he took my keys and went to my car, going through every possible part of it, with hopes that he would find something. When he did not, he came back inside the house, then began throwing everything around in the nursery, emptying the drawers. He continued this rage into the dining room, grabbing all the porcelain figurines I had collected and found dear to me due to many of them being from my grandparents who had passed away. He threw each one of the figurines against the wall, screaming, demanding I give him the money and do it now.

The more I ignored him and his tantrum, the worse he got, by throwing dishes and smashing them on the floor. After he got done searching the kitchen, he came back to the dining room where I was feeding my daughter her dinner and eating my dinner. He then grabbed my plate, threw it against the wall, and grabbed my hair. I tried to kick him and hit him, only to make him madder, but the moment he lost his grip on me, I went to let my daughter out of the highchair. When I did this, he grabbed my hair again, throwing me to the ground. I quickly got up and started to run when I felt his foot kick me in the back. I began crying begging him to stop when he told me that it was too late, that he was not going to let me leave him, at least not alive, and that I would never see my baby again. That is when I blurted out, as a plea for my life, that I was pregnant.

He stopped for a second there and asked me when I found out. I told him that the other day when I went running errands, I had gone to see my doctor and she confirmed it. Eduardo told me that it was bs since he had not had sex with me in weeks. But I pointed out that he had when he forced himself on me the month prior, and that the dates add up. He told me that I must have been with someone else because it could not be his. I looked at him and told him that because of him, I didn't think I could ever trust another man again, nor did I want any sort of relationship with anyone anytime soon. And with my smartass, I grabbed my phone, knowing that I had my way out but that he had not planned on me being pregnant, and I said, "How about we call your girlfriend and let her know that we are expecting again?"

I continued, showing that I had her number stored, unknowingly pressing the call button as I went on and said, "I am sure she will be pleased to find out how it is that you got me pregnant, to learn that due to you raping me regularly, that in that time when you were trying to get me pregnant just 1 month prior, you had succeeded." That she should know what kind of person he is, and how he tried to break me, forcing me to submit to him. How I purposely locked the door to the nursery, to keep him off me, since he had no problem raping me in front of our baby either.

As I said all of this, I looked at the phone and realized she answered and heard everything that was said. When he realized that she heard it all, he grabbed my phone and threw it against the wall. Then grabbed me by the throat, threw me on the bed, and put all his weight into the choke, saying that I needed to die. I tried to fight back, trying to push him off me, but I began to feel like I was fading out as I was not able to get any air, that was until I looked out of the corner of my eye, and saw my baby girl, standing in the doorway, watching her dad choke her mom and crying for me. Crying for her mommy. I took all the energy I had, and for the split second when he looked over to see our daughter, I kneed him as hard as I could.

He fell over off the bed, grabbing his crotch, cursing me.

I ran to the door, picking up my daughter to see him getting up to come after us. The closest door was the bathroom, where I had my curling iron on the counter and plugged in. As I got into the bathroom, I could feel that he was not far behind me, so I grabbed the curling iron to use as a weapon and burn him. When I did this, he grabbed a camera out of his pocket and recorded me. He said that I was crazy, coming at him for no reason and scaring our daughter.

He turned off the camera and started coming back at me, and as he did this, there was a knock at the front door. But the knock was not a normal one, it was a very loud and demanding one. He stopped, went to answer the door, to see the police were outside. The neighbors had heard us, him breaking things, and the struggle after when he had pulled me by the hair and I screamed, begging him to let go.

An officer came into the bathroom, another followed, and she handed my daughter to the officer behind her. The officer then asked me if I was okay, that they were going to help me. That is when I cried, uncontrollably, and told this officer how the fight started, that I was pregnant, showing her the marks on my neck, my bloodshot eyes caused by being strangled, and marks on me from the altercation. All evidence that went along with the statement I gave.

As the officers were taking photos of the marks on me, trying to comfort my daughter, and walking around the house to see the mess he had made, they took him outside to talk to him as well. I stood there, holding up my hair that had blood in it from when he had pulled it, where a large cluster of hair had been ripped out, to see him pull out the camera that he had used just minutes prior, to record me defending myself. I was confused, thinking that there was no way anyone would believe his twisted lie. Then he reached into his truck, to pull out that old bottle of pills, the paperwork from when I went to be treated for postpartum depression, and the prior police report. It was like he had it all ready in case things went south, to use in his defense.

The officers looked over everything he handed them. Called the female officer that had talked to me inside, to go outside. They showed her everything and she then came back in. She asked me if I had been treated for postpartum depression, which I said I had, but that I was no longer taking the medications. She asked me if the doctor had advised me to stop taking the medications, and I told her that she had not but that I was no longer needing them because I was not depressed. She asked me if I knew about the video he showed her, and I explained that I did, that he took that video when I went to try to defend myself after he had just tried to kill me.

The officer went back outside and several of them stood around talking, looking back up at me in the house. She walked back up to the house, as several of the other officers left. Eduardo walked back into the house, not even looking at me, grabbed his keys, and left. The officer then said that Eduardo did not want to press charges on me and that I had left marks on him as well. That he had scratch marks and that his story was different from mine, and he had the video which supported his claim. She then continued and said that he was advised to stay somewhere else for the night to let things cool down before coming back and that I should probably go back to my doctor because Eduardo could request a court order for me to be placed on a psychiatric watch.

I was shaking. And as the officers drove off, I felt once again defeated. I sat there, comforting my baby, staring off, trying to figure out what had just happened, realizing that he continued to get away with everything and knowing that I needed to protect my daughter.

That night seemed to be a long one. Every noise woke me up to think Eduardo was back and was going to finish what he started. I did not have the law on my side, to protect me. I did not have my own family there to help me. So, when morning came, I called the apartment complex and asked if I could move in sooner. The manager said that I could, but all she had at the moment, that was ready, was a little smaller apartment, and one that was not close to the office like I had wanted for my own, peace of mind. I took her up on the available apartment, called the cousin and some of my other friends, and by the end of the afternoon, I was moved out and moved into a place that was mine, away from him.

I felt free, liberated once again, and in a place that would allow me to move forward. I vowed to myself that I would never look back, nor allow what had happened to me, to bring me down or happen again. This promise was one not only for myself but for my daughter and the baby I was carrying as well.

The following night after I had left, Eduardo called me. Demanding that I let him see his daughter, which I told him that we would need to make arrangements for. He also said that he would not claim the baby I was pregnant with, not until he got a DNA test to prove it was his. I told him that was fine with me, and that he was a piece of shit because he knew it was his. But regardless of what he said to me on the phone, I did not let it bother me or bring me down. I was not going to allow him to have any say-so on any part of my life ever again.

A week after I had left, we made arrangements where I would take the baby to one of the babysitters, he would pick her up, and I would get her after I got off of work. We also agreed to the days when I was on-call, that he would keep her. This all seemed to work, I avoided conversation with him, or even going into a house with him. That was until I got a call at work. My daughter had been with him for the past two days and one of his cousins was watching my daughter. She called with concern saying that my baby had a fever and a lot of rattling in her chest. I left work to pick her up and take her to the doctor.

We had switched pediatricians after her stay in the hospital when she was just a couple of months old and were incredibly pleased with the choice of doing so. The new doctor was extremely sweet, had been in practice for many years, and had a great reputation. So, when I went to take my daughter to be seen, the moment he heard her cough in his waiting room, he came in and asked to have her brought back to a room. He went and did an exam and then asked me to come and listen to her chest. I could hear fluid in there, and he then had an O2 test done on her, along with a chest x-ray, to only confirm what he was thinking, that she had pneumonia.

The thing was, with the diagnosis, she needed to be watched very closely and given treatments every few hours, but due to the RSV going around, there were no single rooms at the hospital. That if we went there, she would have to share a room most likely with another child who had RSV, which could be dangerous for her. So, the doctor suggested that I could do the treatments at home and ask for help since someone would need to sleep with her sitting up to avoid her choking on the access fluid in her lungs. During this, Eduardo showed up. The God Mother had called him to let him know that I was there and that the baby was sick. He had walked in as the doctor suggested I have someone help me to care for her, so she could get better, explaining that the care would need to be round the clock for at least the next week. Eduardo then said, without talking to me, or considering anything, that he would be there and help me.

I felt hot in the face, I was not going to be doing this with Eduardo. Then the God Mother came in, mentioning that we needed to do what was best for the baby and to put our differences aside. I agreed not wanting to argue since she already had the idea that I was crazy, and as we left Eduardo said that he would come by my apartment after grabbing some things.

I was given the prescriptions for the medications along with some medical equipment that I needed to pick up. I told Eduardo that I would be at the apartment after stopping by to drop off the prescriptions and pick up the equipment.

When I got done and arrived at the apartment, Eduardo was there waiting for me. He agreed that he would sleep on the couch and that we were only doing all of this for our daughter's sake because she needed us to work together, for our baby to get better.

As we walked inside, he mentioned that he had received some letters from the bank, saying that since the mortgage was not being paid, they were going to be foreclosing on the house soon. I looked at him, confused since we had only had the house for not quite a year. He said that he had hoped to get the payments caught up, but the money I thought was being used, was not being used to pay the bills. That the lights, and gas were off as well. I asked him why he had the baby there if there were no electricity or gas, and he said that he had been staying with his brothers for the past few nights. I was too angry at that point, knowing my money was completely wasted all for nothing and wanting to know what he did with all the money. But I needed to focus on the baby, get her better so he could leave.

After almost 2 weeks, we had to take our daughter back to the doctor. The doctor said she was doing better but would need more medicine. We got back to the apartment to drop Eduardo and the baby off, and I left to pick up the prescriptions at the pharmacy and run to the store for some groceries. I had not been gone a long time, but when I drove up to my apartment, I drove up to Eduardo's brother and 2 of his cousins, unloading the brother's truck into my apartment. The fucker had pulled another fast one on me and I was floored.

The brother did not make eye contact with me, and for good reason, because I was pissed. I came out of the car yelling for them to leave, to take everything out of my house, and leave. The brother and cousins got back in their vehicles and left, but left, leaving everything in my apartment. When I walked in, Eduardo had a smirk on his face, but he was holding my daughter, giving her a breathing treatment, so I went to the room. I could not believe what was going on. I left to walk to the office, but it was a Friday, and they left the office early on Fridays.

When I got back to the apartment, Eduardo was carrying my daughter as she slept, and he was unpacking some of his things. I went to get my daughter and lay in the recliner with her, so I could think and figure out what to do. He walked around the apartment, placing his things around it, smiling, acting as if he owned the place, which just made me madder and madder. But I decided to not let it bother me because I knew he was not on the lease, and come Monday morning, I would have the management remove him from the property. Until then, I would avoid conversation with him, only to discuss things that had to do with caring for the baby and that was it.

The plan seemed to work, and come Sunday morning, my daughter was up playing, running around, and laughing again. She still had a cough but had her color come back, and her sweet disposition came back as well. I felt like come Monday, she and I could continue to move forward, and I could be done with him.

When the time came for the office to open on Monday morning, I was waiting outside for them to open the office. The apartment manager pulled the file and then asked when Eduardo came to help me. I told her that it had been for 2 weeks. She then got a highlighter and selected a section on the rental agreement showing that after someone had been in the apartment for 2 weeks, they are considered tenants. She then advised that I could have him evicted, but that could take 30 days or longer, and it had to be done through the courts.

I felt as though I was moving backward. Like everything was going to start over again and again, and I was not going to allow that to happen, I had vowed to myself, my daughter, and the baby I was pregnant with that I would not allow that to happen again. She knew some of the situation I had been in and suggested that in a few weeks, she will have another unit open up, a one-bedroom this time, and said I could move into it if I was interested. That she would then deal with him from there. I found the thought of another 3 weeks to be 3 weeks too long, but it was a better solution than me not having one at the time. So, I agreed. She told me that she would waive the deposit, that I would just need to pay the first and last month's rent and we would transfer the paperwork to a different unit.

On my way back to the apartment my mom called. She said Eduardo had called and had asked for help with paying his phone bill on Friday and that she had but that I would need to get the money from him to give to her when I went to visit for Thanksgiving. I was confused on the call because I was unaware that he was still in contact with my mom, but apparently, he was, and she had just paid his bill for him. I then felt even more confused, because I was trying to figure out why he was not paying bills, where all the money went? So, when I got back to the apartment, I told him that my mom called. He said that she had given him her credit card info, so he could pay the bill over the phone but that he would give me the money to pay her back. He then said he had to go to work and would see me later.

I took the baby to the doctor, to have her checked again and hopefully cleared. When I got to the office, the God Mother was there, and she said that she was happy to hear that we were back together. I ignored her and went into the appointment. After the doctor cleared the baby, I decided to call the brother's wife. I asked if I could talk to her about some things. She stopped me and said that she was quite sure that it was about the other woman. I said that I was not sure what she meant. She then went on and said Eduardo had been by to borrow money for diapers and asked for a loan to pay some bills. Apparently, he had given all his money to that other woman for her bills and to help her with her kids.

I told the wife he never bought diapers, and that he had never bought anything for our daughter since the day she was born. He had never used any of his own money for really anything, that everything we had, all bills, had been paid for with my money. I asked her what day this was, and she said it was in the middle of the week prior, that he said he was fixing to lose the house, and they told him they would give him money for diapers but that was it. That is when he asked them to help him move since he was going to lose the house. I told her, "thank you for the information" and I informed her he did not buy any diapers that day, instead, he bought a video game, and I knew because I had bought diapers the day before and noticed him playing some new game on my XBOX.

When I got back to the apartment, I was livid. He was a liar, a cheater, and a man that I honestly did not want around my kids. He had been giving all our money to the other woman, he had forced me to purchase a home we were now losing just as fast as we got it. That, in just a little over a couple of years, so much had happened, which was more than I could have never imagined happening to anyone in such a brief time. I went into the room and grabbed some boxes that I had in the closet, and began to pack up, once again.

As I packed, I can remember thinking that I could not wait to get away for a short break from all this madness when I went to visit my family for Thanksgiving. I looked over at my daughter playing on the floor, questioning myself on how could I save her from this madness, and how could I protect my unborn baby from this as well? I then went on to think about the vacation, how once I got back, I could move right into my new apartment and just let him stay there until the complex evicted him. Thinking that he was pretty much out of luck and would hopefully just give up.

The Nightmare Next Door

As the countdown was on for Thanksgiving, I was feeling more and more excited. Excited to see my old friends and family back home, and excited about the fact that once I returned, I would be moving again. My dad had requested that I pick up some pies from one of his favorite bakeries and had placed an order there at the bakery to ensure he got the pies he wanted. He also asked that I pick up a few other items before driving down to see them.

Eduardo knew about the vacation since I had been planning it for the past few months, and until we got closer to the day I would be going, had not voiced his concern or protest to stop me from going. When he finally said something to me, he seemed to act as if he had no idea that I was going or thought I would not go for some reason.

This protest turned into an argument, where Eduardo told me that I was not to go. Informing me that if I did go, I was not allowed to take my daughter with me. I told him that he had no say so in anything that I did, that we were not a couple, and I could do as I pleased and explained that I would only be gone for a few days, in which he would be working anyways. That is when he struck me. I was caught off guard feeling like he would not dare, but he did, and he did it again and again, knocking me to the floor.

When I was on the floor, I feared him kicking me in the stomach, instead, he kicked me in the back with the steel-toed boots he was wearing, sending pain that was unlike any other pain he had inflicted on me which could be felt at the tips of my toes and fingers. As I tried to grab my back, he then stepped over me, kicking me as hard as he could in my stomach and groin area. Leaving me trying to gasp for air, while feeling a pain that I had never felt before. Something that I can honestly say was worse than labor pains and left me feeling the effects of the blows for years to come. Where the pain in my tailbone, still causes issues, even after nearly 18 years.

He went to the room and left me there, curled up in a ball on the floor, trying to recover from what had just happened as I cried. I got up and went for my daughter who was in her room crying for me. I took her to the kitchen to make her something to eat when I had a wave of nausea come over me. He walked in as if nothing was wrong, grabbed my daughter, and sat her on his lap as he fed her the dinner I had just prepared for her. I could not eat, and as the evening went on, I started feeling sharp pains in my lower back.

It felt as though there was a hot knife in my lower back where he had kicked me, and the excruciating pains continued throughout the night, some coming in waves and lasting for what seemed an eternity. The next morning, I got up to my blankets being covered in blood. I went to the bathroom and realized that I had had a miscarriage. I grabbed the blankets, put them in the washing machine, scrubbed the mattress, then I went to get my daughter dressed and drove her to my friend's house. My friend had her mom watch my daughter while she took me to the hospital, both of us not talking but knowing that I lost the baby I had been carrying. When we got to the hospital, they took me to a room in the triage. The doctor came in, examined me then ordered an ultrasound. She then explained that I had indeed had a miscarriage and that they would need to do a DNC to make sure that everything came out to avoid infection.

My friend stayed by my side the entire time during the procedure, offering the support I needed. My back and groin still had the pains from the kicks I received the day prior, a large bruise had formed on my lower back and as they went through with the procedure, I could feel it all. The thing was, even though I had lost the baby, I felt a bit of relief. Even today when I think about it, I realize that it sounds bad to say such but to bring another innocent child into the life I had, was not fair to that child. It was not fair to the daughter I already had, and I felt relief in knowing that Eduardo was not going to hurt another child and that the child I lost was going to be in a better place by not being brought into the nightmare that I had brought its older sister into.

After leaving the hospital, I went back to my friend's house where we talked. I told her about the new apartment and how I could not stand seeing him every day. She then insisted that we go out for a lady's night when she would be off next, to let off some steam and celebrate before I went on vacation, the freedom I would be getting once I got back.

I decided that I would take her up on her offer of going out. I also decided that I would not give him the satisfaction of knowing that I had lost the baby, or that he might have played a part in me losing it. I did not want to tell him anything that was going on in my life.

When I arrived at the house, Eduardo was there waiting for me, asking me where I had been with my daughter. I told him that what I did, was none of his business, and if he wanted to worry about someone, call his girlfriend who he has been supporting. He got up, got in my face, and grabbed it, saying that I was an ungrateful bitch and that my mouth was going to get me in a lot of trouble. I just stared him in the eyes as he did this, not saying anything or changing my expression, not showing him any fear.

For the next couple of days, we did not speak to one another, I avoided the chance for a confrontation as best I could. Making sure I was never in the same room with him for any extended periods, taking my daughter to the park or my friend's house to play with her nieces when he was at the house, and during the day, enjoying every moment that Eduardo was not there.

Then on the afternoon that I was to go out with my friends, I let him know that I would be going out with friends that night and that he was to watch our daughter. He did not say anything to me about that, instead, he sat on the couch and played some video games.

A few hours later, my friends showed up to pick me up. Eduardo answered the door and told them to go out without me, that I would not be going. My friend laughed at him and told him to get out of her way as she pushed her way into the apartment and to my room. At this time, I had not figured out what I would wear, so she and my other friends who came over, picked out some clothes and insisted that I looked too hot to not go out. As we walked out of the bedroom to the living room, he was standing there, blocking the front door. He told me to get back in the room and demanded that my friends leave, that is when my friend, who was only 4 foot 9, got in his face.

She was a woman, who was not one who allowed anyone to tell her what to do or try to push her around, and when he tried to order everyone around, she told him to move and have a seat. He then tried to tell her that he was only going to say it one more time, that I was not going to be going out with them, and for them to leave. That is when instead of arguing or asking him to move, she decided to go out the back door, and climb over the balcony, which was not a tricky thing to do since we had a bottom-floor apartment. The rest of us quickly followed her, trying to hurry and get out before he went to grab me again for any reason. Once we had got outside and around to the front where the cars were, we all let out a laugh, running to the cars and hurrying to get out of there.

As we went to the first club, I felt freedom, even if it was just for a fleeting moment, I felt like I was invincible. I had many admirers at the clubs, buying me drinks, asking me to dance, and wanting to hang out with the group of girls. I felt like a woman again, being admired by men, which made me feel pretty, even after all the horror I had been through and how down I had felt just months prior, I felt like a human being again.

During the night, I had one gentleman who I had danced with many times, and for the majority of the night, had talked to me. He was a very good-looking, well-built, Sergeant in the Air Force who was there with some of his friends from the base a few towns over. After talking for a while, he invited his friends over to introduce them to some of my friends. Making the night one that was worth the small confrontation. Once the club had called the last call, we all decided to walk over to the IHOP, where we got some coffee and food. We laughed, talked, and had a lot of fun, being young adults. Where some in the group talked about their young children, showing me that you can enjoy life even with kids. Giving me the realization that the life I had been living, needed to be left far behind, and even with being a young single mom, I could still have a life that I could enjoy.

After eating, we were all heading out and ready to say goodbye, when this good-looking soldier who I had been hanging out with and talking to, grabbed me to give me a good night kiss. I had to stop him, explaining that I was not ready for that, and was not sure when I would be ready for any sort of affection from a man. He looked at me and told me that was okay, that he enjoyed my company and wanted to know if we could keep in touch, become friends if nothing else. I agreed, and with that, he offered to drive me to my apartment.

When we drove up, I could see the curtain move, making me realize that Eduardo had been waiting for me to come home. We sat in the parking lot as this man could see me get uneasy, and that is when I explained the situation, not going into the details but letting him know that Eduardo and I were no longer together, but that he would not leave. This guy offered to help Eduardo leave in a joking manner, and I then explained that after the Thanksgiving break I was moving into another apartment there at that complex. He gave me his number and I gave him mine, asking me to call him when I got back.

As we talked in the car, we could see Eduardo peeking out, watching us. This man got out of his vehicle, then insisted he walk me to the door. I agreed to let him, and as we walked to the door, he asked for a goodnight kiss, loud enough to let Eduardo hear. I giggled and decided to give him that kiss, not caring if Eduardo saw it or not. We then said goodnight and I walked inside.

When I walked inside, Eduardo was standing by the window, watching the guy I had just kissed drive off. He then insisted I tell him who that was, and I just kept telling him it was no one. I then went to the room, locked my door, and went to bed, not minding anything that Eduardo was trying to say to me on the other side of the door.

The next day, we did not talk much, in fact, I tried to avoid any sort of interaction with Eduardo. Then the day came that it was time for me to get ready to go on vacation. I had been very vocal about the vacation; when I would leave and when I would be back.

Eduardo had to work over Thanksgiving, so I did not consider anything that had to do with him over this time. I knew that he would be staying at my apartment, but also knew that once I got back, things were going to change again, and I looked forward to that. As I went around the house getting things for me and the baby to take with me, Eduardo stopped me. I was coming back out of the room, when he stood, blocking my way in the hall.

He got in my face and asked me what I thought I was doing. I looked at him, rolled my eyes, and told him to move. He did not, instead, he got right in my face and yelled, asking me what I thought I was doing, then slapped me and told me to show him some respect. That I did not show him any respect and that I was a whore who slept around with every man I saw, and that I was pregnant with another man's baby because I was nothing but a dirty whore.

I told him that he needed to go, that he was going to be late for work. He then grabbed me by the neck and told me that I better be there when he got home, that he was not done with me, and we had unfinished business we needed to tend to. With that, he tried to kiss me, and got mad when I refused him, saying, "You can give it up to anyone now huh, you are just as common as the whores who walked the BLVD."

He let me go and I stood there, frozen, scared of what he was going to do next, instead I heard him grab his keys, and the front door open and close.

I knew he would not be off until that evening, so I spent the day hurrying, running errands, packing my things up in boxes, and hiding the boxes in the storage closet that was on the balcony that I could get to easily when I got back.

While I was out picking up the pies my dad had ordered, my phone rang. It was Eduardo asking me what I was doing, why I was not at home? I told him that I was at the store picking up some things and would be home later. He kept on calling every 10 minutes it seemed, asking the same questions. He then called to say that his brother needed to borrow a stroller from me and to meet him at the apartment. I was headed back to the apartment at this time, so I agreed I would meet him.

When I arrived, I went to put my baby down for a nap while I finished packing our bags, when a knock came on the door. I figured it was the brother coming for the stroller, and I yelled out saying that it was in the storage closet on the balcony if he wanted to meet me out there. I did not hear a reply from the brother, instead, I heard someone say, "Mam?"

I went to the living room to see who it was, and since I had left the front door open, I saw a police officer peering into my apartment. I asked him what I could do for him, and he asked me if I was going somewhere. I told him that I was, that I was going to visit family for Thanksgiving, pointing to the pies I had just picked up that were still warm from the bakery. The officer then asked me my name and informed me that he was there to serve me papers, handed me the papers, then left.

As the officer left, I just stood there confused as to why I was being served with papers, that was until I looked down and saw that they were an emergency order for temporary custody. Stating that Eduardo swore to a court that I was going to kidnap our daughter and leave the state to never come back, trying to stop me from going for Thanksgiving. Giving him temporary full custody of my daughter until we went to court, or I had a lawyer to contest the orders on my behalf.

Along with the order of temporary custody, Eduardo had also voiced concern for his own life, stating in the paperwork that he had given a letter to his brother, that if something were to happen to him, that I had something to do with it. He made claims, sharing that I had friends whom he feared, who would be willing to do my bidding for me. And in the letter that his brother held onto for safekeeping, he had the names of those who would be responsible, if something were to happen to him or he was to disappear.

After reading the papers over, I called my parents. I talked to my dad this time and told him a lot of what had been going on, the abuse (no details) but stated that Eduardo had hit me earlier that day and threatened me before he left and that I was scared that threat was him saying he was going to finish what he had started by killing me. My mom got on the line, and listened as well, she then called a cousin we had who was a lawyer and explained to him what I was served with.

My cousin then called me to explain that since we had not gone to court and because I was not attempting to leave for good, just a vacation which can be shown as had been planned from my work where I took off months in advance, that I was not leaving like a thief in the night as he put it. He said that Eduardo must have hired a lawyer and that they put an order because Eduardo must have portrayed to this lawyer that I was leaving town, with no plans of coming back. I then told the cousin about some of the abuse, that I had got an apartment, lost the house, how he weaseled his way into my new apartment, and how I had a new one-bedroom apartment set up once I got back.

My cousin said that was good because the apartment complex will have the new lease showing that I never had intentions of leaving the state for good, as he put in the papers, that I was going on a vacation as planned and coming back. As I had been on the phone with my cousin, my parents had made several phone calls, one to a lawyer that the cousin had suggested we call, and other calls to my family, that were still in the area.

When I hung up with the cousin, my phone rang again. It was my mom, letting me know that they had gotten in touch with a lawyer that was local to me, giving me this lawyer's info and then informing me to get out of the house right away. Take whatever I needed and head to one of my cousin's houses that lived in the town I was in and that I should be safe there until they could figure out what to do next.

I hung up the phone, called the lawyer my mom had given me the number for, and spoke to her, as I did this, I ran around the house frantically, grabbing clothes, diapers, baby food, everything that I could easily travel with and live on for a short while if needed. The time was going by way too fast, and I was scared he might get there before I left.

I was going around grabbing just the necessities, filling up my car. The lawyer said I could leave town, but to be careful because after talking to Eduardo's lawyer, she was concerned since he seemed to have the courts believing that I was leaving the state and kidnapping my daughter, never to come back. She told me that we would be furnishing proof of the planned vacation and the new apartment after the break when we went to the courts to plea my case, but that nothing was stopping me from taking that vacation, but Eduardo, if he got there to stop me. And with that, I continued to pack and then got in my car to head to my cousin's house.

I arrived at the cousin's house, sitting in their driveway, thinking that I was not sure if going there was a clever idea. They had a family, a child that was just months older than my daughter. That is when my dad called, saying to not go there, that Eduardo knew where this cousin lived, and I agreed that I did not want to expose my cousins to the mess I was in. My dad then asked me to go to my grandma's house, his mom's, a lady that I did not know well, but that Eduardo did not know either.

During the drive to the outskirts of town where my grandma lived, my dad called again, telling me to turn around and just get out of town. By this time, it was starting to get dark out, which was a lot later than I had planned on heading out for, knowing that I had an 8-hour drive. And as I began getting further and further away from the town, my mom called saying that she was getting me a room in a town that was just an hour up the road, and for me and my daughter to stay there for the night. She then advised that I do not answer any calls unless it was from my parent's house.

I arrived at the hotel, got my room, and went to get some food for my daughter. I had noticed that for the past few hours, my phone rang constantly, knowing that if it was him calling, that if my family needed to call, they would not be able to get through to me. So, after picking up food for my daughter and getting her cleaned up and ready for bed, I called my parents from the room, letting them know the number so they could call me. That is when my mom informed me that they had been trying to call because Eduardo had called them, numerous times.

She continued, explaining to me that my dad got on the phone after the fourth or fifth time when Eduardo was continuing to call, and he threatened to kill my dad. She went on and said that after Eduardo did that, he called back a few minutes later, voicing many threats and when my sister got on the phone, a teenage girl, he threatened her as well, promising to make her show him some respect. My mom then let me know that Eduardo went to my cousin's house and had somehow found my grandma's house as well, going to every house he thought I might have been at, to hide from him.

I felt so uneasy, but also relieved. I did not like the fact that Eduardo was calling, driving by harassing, and threatening my family, but I was not there for him to finish off either, as he warned me to be earlier that day. I also felt some solace in knowing that now Eduardo has shown his true colors to others, that I was no longer alone in this fight I was about to take on.

The next morning, I got up and took my daughter to the lobby of the hotel for breakfast. After eating, we went to the room, grabbed our bags, checked out then headed back on the road towards my hometown to see my parents and old friends. I had kept my phone on silent that night before, due to the nonstop calls that appeared to have gone on all night long. Eduardo had also left several messages, filling the voicemail box, but I decided to not erase them so that he could not leave anymore. In his messages, they went from warning me to go back home to him with my daughter, to him begging me to come back and talk to him. He had shown a broad range of emotions in each message, to where I could hear in his voice that he knew he had not won as he might have thought he had.

I called my family from the hotel before leaving, letting them know we were back on the road and that I would call when we stopped for gas. I decided to turn my phone off, so as to not waste the battery from all his calling that day in case I needed it for any sort of emergency. As we continued that drive, I felt the fears, the uncertainty I felt over the past couple of years, leave one tiny bit at a time. To where I could feel that weight I had been carrying, lifting from my shoulders, and a new door opening in my life. A door that was not going to include him no matter what, and where I was going to protect my daughter from the monster as well.

Later that morning, we finally arrived at my parent's house. My family came running out the door, with tears in their eyes, to come and embrace me and my daughter. I could see that they too were stressed out and fearful from the events that had unfolded less than 24 hours prior. Where my dad hugged me, crying, saying that he wished I never had to go back to where that monster could get to me or my daughter. Saying that he had wished I would have reached out for help so much sooner.

As he did this, I looked to my mom, whom I loved, but who for a while there, had sided with the monster, believing the lies that allowed him to put his hooks in me deeper and deeper. But she did not know better, she was not there to see firsthand what was going on, and Eduardo had called her regularly, using the evidence of me going to a doctor for help as his way of proving the stories he told others. I also did not hold that against her, because I knew that she thought what she was doing was in our best interest, and now that she knew, I did not want her to feel guilty for anything, because Eduardo had made me believe things that were untrue as well. And I was just glad to be with my family, even if it was only for a few days, we were where it was safe.

As we walked into my parent's house, the phone rang. It was Eduardo, which is when my family explained that he had been calling nonstop day and night, and regardless of them having their home phone be also a business phone, they were not answering. Instead, they let their machine pick up the messages, which he did not leave any, instead, he would hang up and call again, and again.

I walked my daughter upstairs to the living area my parents had set up for my daughter and me to use while we were there. They had baby gates, blocking the stairs, knowing that we had a walking toddler on our hands, and keeping my daughter safe while we all visited upstairs. My sister was very excited to see her niece and insisted she take her to let me sleep since everyone could see the stress and fear I had on my face, noticing the bags under my eyes, and the red eyes from lack of sleep and crying. I took her up on the offer and went to sleep on the sofa sleeper that my parents had set up for us to use while there.

A few hours had passed after I fell asleep, and I woke up feeling very refreshed. I could hear others downstairs talking, and as I walked down, I was rushed up upon by some of my old friends, who were embracing me. Telling me how much they missed me, how adorable my daughter was, and that they too, were all there for me.

The presence in my parent's house was a very welcomed one, one that I did not want to ever leave, knowing that when I did leave, I was going back to the horror that awaited me. Knowing that he was given the time to plot and that he was beyond livid at the fact that he was not given the chance to finish me off like he had promised he would do before I left. That I had family, who were still there for me, regardless of how hard he tried to isolate me from having anyone on my side. And knowing that I refused to talk to him so that he could somehow convince me to go back, and that I had gone against the orders he had made, thinking he had the upper hand.

As my family, friends, and I sat around, they all asked to see the paperwork I had been served with the day prior. My mom called the cousin who was a lawyer, letting him and the rest of the family know that we were safe and there with them, and reading over the entire order that was served to me. My cousin explained that I would have a fight ahead of me because Eduardo had one-upped me by going to the courts first. That his claims were not all valid, but that he might have something up his sleeves that could cause a lot of issues for me in the near future. The cousin let me know that he was there for me, as was the rest of the family, and to reach out at any time I needed them. I thanked everyone, feeling loved, and feeling like I was ready for whatever "he" had waiting for me.

By that late afternoon, the phone calls had stopped, and Eduardo was no longer trying to call my phone or my parent's phone. Then the phone rang after about an hour of silence, and to my surprise it was a group of my friends, asking me to come and visit them, to catch up on things and to bring my daughter by for them all to meet.

My family insisted that I go out, meet up with my old friends and try to forget about what was going on, to enjoy the time I had there. I took them up on the offer to head out and bring my daughter to meet some of my childhood friends who were extremely excited to meet my baby and see me.

As I drove down the mountain that my parents lived on, I had a feeling of knowing that I never wanted to leave that place again but having a dark feeling of also knowing that I had to leave in a few days to return to the nightmare that awaited me.

I arrived at a friend's house where a large group of close friends all gathered, to greet me, give me lots of hugs, and show me that they were there to support me with what was ahead. The feeling I had was that I was home. Home where I belonged, with the people I cared about and loved most the people who knew me best, and the people who made me feel safe, even with all the darkness I had in my life.

The love that everyone showed me, and my baby, was exactly what we needed. Where my daughter was treated like a little princess, getting hugs and lots of kisses from everyone who awed over her adorable dimples and curly hair. They had gifts that they wanted us to have, knowing that it might be some time before I could go back and see them all again, and all of us, not knowing, what I had waiting for me when I got back.

I had plenty of offers from some of my friends, who once I had told them some of the horrors I had endured, showed them some of the marks I still had on my body, to help me take care of things. To take care of Eduardo, to make sure he never put a finger on me or my daughter ever again. I had one friend, Jay, the one who was like the big brother of our group of friends, who while I went into some of the details of what I had gone through, had disappeared to only be found in his room by his wife, packing a couple of bags and insisting that he leave right then. Angry and told his wife that he was beyond livid at what Eduardo had done to me and subjected my daughter to. As if it was his little sister going through the terror, and his niece being the innocent witness to it all.

The idea of letting my friend go with a few others to take care of Eduardo once and for all was one that I had to admit I had found to be a solution, but one that I could not allow to happen. I could not allow my friends to put themselves and their families in any sort of harm or trouble. And I explained that to them, where I understood their intentions but that I had to do what was right. Sharing with them the rest of what the paperwork I had been served with said, where he mentioned a letter with names of those who would cause harm to him if something were to happen to him. That, if something happened to him, his brother had this list with names, most likely all their names on it.

My friends all looked over the paperwork and laughed, saying that Eduardo was something else, which I was very aware of. Then told me that they have friends all over, ones who were nomads of sorts, ones who no one would ever see, nor find if something were to happen. And that all I had to do, was give them the word, and they would take care of the rest. I again found the offer, one that was somewhat tempting, especially as I would think about the rapes, the beatings, his threats on killing me. But I thought that I could handle going to court and that in the end, my daughter and I would be okay, going the legal route with everything. Not involving others in the matter and causing unnecessary drama in their lives.

We continued with the party at my friend's house, where the kids all played, other babies my daughter's age were there playing with her, and where we enjoyed lots of great food and conversation. When the time continued to go by and get late, I knew I needed to get back to my parent's house, I gave everyone hugs, thanking them for everything, as they each said that they were always there for me, that they were just a phone call away, giving my daughter kisses on the cheek before we left.

The drive away from their house was one I took with a heavy heart, not wanting to leave that safety I felt there with them. Knowing that in just a few days, I would be back in the same town as Eduardo and facing a different kind of fight with him, one that was going to take place in the courts.

The next day, my family, neighbors, and some friends that lived up in the tiny mountain town my parents lived in, all enjoyed an all-day Thanksgiving feast. Sitting around, talking, and laughing. One family friend, who was a psychiatrist asked to speak with me. He let me know that my parents had filled him in on some things but asked some questions that he requested I answer as honestly as I could. As I answered his questions, about both myself and Eduardo, he looked up at me and asked me if I felt like I was in danger. I told him that yes, I did, that anytime I saw Eduardo, heard his voice, or would see that he was calling, I felt fear come over me.

That is when he explained that I was in an extremely dangerous situation, that from what he had gathered from everything he has heard, Eduardo seemed to be a textbook, Narcissistic Sociopath. Explaining that this type of person is one to avoid, having a dangerous mindset, one that is only self-serving without regard to anyone or anything else, and that trying to be civil with such a person can be almost impossible. That Eduardo most likely did plan everything that had happened very carefully, and that he found me as the target he had been seeking. Where he seemed to be delusional, creating a fantasy of sorts, giving him a grandiose feeling where he appeared to be some great man by others, all while tearing me down. Doing whatever Eduardo needed to do to make this persona one that was in his favor, which was a dangerous one, where I was the object of the obsession to making "his" fantasy a reality.

The stalking and following me, even before we became romantically involved, was his way of getting to know my behaviors and finding how he could get to me and execute his plans. He went on and explained that the feelings I had after having my daughter, where I felt as if I was depressed, were most likely due to the isolation and treatment I had endured. Which, with the hormones that occur after having a child, can turn into feelings of hopelessness and despair, especially with what I had been through. And that due to Eduardo's calculated ways, he most likely had planned on and even made things harder for me to try to drive me to have a breakdown, making me feel as if there was something wrong with me.

As he went on, I felt as though he was a mind reader, explaining how his guess on a diagnosis of Eduardo, was as if he had been there, watching from behind a screen, because the explanation of behavior was spot on. He then told me that when I got back, to try to avoid Eduardo, because everything he does is calculated, and he has most likely already planned out his next move and to be careful.

After that talk with the family friend, I thought about everything he said and realized that I was dealing with, more than I had realized. Which scared me, but also gave me the upper hand in knowing that Eduardo was planning his next move and that I was going to take everything he did or said from then on, as nothing but things that Eduardo had carefully planned out, and not play his game anymore. I thought I could go at the fight ahead with what I knew, thinking that maybe I could outsmart him. That when I got back, he would be forcefully removed from the apartment, and I would not allow him into my new apartment.

The vacation seemed to go by a lot faster than I had wanted, but when it was time to head back, I was ready, or at least as ready as I could be. I had gone Black Friday shopping with friends the night of Thanksgiving and enjoyed taking my daughter to the park that I and many others from the community designed and built. Trying to take advantage of every joy that I could find there with friends and family in that brief time. But when it was time to go, I had a plan set in my mind that I thought about during my time back in my hometown. Where I was to head straight to the leasing office, pick up my new apartment key, move, then go to meet with the lawyer my family had hired the following day. Which all seemed pretty straightforward at the time.

When I got back, I did go to the office, I did get my key, and right away went to get my things from my apartment, knowing that Eduardo was unaware that I was back. Or at least I had hoped as much. As I went into the apartment, he was not there, so I began grabbing the boxes I had stored in the outside storage on the balcony. I then went to grab as much as I could from the apartment when Eduardo showed up.

Eduardo did not show up alone either, instead, he had the police with him, and demanded that I be removed from my apartment and that I was stealing from him. I showed the police that I had a rental agreement, that I was the only one on that agreement showing that it was my apartment. That is when Eduardo furbished another rental agreement, where he had me removed from the agreement and had the apartment put in his name. The officer looked over both of our documents and asked me if I had things in the apartment, which I said I did. As I talked to this officer, Eduardo had called his lawyer, trying to get an order to have me removed and trespassed from the property, when the apartment manager showed up.

She explained that the apartment was originally mine, that Eduardo had moved in, and due to the 14-day stay that made him a resident as per the rental contract I had signed, I had gone and paid for another apartment, one on the same property that was only 3 buildings away. Showing the officer, the new agreement. She also went on and explained that they did try to evict Eduardo after I left for my vacation, but that he made arrangements, paid a new deposit, and signed a new lease, which now made him the tenant of my old apartment. With that, the officer told Eduardo that since I was a resident in the same complex I could not be trespassed from the property, but that Eduardo could put an order to keep me a certain distance from his front door. Which Eduardo said he wanted to do. The officer then told me that I had exactly 1 hour to get my things from the apartment, and in that time, he would remain there to ensure that we remained civil. As the officer said this, Eduardo's brother drove up and offered to help me with my furniture.

As the brother and I tried to get as much as we could out of the apartment, Eduardo just stood there, watching, not offering any help, watching as his brother put my bed and furniture on his back going up and down the stairs to my new apartment. Eduardo then tried to tell the officer that I had kidnapped my daughter and showed this officer the orders he had me served with the day I left for vacation. The officer looked over this paperwork, then explained to him that since we had not been to court, and that I had my daughter there, seeing I had not kidnapped her as far as he could see, and that the matter was a civil matter.

This reply from the officer made Eduardo livid. He then went around following me, trying to tell me what was mine and what was not mine, and saying that I was not allowed to take anything of our daughters with me. I then told Eduardo to back off and that he never paid for anything that was hers and that he was nothing but a joke. He tried telling the officer that I was stealing, to which the officer asked him for proof that the items in my old apartment were his, which he had none. And as the time was getting closer and closer to the hour mark, Eduardo decided to remind me how much time I had as I walked in and out, hurrying to grab whatever I could. Not being able to get to the master bedroom because he claimed he left the key at work, where my computer was, my birth certificate and other important documents were stored in a filing cabinet.

I felt good knowing that I had gotten mine and my daughter's clothes out, most of my furniture out, and his brother was there to help me. Because with him there, I was able to grab some of my dishes, some of the pictures, minus the ones that were in the albums in the master bedroom that was locked. And I felt relief in knowing that I was able to do all of it, without him touching me, and in front of witnesses.

I felt good about the move, which was until I had settled in later that day, and looked out my window, to see him standing by his truck, staring up at my apartment. Not doing anything, just standing there staring, with a smirk on his face, leaving me to the realization that regardless of me moving out and getting my place, I was now living next door to my own personal nightmare, the monster who had tormented me.

Preparing for Battle

That first night in my new apartment, I had a tough time sleeping. This was because, every time I looked out my window, I could see Eduardo just standing there, only leaving on occasion, but returning to his post. Watching me from below. This went on until about midnight that night, and even after I had not seen him standing there for some time, I still felt uneasy.

When morning finally came, I found that I had fallen asleep on my couch, waking up to my daughter not crying, but calling out for mommy. I went to the room to get her up, start breakfast and get us both dressed so we could head out to meet my lawyer, to see what our next move would be. I must admit that the first meeting was one where I was a mess. I was shaking from the idea that Eduardo could possibly take my daughter from me, and that I would be going to court with him very soon.

As I walked into her office, the receptionist greeted me, telling me that they were extremely glad to meet me, and walked me back to the lawyer's office. She then offered to take my daughter to another room where she had some crackers and toys to keep her occupied with. My lawyer stood up, to shake my hand, but when she saw me shaking, she instead hugged me, assuring me that I was not alone in this and that she was going to fight for both me and my daughter. She sat me down and handed me copies of the papers she had on her desk, along with a highlighter. She asked me to follow along with her as we read over a new set of orders, ones that she said once I approved of them, she would be faxing to Eduardo's lawyer and walking directly to the courthouse to have filed.

The new paperwork went on to contest the temporary orders he had me served with, demanding new temporary orders be put into place. Showing proof of his deception to the courts, with copies from my work on the request for vacation time that had been filed 6 months before the Thanksgiving break, copies of the apartment lease contract, showing my intentions on not only coming back but to only leaving him, not leaving the state and no evidence of kidnapping my daughter. As we went over everything, she had her assistant phone Eduardo's lawyer, to inform him of the new paperwork we were going to file and fax over, to which the lawyer agreed, seeing that we had the evidence to counteract Eduardo's claims.

Before we finished up, my lawyer informed me that Eduardo did have a restraining order put in place, which kept me from going to his front door. Since we shared a parking lot at the complex, he could not keep me from parking anywhere. She then explained that the new temporary orders, were just temporary until we went to court, but that they gave me 50/50 custody until then. Where I would have my daughter on my days off work along with every other weekend, and Eduardo's lawyer would be sharing this with him as well as serve him these papers since she was going to leave the office after I was done to have the new papers filed on my behalf. She also informed me that it might be in my best interest, to hold off on school, until after we went to court.

As I left her office, I felt like I had the upper hand, that I was not going to back down and, in the end, I would win. Knowing that I also had the uneasy feeling that Eduardo would have my daughter alone with him 3 days a week, which he had never had before since I was always the one to care for her since the day she was born. Where he helped very little, never had changed a diaper, made a bottle, fed her without guidance, or did anything other than watching her when she would sleep on occasion. Regardless, I knew that I had to abide by these new orders I just agreed to put in place and hope for the best outcome when it came to my daughter and her wellbeing.

After my daughter and I left, I decided to head to the store, to pick up some groceries that we would need at my place. We got back, and I put my daughter in the playpen, so I could unload my car. When I went up the stairs and walked into my apartment, Eduardo was in there, taking a photo of my daughter in her playpen. I demanded that he leave, and he told me that the orders had only been in place for less than an hour and I was already neglecting my daughter. Eduardo then went to sit on my couch and ask me what I was going to be making for dinner as if he was inviting himself. As he did this, the guy who lived in the apartment directly across from mine saw and heard what was going on. He peeked in and asked if I was okay when I said that my ex was just leaving. When I said this, Eduardo got up, with a smirk on his face, then as he walked out, he looked my new neighbor up and down, laughing as he walked down the stairs to go back to his apartment.

I thanked the neighbor, who told me that he was there any time I needed anything. I then called my lawyer, telling her what had just happened. How he just walked into my apartment without my consent, took photos of my daughter as I unloaded my car with the groceries I had bought, and until my neighbor showed up, was making himself at home, inviting himself to dinner. I asked her how that was fair, knowing that he had a restraining order on me to not even go to Eduardo's front door. She agreed that it was not okay nor fair, and told me she would call me back shortly.

My lawyer called back after a brief time, told me that the restraining order had been lifted, that she spoke to both Eduardo's lawyer about the recent incident and the judge who granted the restraining order, and they all agreed that what Eduardo had done, violated my rights and privacy. She also informed me that I would still need to follow the temporary orders, regardless of his behavior, but to keep a journal of his actions so I could use that in court.

When the day came for Eduardo to take his 3 days with my daughter, he did not show up. He did not call nor did his lawyer call to say that anything had been changed. Which left me with having to call into work, due to not having made prior arrangements for my daughter to be watched after. I called my lawyer to let her know to which she was perplexed as to why "he" had not come for my daughter. The next two days, he did the same, not coming to get my daughter during his time and leaving me to have to call into work since I had not planned on such an incident happening.

Come Monday when I called my lawyer to tell her what had happened, explaining that I had to miss work for those 3 days as well. She then stopped me, and said that was it, Eduardo was doing it all on purpose, hoping I would lose my job and in hand not be able to pay for a lawyer. She laughed and said that he had no idea, no idea that I had a good family backing me, and that she has talked to several of them who are covering all my fees and have also pledged, ensuring that no matter what, my daughter and I were taken care of.

She told me that she was going to note all of this and let Eduardo's lawyer know as well and that if he continues to not pick up my daughter on his days, he would lose. Within minutes she called me back, letting me know that Eduardo's lawyer had him in the office, and he claimed that the new temporary orders were too confusing for him. He said that he was unaware that he was supposed to get my daughter on those 3 days, and that his truck had broken down, so he had no transportation. I told her that he was full of it, which she agreed because the orders were pretty straightforward, and he lived just 3 buildings away from me, which was just a short walk out his door, down a path, and up some stairs. So, the whole no transportation thing was a joke.

After that call and thinking about things, I realized that Eduardo was trying to pull out all the tricks he had and was running out of them, or so I hoped. That he probably did not anticipate my family being there for me after everything, nor me getting a lawyer as fast as I did. And that when he realized I had got another apartment, Eduardo thought he could somehow have me trespassed before I even moved in, not knowing that I secured the apartment as soon as "he" had weaseled his way into the one he was now living in. Making me feel a little better about everything that was going on, but also knowing that I needed to watch out for what he had planned for me next, which would come sooner than I had anticipated.

My week with my daughter went on with really no issues from Eduardo other than him bringing that other woman and her kids to my old apartment. Which was just annoying to see, knowing that she was apparently willingly falling into Eduardo's trap, even after that scene at the restaurant. But also keeping in mind what he did to me, wondering if he was doing the same things to her, taking over her life before she could blink.

Then on the day he was to come and get my daughter, he showed up in that other woman's car, with her and her kids. The kids ran into the apartment when they saw me standing at the bottom of the stairs of my apartment to hand my daughter over to him for his time. As the kids ran into the apartment, Eduardo grabbed the other woman and kissed her, then looked at me smiling, and told her that he would be right back. I found the incident unsettling, knowing that Eduardo was trying to get under my skin, but I did not let it bother me. Instead, I felt a little better thinking that my daughter would at least be watched after knowing that there was someone else there and that she had kids of her own.

I walked back up to my apartment, after giving Eduardo my daughter for his time with her, to go and change and prepare for work, when I heard a knock at my door. I opened it to police officers being there, with a warrant for my arrest. I was in complete shock, I looked over and saw that the car Eduardo had been in was gone. They confirmed my name and told me that I was under arrest for a warrant that had been sworn in at the courts by, her. The other woman was on charges with harassment and death threats. I felt sick. I mean, at first, I had no idea what they were referring to until they showed me the warrant, which showed that the harassment was phone harassment. And that she had not only pressed charges on me, but that Eduardo had called Crime Stoppers, and collected $500 for tipping them off to where I was and turning me in.

When the police came in to arrest me, one of the officers had recognized me from when he stood by to watch and make sure I got my things out of my old apartment safely. He told me that he thought that Eduardo seemed like a douche bag and asked me how I got myself into all this mess. I explained that I was getting ready for work and the other officer then recognized me from my work, where he had brought patients to me on a few separate occasions. Both officers stood there and told me I could grab some phone numbers and get changed out of my pajamas but that they had to take me in. As I got ready, they asked me about the charges, which I did not deny. I told them what happened, and they laughed then said that the whole situation was messed up and that they regretted having to take me in, but it was their job.

On the way to the jail, we talked, I mentioned that I thought Eduardo had a speeding ticket that he did not pay for. They pulled over to look him up, wanting to help me get back at him for not only the mess I was in but for also the fact that Eduardo got money for turning me in. When they pulled up his name on the screen, I felt a bit of contentment, regardless of the fact I was going to jail, knowing that he too would be getting an unexpected visit from the police. I told them that he had to work that day, so they could find him there. They promised to go to him after they got done at the jail, and when we arrived at the jail, they let the guards know my story, to where everyone treated me well considering I was in jail.

Within minutes of arriving, they asked me if I could make bail because as soon as I did, they promised to process me out. I said that I could but would need to make a long-distance call to my parents to get the money. They explained that they could not allow that, but that one of the guards knew my boss and said that I could call my work, explain things and he would back me up and that maybe my boss could call my parents. So, I agreed, and with the strange ways things were going, that plan worked. My boss said she had to put me on speakerphone because no one was going to believe why I was calling into work that day and not able to make it. Since she also happened to be the one who was there the night that woman had called me, over and over again, where I finally had it and left the messages that landed me in jail. She along with others from my work who heard the call were all in shock at what was going on.

After calling my boss, she made the call to my parents who then called my lawyer who got a bondsman and came to bail me out. The time to get the bondsman to the court took the longest because apparently, they were busy that day and I was towards the bottom of the list, making my stay in the jail a few hours longer than I had anticipated. But once the bondsman showed up to show that my bail had been paid, he explained that I needed to go with him to his office and sign some paperwork then he would take me to my house. By that time, I did not care what I had to do, I was livid and ready to go home since I had already called into work. I felt dirty from the jail and was ready to take another shower and just go to bed.

The next morning my lawyer called to let me know that she would set up the court date for the harassment charges, but first needed me to explain what and how that happened. I told her the story, and just like everyone else who I have told then and since, she laughed, in disbelief of how it happened and agreeing that she too would have said the things I said but probably worse. But the fact of the matter was, I called the woman more than twice, leaving vulgar and threatening messages, which is why I got the charges I did. As I got up, I went to take a jog to pick up some coffee, and when I went down the stairs, Eduardo seemed to have a look of shock on his face seeing me at my apartment and not in jail. I pretended that I did not see him and jogged my happy ass to get my coffee and treat myself to a donut while I was at it.

Later that day I had to go to work, and as I walked in, I was greeted by my coworkers with a welcome back from the slammer mini party, as a joke. None of my coworkers could believe that I had been arrested, nor that she had pressed charges on me for that. My boss asked me if I was okay, and I told her I was, but that I vowed to never leave a voice message again, which I have kept to this day when it comes to personal calls. With that, she laughed and agreed, saying that she and everyone else will be thinking twice before ever leaving a message again too.

The following day, I had to meet with my lawyer. When I got to her office, she looked at me shaking her head. She said that this was a first for her, but that they were charging me with harassment, threats of bodily harm, and death threats. She then went on to inform me that Eduardo also got a visit that day from the police but that due to the ticket price, he was allowed to pay it and leave. Which she agreed sucked since he probably used some of the money, he collected for turning me in to pay that ticket. From there she told me that we needed to discuss the court dates, for not only the custody hearing but also for this. Explaining that she was going to push the court date for the charges on me out, so that they cannot be used against me in court, guessing that he was probably hoping to be able to have these charges as ammo against me.

My lawyer then went on to explain that we had a big fight ahead of us, that the lawyer Eduardo had hired liked to play dirty, and she was not scared of getting dirty, but that I needed to be prepared. We made plans to meet up again after the holidays, and with that, I left her office.

The following days, I was off for what was my Christmas holiday, but due to my time with my daughter being the days before Christmas as per the orders, I was celebrating that Christmas a day early with just myself and my daughter in my apartment. The time was an extremely sweet one, where I had picked up many toys for her, as did others, knowing that in the hurried move, I only grabbed the necessities, leaving all but her favorite stuffed animal and lovee behind. It was an unusual way of celebrating for me, where I was not with my family as I had hoped to be, but due to the timing of the holiday that year, it was what it was, and I was determined to make it the best for both of us.

I took many photos, marking the occasion, as being the one that was our first Christmas together, the one where I was free from Eduardo's control, where I was starting over again with my daughter, ready to take on the road we had ahead of us.

The time seemed to go by fast, because after my Christmas time with my daughter, she went to spend the next week with her dad. I took that time to work, keep my mind busy, get the holiday pay for both Christmas Day and New Year's, and prepare for my next meeting with my lawyer. When the day came for that meeting, my lawyer seemed to have a somewhat annoyed look on her face as I walked into her office. She then pulled out some papers that were in a folder and said that we had one more thing we needed to discuss. That is when I saw them, the papers we had signed when we went into file for a marriage license. I right away told her that we never went through with it, that we only applied for the license, that Eduardo forced me to do it but that I was glad we never went back to get the license.

She looked at me, waited for me to quit talking, and explained that when we applied for our marriage license that the license, we had gotten was a Declaration for an Informal Marriage License, which is a Common Law Marriage. I told her we did not, that we had just applied for a marriage license, but she showed me that it had been completed and the document I signed was indeed an Informal Marriage License and explained that I would need to file for divorce before we could go any further with the custody case. She went on and told me that Eduardo's lawyer was the one who came across the marriage license and that Eduardo voiced that he wanted to get the divorce over with quickly, so he could marry that other woman. Letting me know that, over the holidays, he had proposed to her, and she accepted.

I told her that I had no problem with that, and she got on the phone to set up a court date for the divorce. Surprisingly enough, we were able to get in the court within a week, and I said that would work for me. As she made the court date with the judge's secretary, I looked at the license, saw my signature then looked over the document, realizing that I had not read that document before signing it, feeling like the biggest idiot in the world, for not knowing that an Informal Marriage was even such a thing.

When we arrived at the court the following week, I saw Eduardo there and felt very uneasy. He stood there, staring at me, watching as I walked to talk to my lawyer, as I went into the bathroom, and as I walked into the courtroom just ahead of him. My lawyer whispered to me the creepiness of Eduardo's stare towards me, and I just looked at her and said that is the way he was with me. As we were called up, I, as well as both lawyers, expected the so-called divorce case to be a pretty clear-cut one, but once again, we were all wrong.

When I stood up, Eduardo insisted I go ahead of him, and he held the little swinging door open for me as well. The judge asked us up to his podium, following by asking me why I wanted the divorce and if I was going to agree with his judgment, I explained that we were no longer together, and I said I would agree, then asked the same of Eduardo. That is when Eduardo said that he did not agree to the divorce, saying that he was going to refuse it. Making myself, the judge, and both lawyers gasp as to what he had just said.

The judge then looked at me, and asked me why I wanted a divorce, to which I replied by pointing out that we were no longer together, he had a new girlfriend and was planning to marry this new girlfriend soon. The judge raised an eyebrow and looked at Eduardo and asked if what I said was true. Eduardo answered the judge by saying that it was, but that I was his, and he has changed his mind. The judge quickly looked back at the lawyers and then saw the look of fear on my face, when he looked at me and said that he was granting me the divorce.

I felt relief with that judgment and quickly walked back to my lawyer as we headed out of the courtroom, not speaking until we were in the lobby. When we got out to the lobby, my lawyer looked at me and asked what the hell just happened in there, in disbelief of Eduardo's actions. I told her that I had no idea, that Eduardo is obsessed with me, and that I was scared because when he did not get his way, he usually took his anger on me. She asked me if I could have a friend stay with me for a few nights, and I was sure my friend from work would then warn me that Eduardo scared her and that she felt as though we were going to be preparing for a battle.

With that remark, I knew she was right, that when it came to Eduardo, there was no being civil, that all of this was a game to him, and we were going to be going in for a battle.

Shortly after our first time in court, and my small first victory, I received a call. The call was an unexpected one, but it was the Sergeant I had met before the holidays. I found his call to be a welcomed one, and he said that he had seen my friends out, approached them asking why I was not with them, and wondered why he had not heard from me. I explained that after that night we had met, I had a lot going on in my life and had not had a lot of time to think of anything else or add anyone else to the complicated situation. He understood, sharing with me that he too had been married, had twin boys who lived quite a distance but asked if I minded him calling me to just talk or hang out from time to time. I told him that I was okay with that, and with that, we began to talk almost daily.

The talks were nice ones, ones where I could tell someone about my day, whether it was good or bad, and talk about some of the crazy things that Eduardo was doing, like not only following me but following my friends as well. To where Eduardo began following friends after they left my apartment, creeping them out even more than before. Or where, when I had company over, Eduardo seemed to either stand outside looking up at my apartment or would watch us from his window in his apartment, taking photos as we were coming and going. For a second there, I had thought that this man, the Sergeant, would want to run and not have anything to do with me due to the situation, but he did not, and when he would come to town, he would visit with me, take me out to eat, and pay no attention to my stalker who seemed to watch our every move, taking photos, and watching us.

A month after our friendship had started, the Sergeant asked if we could try for a relationship, that he enjoyed my company and that I was easy to talk to, which was not always as easy to do with other women he had met. I agreed to this, but not before asking if he was 100% sure, knowing that Eduardo was always there watching my every move. He said he had no problem with Eduardo, he was not going to allow the intimidation to bother him, and that as long as he was around, he would not allow Eduardo to bother me either. That reply seemed to be one that I needed to hear, it was like I had a person that was not just another friend on my side, but a man who was there to protect me in a way.

In the following weeks, we had decided that we would only date on the days I did not have my daughter, because I was not feeling comfortable with bringing my daughter around anyone new. This new guy respected that, and I was happy for the first time in an awfully long time when it came to having a relationship.

He would have me come out to the base to spend time with him out there, out of town, and away from prying eyes most times. Until one weekend that we had decided to have a sleepover at my apartment. We planned a weekend of going out with my friends, and some of his friends from the base came into town, staying at a hotel, to join us as well. Making the weekend one that I had looked forward to having and was enjoying.

Come Sunday morning, the Sergeant had to head back to base for his shift that was later that day, so he ended up leaving as the sun came up. After he left, he called once he got back on base to wish me a good day and tell me that he enjoyed the weekend and looked forward to many more ahead. As I said goodbye and began to get ready before meeting with Eduardo later that day to pick up my daughter, I heard a loud knock at my door. I had been in the shower and yelled for whoever it was to wait a minute.

That is when I then heard what sounded like a large crash in my living room. I grabbed my robe, ran out of the shower to see what had happened, when Eduardo came rushing in, going right past me to my bedroom, demanding to know where the guy I was seeing was, and saying that I was not going to get my daughter due to having a strange man stay over. Telling me that he had taken pictures of all the guys who had been at my apartment that weekend and was going to show the courts that I was nothing but a whore and endangering my daughter by having these strange men coming and going.

As he went on, my neighbor came in with a baseball bat, demanding that Eduardo leave and leave me the fuck alone. The neighbor had been woken up to the loud crash as Eduardo had busted my locked door open and heard Eduardo yelling at me.

When the neighbor came in, Eduardo then pulled out his camera and took a photo of the neighbor, trying to say he would use that as evidence as well, saying I had guys coming after him. I stopped him as he talked, and explained that first off, I was dating only one man, a military man in the Air Force. Second, those guys who were at my apartment were staying at a hotel, were friends who came to town for the weekend and only came over to visit at my apartment before we all went out to meet up with my other friends. Explaining I would be calling the cops on Eduardo for breaking my door down, and my neighbor was there because he knew that my ex was a douche bag.

Eduardo then tried to claim that it was my word against his and that with the photo of the neighbor coming at him with a bat, he would claim that the neighbor broke down the door and that he came to my rescue to only have this guy come after him. My neighbor looked at me then at Eduardo and told him to leave, and he was not welcome, to which Eduardo tried saying my neighbor had no say in what he did. I stopped Eduardo told him to get out and that he was not welcome.

As Eduardo walked out and down the stairs, my neighbor stood there, then asked me if I was okay. I told him I was, and he said he was going back to bed, but that he would leave his door open in case Eduardo showed up again, he could hear me yell for him if I needed help. I thanked him, went, and got dressed, then went to clean up all the pieces of the door frame that had shattered on my living room floor.

After picking up my daughter from Eduardo, the guy I was dating called to ask me how my day had been going. I told him about the incident, which upset him. He asked me if I would consider moving out to the base, to be closer, where he would make sure both myself and my daughter were safe. I told him that the offer was a sweet one, but that I was not ready for anything that serious, and I had to deal with the mess that was my own. He then went on to inform me that he had put in a request to be transferred so he could be closer to his kids, and he wanted me to go with him. That he would take care of me, and my daughter and I could get back in school, and even get a job at the hospital that was near the base he was wanting to transfer to. He explained he was aware that it seemed like we were moving too fast, but he put the request in for transfer months before our dating, and he had received a reply granting him his request when he arrived for duty that morning. Informing me he would be relocating in 6 weeks.

I told him that I was incredibly happy for him, I knew he missed his kids dearly, but I had to stay where I was, due to the court orders. Which stated that until we went for custody, I was ordered to stay within a 100-mile radius of the town I lived in. He said that he understood but asked if we could continue to see one another until he had to leave, and even then, keep in touch because as he put it, I was one in a million. I was honest, true, a beauty like no other he had met, and a woman he wished he had met sooner, before I had met Eduardo, to have prevented all the drama I endured from ever happening to me.

I agreed to continue dating until he was to leave and even remain friends after. But found those 6 weeks, went by a lot faster than either of us had wanted. On the day he was leaving, he hugged me, and told me that if nothing else, he was so glad to have gotten to know me. That he would cherish the time we had together, and I was one woman he would never forget. I was sad to see him go, not knowing if I would ever see him again but happy in knowing he was going to be happy, being with his kids again.

After the Sergeant had left, I felt somewhat alone again but was also very careful about the idea of dating. I had lots of admirers who voiced their wants for dating, and even got a MySpace account, to connect with friends, keep in touch and meet new people. And after a month of turning down guys who approached me for a date, I found one who I had casually dated when I had first moved to the area.

At the time we had dated prior when I was in nursing school, he was in the Police Academy and had since graduated. He was now, a local police officer, and was one that I remember getting along with well. He had found me on MySpace and began to pursue me in a relationship. As I did with my previous relationship, I let this man know about what was going on in my life, and the ex who stalked me regularly. He said that he was not scared of that, and if Eduardo tried anything, he would ensure I was safe.

We began to date, going out to dinner on the days I did not have my daughter, and even enjoying nights in, which we would rent movies. He did notice the ex, who watched when he would drive up, go in and out of my apartment carefully, and found Eduardo made him feel uneasy. As Eduardo did with everyone else who came around me, Eduardo took photos, and even wrote down the license plates of those who visited me. Following them to their houses and taking photos of them and their homes.

This stalking towards him did change his mind about wanting to pursue a relationship with me, which was a bit of a letdown for me, but one I understood. When we decided to put the brakes on the relationship and go on as being just friends, he let me know that he would be there for me if Eduardo tried anything, but the drama Eduardo was causing with me and trying to stir up with him, was something he did not want to deal with. Especially with him being a police officer and having the idea of this guy, who watched our every move, possibly jeopardizing his career by twisting things around, as Eduardo did often.

I went on from that relationship, knowing no matter who I dated, whether it be military personnel, a police officer, or anyone for that matter, Eduardo was going to harass them. Take their photos, watch their every move, and make things extremely uncomfortable for those who came around me. I later found out from a meeting with my lawyer that Eduardo had shared many photos with his lawyer, license plate numbers of everyone he saw visit my apartment, and even gave the lawyer addresses to many of my friends. Along with those, Eduardo had a notebook that he wrote things down in, which had claims of many men coming and going, my neighbor threatening him, and Eduardo being concerned for his daughter's safety. Trying to prove that I was a woman with loose morals and not a good mom. Showing things on my MySpace where guys had left messages on my page, hitting on me, claiming that I was sleeping with all of them.

I found that trying to date was ridiculously hard to try to take on and was nearly impossible. I knew that due to the uneasy situation I was in, I would be straightforward with guys who took me out, on the first dates. I would let them know I had a crazy ex, who stalked me, and pretty much anyone I associated with, and that if they chose to walk away and never look back, I would not hold any grudges. But I knew this was the best way to approach any sort of new relationship, before getting close to someone, to let them know where the door was and there would be no hard feelings.

I also found that keeping friends around was becoming a very trying thing to do, where I had many friends who were scared off by Eduardo, all but a very select few. One of which, happened to be one who was not scared of Eduardo, and even with her being as small as she was, she had no problem getting in his face when he tried to intimidate her. But regardless, his obsession was becoming scary, even if I was not in the same house as him, I feared him.

I think aside from him breaking my front door down, him trying to run my friend and me off the road, while I had my daughter in the car, was where the fear came into play. Where I saw that regardless of what Eduardo told or how he portrayed himself to others as being the loving and doting father to his daughter, he knew she was in the vehicle at the time, and had no remorse, in the game he was playing of trying to push my friend's vehicle into a ditch.

It all started when she had come to pick me and my daughter up for a birthday party at her house for her niece. They were having the party across the street from her house, and during our time trying to have this kids' birthday party, Eduardo drove around the park several times, staring us down as he drove past us. Making others at the party extremely uncomfortable. That was until my friend's brother and his friends showed up, and as he drove past, they all stood up, letting Eduardo know he needed to keep driving. At the time, we all thought that he had left, and we would not be seeing him again, at least not at my friend's house that day. And it seemed as if we were right until the party was over and my friend and I, along with my daughter, were headed back to my apartment.

We had gotten only one block from her house when I saw Eduardo, and he had seen us as well. I informed her that he spotted us, and as I said that we realized that he was behind us. She did not like the idea of him following her again, as he had done on so many occasions before when she had left my apartment, so she turned down a backstreet, which he followed. She then went to get back on the main road, and as she did this, he came upon her vehicle quickly, tailing us very closely. So close to where he lightly tapped her back bumper. She tried to get in the other lane to let Eduardo hopefully pass her, when he jumped in the lane as she went over and sped up, pushing us off to the side. My friend had control of her vehicle and tried to slow down, allowing him to get ahead of us, but as she did this, so did he.

Eduardo then got to the side of the car, where he could see me in the passenger seat, and tried to swerve his vehicle into us, once again pushing us into the side of the road. My friend then once again, turned down a side street as to ditch him, when he quickly found us, not slowing down as he got closer and closer to us. And Eduardo continued this until we arrived at the apartment complex, whereas we turned in, he tried to once again, push us off the road, pulling in front of us and slamming on his breaks. We got around him, parked, and as I grabbed my daughter, we ran up the stairs into my apartment, while Eduardo got out of his vehicle, and laughed.

I got on the phone to call my lawyer and inform her of what had happened. She agreed that the behavior was extremely dangerous, especially since he knew my daughter was in the back seat but said all I could do was note the incident and have my friend make a statement as well.

The following day, it was Eduardo's time with my daughter. As we made the exchange, I let him know that his reckless behavior put our daughter in danger, which he denied even took place. He then decided to inform me that he would be getting married in a couple of months, to which I congratulated him and walked away, in disbelief of everything and furious at the fact that he had no regard for his daughter's life but that I had to allow him his time with her.

A week had passed, and my friends from the hospital I worked at were throwing a birthday party for me at one of their houses. They made it a fun, princess party for me, to cheer me up, since I was still shaken up, knowing that my daughter had to go to him, and until we went to court, there was nothing I could do to protect her from him. The party was on a day that I had my daughter with me, and it so happened to be within walking distance of my apartment. With that in mind, I decided to enjoy a couple of beers with some of my friends, who were not on-call that night, and others who were on-call hung out to pass the time with good company.

A couple of my friends had come to my apartment to walk to the party with me, and shortly after arriving, my friend who was hosting the party for me, asked if I knew anyone who owned a red truck. I told her that I did not know anyone in a red truck but went on her balcony to see what it was she was referring to. She then pointed to the empty lot behind her apartment, and beside the tree, there was a red pickup truck with someone sitting in it.

We found it to be odd, but I had never seen the truck, nor could I see who was in it, so I was quite sure it was not Eduardo. That was until a couple of friends said that when I was in the dining room drinking a beer, they swore they saw flashes from a camera. I felt bad for the idea I had brought my drama to the party they were having for me, and instead of staying as I had planned, I told them I was going to head back to my apartment and call it a night. They understood and insisted they all walk with me, just to be safe. As we walked, we noticed that Eduardo was not at his place, so I felt better about being able to go to bed early, without him seeing me.

The next morning was Eduardo's day, and as I walked my daughter down the stairs to go with her dad, he drove up in the same red truck that my friends and I had seen outside of my friend's apartment during my party. I felt sick, knowing that he was stalking me, even from my friends' houses who did not even know him. As I went to take my daughter to him, one of my friends drove up, the friend who Eduardo tried to run off the road, who had also been at the party the night before, and when she saw the truck, she was floored as well. She walked up to me and asked me to please tell her that was not Eduardo driving that truck, and when I told her that it was, she explained that after I had left the night before, one of my friends who had been at the party had got called into work, and as they drove up to the hospital, that truck followed them.

After that, I knew Eduardo was getting increasingly obsessive, not only trying to scare me but also scaring my friends, and people I worked with at the hospital. I had continued to try and live a normal life, or as normal as possible, but trying to date or even go out with friends was hard. Eduardo had gotten a second job as a bouncer at a local Tejano club that stayed open after other clubs closed their doors after the last call, and many of my friends enjoyed going there to dance into the early morning hours. One night that I had agreed to go out with my friends, happened to be a going-away party for one in our group. She had been offered a great position at a hospital that was in another city and took the offer.

We started the night by going to eat at the restaurant that she had worked at when she was in nursing school with us. The manager insisted that we have the dinner there on him, so we took him up on the offer. After dinner, we all went to her condo, where we fixed our makeup and waited for others who did not make it to the dinner, to show up. Once everyone arrived, we all headed out to the clubs, going to the ones that we had enjoyed going to with our friend, where more of her friends waited to see her, say their goodbyes, and dance with us. Come the last call at the final club we went to, many of my friends wanted to continue dancing the night away and were going to go to the club that Eduardo was a bouncer at. I was one of the designated drivers for the night, and as a couple of the other carloads called it a night, my friends convinced me to take them to the Tejano club, to end our night right. I agreed but was scared of seeing Eduardo there. They pointed out the club was huge and that if we saw him, we were all going to just ignore him.

When we arrived at the club, they were right, it was packed and there were several lines to choose from to get in, allowing us to go in the one that was furthest from where Eduardo was at. The thing was, the line we chose, happened to be the line Eduardo's cousin was at the door for, seemed happy to see me, gave me a hug, and told me to have a good time. I felt good about the decision after that, seeing that Eduardo was terribly busy at the door he was stationed at and had not seen us come in. That was until we were on the dance floor, and I was dancing with a guy, to look up and see Eduardo standing, watching us with his arms crossed and a very stern look on his face. My friends saw this brief stand-off between us and decided to surround me and the guy I was dancing with, to try to block Eduardo's view of me. The idea seemed to work because after the song was over, I did not see Eduardo.

In fact, I decided to just let loose, enjoy myself, and dance with several guys to various songs that evening, until I had gone to get a soda at the bar and was grabbed on the arm. I first thought it was another man wanting to dance until I turned and saw it was Eduardo. He demanded I leave and go home, that I was making a fool of myself, and everyone was seeing it, by acting like a whore, dancing and grinding up on various guys. I told him that yet again, it was none of his business what I did and who I did it with and that I was just dancing, so there was no harm there. During this confrontation, Eduardo's cousin came to my rescue, told him to back off and let me be, then ordered him to do parking lot duty. The cousin then asked me if I was okay, to which I told him I was, he then told me to ignore him and enjoy myself, that Eduardo was just jealous that I was dancing with other guys.

I agreed with the cousin and did enjoy myself. I continued to dance until I was flat, worn out, and my friends agreed that they too were done for the night. As we went out to the parking lot, we got to my car, to find my mirror had been pulled off and that someone had keyed the side of my car. I was in too good of a mood, knowing Eduardo had done it, but I could not prove it, and I did not want to ruin my night with another confrontation from him, so we left and went home.

I had tried to forget about the incident and my friend's brother was able to fix the damage on my car free of cost, knowing that more than likely, Eduardo had done it, but that I did not want to deal with him.

I continued to enjoy my time when I did not have my daughter, and on the days, I had my daughter, I looked forward to making memories with her.

One place that I liked going to, was a pizza buffet and gaming center that had a special they ran once a week, which happened to be the days I had my daughter each week. I noticed that when I would go on that day each week, the local football team was there as well, and one of the players had noticed me. He had watched how I would hold my daughter's hand with one hand, and a tray with our plates in the other, trying to get through the buffet line before she would try to dart to the play area. That is when he decided to approach me and offered to hold the tray for me. I accepted his offer and then he invited me to sit with some of the guys from the team. I found the offer to be a nice one, but my daughter liked the movie room where they played cartoons for kids while they ate, so he asked if he could join us. I felt a bit uneasy since I had not brought my daughter around any guys and told him it was a nice offer, but we were going to go and play after eating, and I did not want him to have to leave his friends.

He seemed to understand, but before he left, he came into the movie room and handed me a piece of paper with his phone number along with a cup full of tokens for my daughter to use in the play area. I found the gesture to be a nice one, but I felt strange calling someone who I barely knew. But that did not seem to bother this guy, in fact, he seemed to wait for us each week. And when we would show up in the following weeks, he would meet us at the front, insisting he pays for our meals and buys tokens each time. He even decided to sit at a table next to the one we sat at in the kid's theater area with a couple of his friends, offering to fill our drinks or get my daughter a dessert. He was a very large, well-built man, as well as very good-looking, and on one of the afternoons, he and his friends asked if they could join me and my daughter in the game room. I am sure the site was one to see, me being a lot smaller than these giants who towered over me, but we had a lot of fun. They won my daughter several stuffed toys and let her play or ride anything she wanted, over and over again.

After that day, he insisted I at least give him my number, so he could take me out, and go somewhere nice that was not a kid's place. I agreed, and with that, I decided to take a chance. When we went out, he took me to a nice restaurant, and we talked. I told him about the ex, as I had done with every guy I met who was interested in dating me. He did not seem to be worried about Eduardo, and looking at his stature, I was sure that Eduardo would be more intimidated by him. As we continued to talk, he mentioned the university he had gone to, which happened to be in my hometown. He then let me know that he was only going to be in town until the season was over, then he was headed back to his hometown, and hopefully getting a contract with another team that he had wanted to play for. I explained how I was not looking to date anyone due to the coming court date and the fact that Eduardo took photos of everyone I was around. He respected that and offered his friendship, as well as passes for me and my friends to go to his games anytime we wanted.

I enjoyed that friendship, and we kept in touch, even after the season was over, for several years. Looking back, I realized he was another guy, who was a really good guy, and had I not been in the situation I was in at the time, I might have considered dating him. But I found after the relationship with the police officer, I would take baby steps as I went forward, and not backtrack to the past horrors I had endured.

Do You, or Don't You?

As the time crept along, in a sort of literal form, I found myself seeing the insanity in my life had become, a norm. I tried my best to ignore and disregard the things Eduardo continued to do regularly. After about a month from the time I had decided to not date and just focus on the life I was living, which I had accepted as my crazy world. Eduardo informed me he was moving out of the apartment he had pretty much stolen from me in a way. Letting me know that since he was going to be marrying the Walmart lady, they were going to be moving into a house together.

I found the news a sort of relief for me. I mean, I was overly excited to finally be further away from him and hoping this meant he was moving on and would soon be leaving me alone for the most part. I began to think I could finally move on, and dream of the life I would make for myself and my daughter. Knowing I would still have to deal with Eduardo, but relieved in knowing he would not be living within feet of me and would hopefully focus on the new family he would be gaining. That was until I got a call from my mom.

The call was not an unexpected one since we talked nearly every day, but it was one where she was very unhappy. She began the conversation with a lot of emotion, and once she explained why she was calling, I understood why she was so upset. She let me know that she received her credit card statement, and on it, there were numerous suspicious charges to various stores over the holidays. She explained to me that every single charge was tracked as being shipped to me, but in clothing sizes that were not mine or my daughters, toys for older kids along with other items that I did not have, and that the shipped items had been sent to the apartment I no longer lived in, with my name on the packages. As my mom continued to explain what she had discovered, I realized, as had she, that Eduardo used her credit card months before to pay a phone bill, and he used it again over the holidays to purchase gifts for his new soon-to-be wife and step kids.

At the moment I realized all of this, I asked my mom if she would be going after Eduardo for credit card fraud, and that is when she told me that she could not. That after talking to the credit card company, she realized the apartment had been in my name and I had been a resident there, and all of the orders were put in my name. And it was explained to her that she would have to come after me, even though I had nothing to do with the mess. I offered to have the apartment complex send over the rental agreement showing I did not live in that apartment at the time of the orders, to which she said regardless, it would be hard to prove since I did have a connection to him and that apartment, and he had pulled another fast one, which cost my mom quite a bit of money on top of all of the anger she had for him.

I was livid, as was the rest of my family. I called my lawyer to tell her what had happened and she said we could try to fight it, but it could come back at me due to the orders being in my name and to the address that I had once lived at, and at the time of the orders, I was still legally married to Eduardo which he could try to use against me if we pursued the matter.

After that, I thought Eduardo had hit an all-time low. I mean, he had pulled a lot of fast ones, with the house, car, bank accounts, stealing from my aunt, the apartment, and stalking, but this I thought was the lowest. At least I had hoped it was. That was until about 2 weeks later after the call from my mom, I received a call from a local uniform shop I had an account with where I purchased my scrubs for work through.

I had not been in the shop in months but received a call from the shop saying that my order was ready to be picked up. I asked what they meant, and they said I had been in one week prior, placed a large custom order, and it was ready for pickup. I got off the phone and decided to drive to the shop knowing they had to have been mistaken, wanting to clear the mistake up. Before leaving, one of my friends called, I told her about the call from the uniform shop when she informed me that the Walmart lady no longer worked at Walmart and was now working for a local blood bank. Saying she had seen her at a blood drive at our work just a few weeks prior, and she knew it was her because she not only recognized her but saw the name on the name tag. As she told me this, Eduardo showed up at his apartment with the lady, and sure enough, she was in scrubs. I thought about confronting them, but I could not be sure what I was thinking was true. Because with those two calls and her showing up in scrubs, I was thinking she had somehow ordered scrubs on my account, but I was hoping I was wrong and that the shop had a simple mix-up.

I left after they showed up and went straight to the scrub shop. When I arrived, the lady at the front counter looked at me with a confused look. She said I was not the person who had placed the order, which I knew but still thought they had just mixed things up on their end. She then pulled out the order and showed me that my account had been used for the order, then asked me to verify my identity, which I promptly did. She then went on to verify the phone number that the person had left for the order, and when she showed me the phone number, I realized that the number was the other lady's number. I right away began to shake. The shop lady then told me that she had called me because when she pulled the account info up when the order arrived, it had my number on my account on the computer, but the person who ordered left a different number on a piece of paper.

She continued and said she was also the one who had been there when the other woman placed this order. I asked her to describe the person, and when she did, she had described the Walmart woman to-a-t. The order was a special order due to the other lady's size, where she was noticeably short but had exceptionally large breasts, so they had to customize the very pricey scrub tops. She said the lady showed up and had my paycheck stubs which were how they linked my account since I used my payroll account from my work to pay for any shopping I did at the shop. She said that the lady claimed to have left her ID at home but had the paycheck stubs in hand which they accepted as a form of ID to place the order. That is when I realized, when I had moved out, Eduardo had the master bedroom locked up, which had my birth certificate, social security card, tax records, and paycheck stubs all in a file.

I left the shop and as I sat in the parking lot, I called my lawyer. She said for me to call the police, which I did right away. An officer showed up to talk to me and asked the shop owner to call the number the lady left, explaining to me that the only way they could press charges on her for theft of identity was if she went to the shop and picked up the order. As I stood out front with the officer, Eduardo happened to drive by, picking up a to-go order at the restaurant that was a few doors down from the uniform shop. Eduardo sat in her car for a few minutes before getting out and appeared to be on the phone. I pointed out the car he was driving, and the shop owner said that the car was indeed the one the lady who placed the order had used. Eduardo noticed us talking and looking at the car, but did not say anything, instead, he went in and picked up his food order at the restaurant and left.

Another week later after the incident, I received a call from the officer who had taken the statement from me at the uniform shop and explained that most likely, Eduardo alerted her, knowing what she had done. And because she had not gone to pick up the order, there was nothing I could do.

I once again found myself to be livid at what was going on, knowing that this other woman was trying to use my information around town as her own. After getting off the phone with the officer, I called my lawyer again and told her everything. She asked me if she could pull a credit report on me, saying she had a feeling that this was just the tip of the iceberg. And she was right, when she pulled my credit, she called me in, saying she needed to show me some things and she was right. When I arrived at her office, she had a folder filled with print-offs from my credit. That is when she began to ask me about payday loans and a whole slew of credit cards that had been opened from the time I had first married Eduardo to our date in court when the divorce had been granted.

I began to shake with anger and told her I had not gotten any loans nor opened any credit cards. With that, she started making phone calls, and after a few hours of the two of us going over every detail on my credit report, she informed me that what Eduardo did was dirty. That since we were legally married when he got the numerous loans that were sent to the joint account we had after I had left him, and credit cards in my name, which were all shown to have gone to my old apartment, I was liable for all of them. That I would have to pay each one off to fix my now destroyed credit, and some might be understanding, but most likely they will hold me liable. She then asked me if I would agree to put a freeze on my credit, which I did not hesitate in agreeing to, knowing I was now in a huge amount of debt that was sickening on so many levels because Eduardo did it all knowing that it would be on me.

After that day, I spent the next few weeks, making phone calls, trying to figure out ways to keep companies from garnishing wages, and trying to find a way to make payments on everything he had done. I called my mom and shared the mess with not just the credit cards and loans but also the scrubs. The news of it all made her just as sick as it did me, and we knew this was not the end either.

Over the next week, Eduardo began to move out of my old apartment. He then left some boxes on my stairs when I had been at work. When I opened the boxes, I realized there were some of my documents inside along with my dishes and other items which included some of my old lingerie that appeared to have been worn by the other woman since the top parts where the breasts went had been stretched out quite a bit. When I went to pick up one of the boxes, the bottom fell out, and everything fragile inside fell out as well, shattering everywhere. The noise it made startled my neighbor who came running out to see the mess that had occurred. He then offered to pick up the other boxes that I had not picked up, and noticed at the bottom of each box, they were not only not shut correctly, but they had large cans of juice, weighing them down so that when anyone tried to pick them up the normal way, the bottoms would open, and everything would get destroyed. As we moved the boxes inside and I cleaned up the mess the first box had made with dishes and juice all over the porch and stairs, I just shook my head, because it was yet another dirty move on his part.

A couple of days after that, I noticed that Eduardo was no longer coming and going, which meant he was done moving. The maintenance man knew I had lived there and told me Eduardo had left a lot of odds and ends behind and asked me if I wanted to go through the apartment to get anything that might be mine. I took him up on the offer, hoping to find some of the items I was still missing. And when

I walked in, I saw the huge mess he had left behind for the complex to clean up. There were papers everywhere, trash, rotten food in the kitchen, and some of my underwear strewn out around the rooms.

The grill my dad had gifted him one Christmas had been left on the balcony, which I ended up giving to my neighbor who put it to beneficial use. As I picked up the underwear, I realized that each pair had been worn, having the sickening realization that most likely, she walked around wearing my underwear and lingerie for Eduardo, which just creeped me out. I then noticed some invoices on the ground, which were all the invoices for those orders they had placed, using my mom's credit card. As I continued walking, I found credit card statements crumbled up on the floor, with the cards my lawyer and I had found, all with my name on the statements, mailed to that address after I had moved out months ago.

I grabbed a few items that were my daughter's which had been left in the old nursery and left because I did not want to be in that place any longer. Knowing they were sick, twisted, crooks who were possibly playing out Eduardo's sick fantasies of me by having her wear my undergarments and lingerie. As I was leaving, my friend had shown up at my apartment, I called her over to show her everything, and I told her about the loans, the credit cards, and last but not least, the undergarments and lingerie that looked as if Eduardo had wanted me to see that he had the other woman wearing my things. She too cringed at the sight and shook her head at everything that had been left there, and the mess I now had to deal with in not only being responsible for all the loans and credit cards but for also having to freeze my credit until I went back to court.

As we walked out and back up to my apartment, my phone rang. It was Eduardo. I answered not wanting to talk since my lawyer had advised me against talking to him unless it was for my daughter, but hoping he was calling to give me his new address to where I could pick up my daughter at. Instead, when I answered he said he was calling to let me know the wedding date. I told Eduardo I did not care but needed his address, so I could get my daughter the next day. He went on and said that since he would be getting married in less than two weeks, they wanted my daughter to be a part of the wedding and would switch off a day with me for this event. I agreed to allow it when he then goes on. Eduardo tells me that he was still in love with me, and I could be his "Sancha", so we could still see one another and maybe I could have more babies for him. Explaining since this other woman had her tubes tied and would not be able to have any more kids, he hoped that I would have more kids for him. And if I agreed to this, he would give me whatever I wanted in the custody case and would treat me better as well.

I was in shock and told him no to his twisted proposal as I hung up. I felt like I was going to get sick when my friend looked and asked me what just happened. I looked at her and laughed, then told her what he proposed to me. I then went on and told her Eduardo said all this right after telling me that he would be getting married in just under 2 weeks and asking if I would switch a custody day with him, so my daughter could be in the wedding. The look of shock and disbelief on her face must have mimicked mine, because for a few minutes there, we both just stood, staring off with our eyes wide open, in silence before we both laughed at the crazy proposal that had just happened. I told her I was glad she was there because, with everything that has happened, unless I had someone to witness the madness, I doubted anyone would ever believe it.

The next day when I went to Eduardo's new house to pick up my daughter, I asked my friend to join me, because I did not feel safe meeting with him alone. I was glad she went too due to the fact that when we arrived, he came out without my daughter. Trying to bargain with me on his proposal he made the day before and trying to tell me that I had to agree to his proposal of me being his side chick, having more babies with him, all while he married this other woman and lived as a family with her, or else he would not let my daughter come home with me. I looked at my friend who sat there looking at this crazy man say these things to me when I looked back at him without blinking an eye and demanded him to get my daughter before I make a call to my lawyer. He looked at me then smirked and said I need to think about this all, that he would give me some time, but it was in my best interest, and things would be better for me in the long run if I agreed to his terms.

I got my daughter and left, feeling dirty with the fact of knowing what I knew, what I had seen, and what I was a part of, to where Eduardo somehow thought his approach was reasonable in his twisted and sick mind. My friend then insisted that she go with me for all exchanges from then on due to the things he had said, saying that he made her worry about both mine and my daughter's safety. Telling me she had never heard of, imagined, or even dreamed of witnessing the madness that she had, knowing what she had been a witness to, was just an exceedingly small part of what I had been through.

As time continued to go by, I met a genuinely nice man. He lived a few towns over and owned his own business and home. I found that during my time off when I did not have my daughter with me, it was nice to escape to the country where he lived. Where there were no neighbors, noise, and where I could relax, even if it was only for a day or two at a time. I also found solace in knowing that with Eduardo being a newlywed, he was busy with his new wife, and did not know about nor followed me when I went to visit this new guy I was seeing. Allowing me to feel safe in knowing Eduardo would not be around or be bothering me during those times.

I dated this man for a few months, to where he and I became close and where he asked me if I would consider moving out to the country house he owned. He told me if I did decide to take him up on his offer, he could take care of me and my daughter. I found the idea to be a romantic one, but one that I told him I would need time to consider. I mean, I had not introduced him to my daughter as of yet, and when it came down to things, the distance was nice in knowing that it was only 60 miles away, which I hoped was far enough where Eduardo would not follow me or stalk me. But I also knew if I were to make a move like that, I would have to notify the courts, which in hand would notify Eduardo of where the guy I was seeing lived, and the possibility of him trying to cause issues.

I chose to hold off on moving but began seeing this man more and more. We went to the church his family attended on the weekends when I did not have my daughter, together. He introduced me to his family and friends, and I ended up making good friends with his sister. And everything seemed to be going well until I started to notice some things that bothered me. See, I had met this man at a bar one night when I was out with friends, and every time we were together, I did enjoy a beer or two with him. But after getting to know him well, I realized he drank regularly. Having a beer at breakfast, during his lunch break, and drank until he fell asleep, even more so when he was not working. He did not have a temper or show any sort of violent behavior, but for me, I did not feel right bringing my daughter around someone who drank so regularly. I voiced this concern to the man, and he tried to quit drinking altogether, begging me to give him a chance.

I did give him a chance, and for a while there, I thought that he was getting better with his drinking until I noticed that he was hiding the cans in his truck and dumping them before I would arrive. Knowing even though he would not drink like a fish when I was around, that when I was not there, he drank quite a bit. I explained to him how I knew it was hard to quit, especially for someone who drank as much as he did on a regular basis, but I was also not blind to see the trash cans outside filled to the top with nothing but empty beer cans. Seeing that he hardly ate when I was not around, and even though he was a nice guy, he was hurting himself which I was not going to stand by and watch nor allow my daughter to see.

With that, I decided to quit seeing this man, which was not only hard for me since I was beginning to have feelings for him, but hard for him as well since the feelings were mutual. But I did so in knowing that the choice was the right one, that regardless of what a great guy he was, I did not need any extra of any sort, whether it be drama or the drama that comes with alcohol, possibly getting in the way of my impending custody hearing. The choice was one that upset him a lot, and even though I explained I did not want to be romantically involved, I did agree that we could remain friends. He was okay with the idea of being friends, he wanted more, but said he would work on his drinking issues if I was there for him and would consider giving him another chance in the future.

After calling it off romantically with the new guy I had been seeing, I found the time for the custody hearing was dragging. Due to both Eduardo and I having good lawyers, they kept pushing the court date out. My lawyer said Eduardo's lawyer was doing it on purpose, in hopes I would eventually run out of money to keep her on and have to go to court for the harassment charges which they most likely were hoping to use against me in court. I was okay with this, knowing Eduardo would run out of resources before I did since I had many in my family backing me with the lawyer fees, so I just went along with it, not raising any concerns, that was until I began to notice disturbing things with my daughter.

At first, I noticed bruises here and there, but since she was a toddler, I knew that she was clumsy, so I wanted to believe the bruises were from falling or bumping into things. This idea seemed like a logical one until one day when my daughter came home with a handprint on her back. I had gone to bathe her and when I went to pull off her clothes, I noticed her back and bottom covered in little bruises, then an outline of a handprint in the middle of her back. I went to touch it when she winced with pain. My heart sank. I called my friend who came over to see, and we right away called my lawyer, took photos, and made a report with CPS as instructed by my lawyer to do.

I felt sick, sick in knowing I still had to allow my precious baby girl to go to that house, knowing someone had been hurting her on purpose, that the marks she had were not from falling or being clumsy, but someone had put those marks on her. I then began to think about the times I had to drop my daughter off with Eduardo, where she would scream and cry, cling to me, and hit him so he would not touch her. I put those tantrums at just that, a tantrum, where she just wanted her mommy, but now I started to think about the other signs. Where my daughter not only threw tantrums but where she would scream and yell monster when she saw Eduardo or his new wife.

A few days later, I had a CPS (Child Protective Services) worker come to my apartment where they explained that they had visited Eduardo, showed him the photos, and asked him to explain. She said Eduardo claimed that my daughter did not have those marks when she was in his custody, and then turned around my statements saying my daughter threw fits when she saw me and called me a monster. The worker went on and said Eduardo and his wife showed her papers from the courts on my harassment charges, evidence of me being on medications for depression, and claimed that I was delusional. That I must have left those marks, showing her the police reports from where Eduardo beat me, but where the police sided with him, saying I had caused injuries on myself and left marks on him as well. They said I must be overly stressed out, being a single mom, not knowing how to care for my daughter, and always going out, drinking, and partying, and I must have put marks on her and may have forgotten I did so.

My stomach dropped as the worker continued. She asked to see my apartment, which I had no problem showing her. Where I had no evidence of alcohol in the home, and where everything was set up for my daughter. Showing her my bedroom which had Dora the Explorer bedding on both mine and my daughter's beds. Where there were her toy boxes, her books on shelves, and, where even the television in my room was a Dora the Explorer one, and the worker could see that I had the entire place childproofed as well. During the visit, my friend had shown up, and the CPS worker asked to speak with her as well.

My friend said we both worked at the hospital together and she had known me since I had moved to the area, that my daughter was my world, and I was the best mom she knew. She also said she had witnessed the madness and lies on Eduardo's end, where he harassed, stalked, and where she used to see the bruises from his beatings on me, where he also caused me to have a miscarriage from a beating. The CPS worker told me that she would have to close the case because she saw it way too many times wherein custody cases, parents try to point fingers at one another, and it seemed like this was one of those cases. A "he said she said" case that never ends well, and where the child ends up caught in the middle of it all. As the worker went on to explain things, I realized Eduardo was using my daughter, that he was abusing her, and had once again found a way to get away with the horrible things he was doing. Having no remorse for any of it and finding this to be a part of the game he was playing.

Within an hour of the CPS worker leaving, Eduardo called, and once again asked me if I would take him up on the proposal he had offered to me months prior to being his sancha. He said if I agreed to it, I could keep my daughter, and he would only visit on occasions but would not cause any more trouble for me. That he would tell his lawyer to give me what I wanted and have his new wife drop the charges against me. But that if I did not agree, I would be sorry. I was getting sicker by the minute, knowing Eduardo knew everything that he was doing, and he was putting my daughter in the middle of it all. Before hanging up he asked me, "do you or don't you want to take me up on this once in a lifetime offer?"

I hung up the phone, knowing that Eduardo was not going to stop and that his web was getting harder and harder to navigate through.

A Feeling Like Never Before

The pickups from Eduardo's house became something that I dreaded, not knowing what he was going to do or say. I also felt uneasy with Eduardo coming to my apartment. Where I would arrive on some days to find him in my parking lot, on my stairs, continuing to press me for an answer. Threatening that if I did not come up with an answer for him before our court date, I would be very sorry, and he would make sure I never saw my daughter again. But I had gotten used to this as my new norm when it came to dealing with him and his behavior. I tried to ignore the things he said and would avoid any conversation that was not about my daughter. I also found a bit of safety in knowing that my friend went with me to all the pickups at his house and that my neighbor watched closely when he saw Eduardo at my apartment.

The thing was, I did not feel 100% safe when I was at my apartment. So, I began looking for a place that was gated, where I could insist Eduardo's pickups be done away from my front door.

I found a gated apartment complex that was not far from my work and the nursing school and was able to move in quickly. I was excited to have found it, excited that it was a lot nicer than the apartment I had been in, the fact I would once again have two bedrooms and even two bathrooms, and that it was gated. Where I could keep Eduardo at a distance from my front door.

I was loving my new apartment, everything about it. From the playground and family-oriented environment to the fact, that I had more room and thought Eduardo could not get to me there. That was until one evening when I had gotten off work, and I began walking up the stairs to my apartment, to find Eduardo sitting on the steps. He told me that he had informed the front gate guard we had court orders and if they did not let him in, he would have his lawyer talk to their boss. Which intimidated the guard and the guard let Eduardo through the gate.

He insisted I allow him inside, that he wanted to see where my daughter was staying when she was with me, and I could not keep him from that. I did not want to argue and cause a scene, so I just pulled out my phone and told Eduardo that if he did not leave, I would call the cops. He looked at me and stood there for a few seconds before warning me that I was going to regret everything as he walked away. The next morning, I called my lawyer and she said that I could have Eduardo trespassed from my apartment and have the order saying Eduardo had to meet me in a public place when picking up my daughter. I found this order to be exactly what was needed but also found that before we got it signed by the judge the next day, I still had to go to Eduardo's house to pick up my daughter.

When I arrived at Eduardo's house, I had arrived with my friend in the car she was driving. He came outside with my daughter and a large stack of mail. Eduardo threw the mail into my friend's car and told me I could never say that he did not give me anything, handed me my daughter, and walked away laughing. My friend and I looked at one another as I put my daughter in her car seat. She reached over to pick up some of the mail he had thrown in her car, to find all the mail had my name on it and had been addressed to the address he lived at with his wife.

We gathered the pieces of mail up and drove to my apartment, where we began to go through each piece. As we opened the mail, I noticed credit card statements, and cancellation notices from where I had called the card companies and had the cards canceled, along with some bills. The bills grabbed my attention because they were all utility bills that were all in my name at the address he was living at with his new wife. Each bill had termination notices on them, and as I went through each one, I called my lawyer, telling her what he had done, that he threw them at me and laughed.

My lawyer asked if I could meet her at her office and bring the mail with me. I agreed to go, and my friend offered to watch after my daughter while I went to visit my lawyer. When I arrived at the lawyer's office, she right away began looking over the mail and had me call the various utility companies while we talked to them. We found that Eduardo had found yet another loophole, which allowed him to get away with once again, being crooked and dirty. Where when before he had even moved, he had each utility including internet and cable, put in my name at his new house. That in that time frame when he did this, we had not divorced yet, where his new wife had got the house months prior after leaving her husband, and he had all the utilities put in my name. And Eduardo knew this, took advantage of it, and once again, screwed me over with a slew of bills that were all now my responsibility to take care of. Regardless of if I had lived in the house, the companies we talked to did not seem to care.

My lawyer looked at me and shook her head. She explained that until I pay all these bills off because if I moved to a house, I would not be able to get any utilities turned on in my name. Pointing out I was somewhat lucky having found a complex that included a bill each month for the tenants that covered all utilities and had free cable and internet for tenants as well. But had I moved to a place that did not have that available, I would have found this mess to have to pay on before the companies would have allowed me to have even the electricity that he had run up to nearly $1000, turned on at any other place. And due to this mess, when I do decide to ever move, I will most likely have huge deposits to pay. Pointing out Eduardo never paid on any of the bills, letting them go to delinquency until they were all shut off and he most likely either put them in his name or his new wife's name.

I sat there and looked over each bill, seeing the money that was now owed and realizing Eduardo just continued to find ways, all where he was somehow able to get away with it.

When I got back to my apartment, I told my friend what the lawyer and I found out and she was just as floored as I was. I then went on and told her I needed to finish nursing school, and that I planned on going back after the holidays since we had a court date set that had not been contested as the prior dates had been. And, in order to get past all of this, and be able to provide a good life for my daughter, I would need to be able to make more money in the long run, so I would not have to depend on anyone else.

Later that day, my friend went home, and as my daughter went to bed, I decided to go on MySpace. I noticed I had a lot of messages on there, which included some from guys I had ignored and asked to leave me alone. One of the guys was one that I had met at a club, months prior, and who would not give up on asking me out, which after all I had been through, I was not about to get involved with another obsessed guy. So, I wrote this guy an exceedingly long, detailed message back, warning him to leave me alone and never contact me again. When I hit send, I realized the message had accidentally gone out to everyone who had sent me messages that day, which I did not care about since I was in no place to seek out any new relationships.

I got off the computer to get myself some dinner, what was left from what I had made my daughter that night, and watch a movie. As I went to sit down, I heard a ding on my computer and found I had a new message. The message was not from the guy I told to leave me alone, instead, it was from another man who had received my accidental message. He said he did not realize he had bugged me; he knew I was friends with his soon-to-be ex-wife and had just wanted to see if I would go to lunch with him, just as friends. I found the message to make me laugh, since the message I had accidentally sent out to all the random guys who had messaged me, was a message asking the person to leave me alone, to get the picture, that I had no interest in, and to kindly "fuck off." I felt bad knowing he had no idea why I would send him such a message, so I took him up on his offer for lunch.

The next day, after handing my daughter over to Eduardo, I went to meet this guy for lunch. When we met up, I realized who he was and told him that I hoped he knew I was not interested in dating him, but I would agree to be friends. With that, he agreed. We kept in touch, then one day he messaged me, insisting I needed to meet a good friend of his. He explained that his roommate and I were sure to get along great and that if he was wrong then he would apologize. I agreed to meet with the roommate and when I did, he asked if he could give his roommate my phone number, which I said was okay.

That evening, to my surprise, the roommate called me. I found it to be even more of a surprise once we began talking, because he seemed to be very easy to talk to, and before I knew it, I realized that we had talked on the phone for a couple of hours. The roommate asked if he could take me out, which I agreed to, and with that, he asked if I would not mind meeting him at their house then we would drive to go and eat.

The next day, I felt nervous, which was something I had not felt in a long time when it came to meeting someone new. I had changed my clothes numerous times, then realized I needed to go before I would be late for meeting this guy for the first time. When I drove up, I felt butterflies in my stomach, which was also odd for me, because I could not remember if I ever had a guy give me butterflies on a first date. But I felt some sort of connection after our long conversation the night before and was excited to put a face to the voice. The roommate came out, introduced himself and we got in his truck to head out to eat.

When we arrived at the restaurant, he was a complete gentleman. Opening doors, holding the chair for me to sit in, and starting the conversation easily, were some things I found to be very surprising. That is when I had to tell him, I mean, I was liking this guy, but I needed to tell him my situation before we went any further. As I explained; the ex, the custody hearing coming up, and the issues Eduardo has caused for me, my family, friends, and of course any guy he found I was dating, I finished what I had to say by informing this guy that I would not hold any grudge against him and would understand if when we left, he chose to not pursue anything further with me. He looked at me and asked why I would be worried he would not want to see me again. That is when I told him about when it came to the stalking, Eduardo took photos, and license plate numbers, drove by houses and harassed those who were close to me. Which can be a deal-breaker for many.

As we sat there continuing to talk, the waiter we had came up and whispered to me. He did it loud enough for this other guy to hear, telling me that if he did not want to date me, to let him know because he thought I was gorgeous and was not scared. The waiter walked away, and I was in shock that he had just done that. That is when the guy grabbed my hand and said he was not scared either, and agreed with the waiter that I was gorgeous, and if I was okay with it, he would like to see me again. I looked at this man, waiting for him to change his mind when he asked for the check and asked if I wanted to go for a walk before heading back to his house. He said he had to work that night, but on his break, would love to be able to call me. It seemed like he would say exactly what I was thinking, how he felt this connection with me, something he had never felt with anyone before, especially someone he had just met and enjoyed my company.

When we got back to his house, he walked me to my car and asked me if he could kiss me. I gave him the okay, and with that first kiss, I felt euphoric. I mean, I had kissed many guys in my lifetime, but never once had I had a first kiss feel so right or leave me feeling euphoric like that either. I do not think I had ever experienced so much of a bond with a person I had just met, and for a second there, I felt scared thinking this was too good to be true. That this does not happen to people, the whole love at first sight, or falling for a stranger I had just met, but I could not help the feelings I was having. And when he called me that night like he said he would, I was beyond happy to hear his voice.

This man worked as a truck driver, he worked for a local company and hauled trailers from yard to yard, and around the local region. We talked for hours that night, to where I ended up falling asleep as he told me goodnight, asking me if he could call me in the morning when he got off work. Which I of course agreed to. And with that, we continued with the phone calls, which lasted for hours each time, where I was feeling like I was falling head-over-heels for this man but trying to go at the relationship ahead with caution. Thinking that this type of thing only happens in fairytales and movies, I was sure I would wake up and find it was not real. But to my pleasant surprise, it was not a dream, and it was happening.

I shared more with this man than I had expected to but found the conversations so easy to have. Where he shared how he had been from California, how at age 3 he was taken from his mom who was a prostitute then adopted at age 8. How the family who adopted him, also adopted 3 of his younger biological siblings as the state of California would come to find them. And how his youngest sister was adopted at just 3 months old when the authorities found his biological mom and a friend dead after an overdose. Describing how his sister had been left in a car seat for a few days before she had been found, his adoptive family did not hesitate in adopting her when they got a call from the hospital saying that they had found another baby his bio-mom had had.

He explained that his biological mom was a biker babe and was told that she was biker property for many years, and he had three other siblings that were out there. One who he had met ended up being raised in the foster system along with an older sister and younger brother who were raised by their biological dads or their dads' families. He shared how he had an awfully hard relationship with his adoptive mom, and at age 16 moved out of her house to live with an aunt and uncle where he lived until he finished high school then went straight from high school to the Marine Corps. After being in the Corps, he came back to the states and became a truck driver, moved back to California, and met his ex-wife. He had married her after being intimidated by her large Italian family, who urged him in a not so gentle way to marry her since he had been seeing her.

He shared with me about how his relationship with his ex-wife was not a loving one, and he had left her at one point only to be forcefully dragged back to her by some of her uncles. He then decided to be an over-the-road truck driver to avoid spending time with her, only to come home early and find her sleeping with another man, which allowed him to leave her without anyone trying to stop him. He told me how he wanted children but was so glad he never had any with his ex. To which I shared with him that I had honestly not thought about more kids and shared some things about my ex.

I felt so at ease talking with him, and I told him about how I had been raped when I was younger. How I had been on a camping trip with friends when it happened, one of which was a girl I grew up with. I was given many drinks and passed out in my tent to wake up to one of my friend's boyfriends on top of me, raping me. I explained how I later found out that he had bought my virginity from a childhood friend, who exchanged me for drugs.

I had told friends and even went to the friend whose boyfriend had raped me, only to be told that I was lying, that was until I found out I had gotten pregnant as a result of the rape. That when I found out, I had a guy friend who was dear to me, who seemed to allow others to believe he was the father of the baby, seeing how I had been treated and how I was being threatened. But when I chose to terminate the pregnancy, my friend did not agree with the choice, and we parted ways. To find even after it was all said and done, the man who had raped me, made threats towards my life, leaving a large group of my friends, to be protective over me, only to have one get shot in the head during an altercation with my rapist and his friends, where the bullet was meant for me. I later found out that the childhood friend who had me raped also set it up for me to be shot to keep my mouth shut about the rape.

I told him about how after everything had happened, the girl who had dated my rapist along with her friends, tormented me. They made my senior year of high school, where I was originally excited to be graduating a year early, become the worst year of high school. And due to it all, I had turned to drugs to numb myself for a brief time. The time that was a very dark time in my life, until I was given the chance to leave and start a new life. To which I did and met Eduardo shortly after.

A week after that first meeting, this new man had some days off and asked me if I wanted to watch a movie at his house. I agreed since the movie was going to be in the afternoon and he said he would like to take me out for dinner after the movie, saying that he wanted to spend the entire day with me. I was on cloud 9 with the idea, and could not wait to see him again, which was a whole new feeling for me. We spent the entire day together, we watched the movie he had picked up, went to dinner, and as it began to get dark out, he offered to pick up another movie and have me stay later than I had planned. I agreed to this, and as the evening went on, we began to kiss.

We kissed through the entire movie, and as we continued, he picked me up and carried me to his room. I was not objecting to fact that we might have been moving too fast like I had done in past relationships, because everything felt so right, and it was like we were in tune with one another. Everything I wanted him to do, he did without me having to say anything, and as the night went on, we made love. We made love like I had never made love before. I mean, it had been months since I had been with a man sexually, but this was unlike any passion I had ever felt. Where everything from his kisses to his touch, was in sync with me, and it was like we were dancing, a dance of passion and lovemaking through the entire night. Something I had never done with any other man in my life.

Come morning, I found myself waking up in his arms, and instead of feeling any sort of awkwardness that can come from a one-night stand or something that might move too fast, I was once again feeling euphoric, and he seemed to feel the same. He embraced me, kissed me as we both woke up, then insisted I relax while he made some breakfast. As I lay there, daydreaming of the night before, I began to feel the fears of Eduardo and the control he still had over me, slowly beginning to disappear. I had to stop myself and remind myself that this was all happening too fast, and I was sure it would end. But it did not.

This man treated me like a princess. Where when I asked for things or mentioned things, he replied with a "Princess Bride" phrase, which happened to be a favorite of mine, saying "as you wish" to any of my desires. He called me when he was working, or we were not together, knowing I had a daughter and respected my rules on not bringing men around her. He would call on the nights I had my daughter, knowing the time I would put her to bed, ask me about my days, as I did the same with him. No matter how many times we talked on the phone or saw one another, we seemed to have so much to say and shared a passion like no other I had ever experienced.

On Thanksgiving, just a month after we started seeing one another, he knew that I was sad about having to allow Eduardo to have my daughter that year and that I signed up to work for the holiday before we had met. We had talked the day before I went in to work the night shift, and he informed me he would be spending Thanksgiving at his roommate's family's house and would call me later that night. I had expected that call, but to my pleasant surprise, instead of a call, he arrived at my work that evening, with a plate filled with food from the Thanksgiving he had attended, along with a bouquet of flowers. I took my break at the time he showed up, so we could talk, and I could eat the feast he had brought me. After I got done and had to go back to work, he kissed me, and that is when it slipped out. After the kiss he said it, and he told me he loved me.

This caught me off guard because I did not expect someone, I had only been dating for a month to say such a thing. But I too felt the same, I felt as though this relationship was different from any other, I had, and instead of telling him how I felt, I just gave him another kiss and went back to work. As I walked in, my friend noticed the flowers and smile on my face, then warned me that she wanted me to be careful, knowing what Eduardo had put me through. I told her about the dinner he brought and what he had said, and she told me that she worried about me, and wanted me to be careful. I had not introduced her to this guy yet but promised to do so soon.

As the days went on, I was feeling like I was living in a dream, so happy to be around this man, and wanted to always be with him. Then one day, I needed a sitter. Since I had been working nights, my friend usually watched my daughter for a few hours in the mornings, so I could sleep, but on this day, she had to go out of town and would not be able to watch my daughter. I was exhausted from working the night shift and needed sleep but could not sleep with my daughter up and playing. I had been on the phone with this new guy, and he could hear the frustration in my voice, that is when he offered to watch my daughter. He said he could come to my apartment and watch her in the living room while I slept, that he had come from a large family, and even helped his roommate with his kids when they would come to visit. Sharing with me how he had a lot of experience with little kids. I felt torn, but I was so tired, and after thinking about it, I took him up on his offer.

When he arrived at my apartment, my daughter was excited to meet him, since she had not met many of my friends, other than the ones who I worked with. We had been watching cartoons and coloring, and he sat down and right away asked if he could join us. My daughter was so excited to have someone new to color with since I was sleepy and not being very much fun. I told him where her snacks were, showing that I had made a lunch that was in the fridge for her to have later, showed him the remote, where her art supplies were when he insisted, he would be just fine and walked me to bed. The two kissed me, and I could hear them as they went to the living room to color and watch cartoons. That is when it happened, I heard my daughter ask him for a hug, and she told him that she loved him. My heart melted because I could hear him tell her that she was so sweet, and he told her to give him a big hug.

I fell asleep shortly after that, then woke up to silence in the house. I got up and quietly went to the living room where they had been at last. There were plates and cups on the counter from the lunch I had made, and I looked over on the couch to see him reclined and my baby girl snuggled upon his chest as the two napped. He opened his eyes and saw me watching as I took a quick photo of the site I had seen, which made my heart flutter. I offered to move my daughter when he said that she was okay but patted on the couch for me to sit next to him. He then put his free arm around me, kissed me on the head, and fell back asleep. I sat there, staring at the two sleeping, not wanting to wake my daughter and ruin the moment. That is when I realized it, I was in love. I was in love with this man I had only known for a little over a month, but the feelings were real, and I was fairly sure he felt the same. Everything about him, the situation, just felt so right, like it was always meant to be in some sort of way.

I looked forward to the days and nights I would spend with him, and on the times when I was off work, he asked me if I would like to stay at his house, knowing how I always had a fear of Eduardo showing up at my apartment when I was alone. I found the invitation one that was simple to accept, and with that, I found myself spending more and more time with this man. Where everything about him felt as if I had known him my entire life, which before I said it to him, he told me that is how he had felt as well.

On the days and nights where it was just the two of us, we not only enjoyed sharing our time together, but I found the lovemaking to be an experience something I never imagined possible with a man. I had dreamed of such a feeling, but until then, had never felt such a connection. A connection that was both of an amazing friendship we were developing along with a soul connection that was felt in his touch, his presence, and in the lovemaking we had. I realized that I could love and be loved at the same time, whereas before meeting him, I felt as though I was somehow damaged and that something like this was never going to happen to me.

Then came the day, when he went with me to pick up my daughter at Eduardo's house. The day when the two would come face to face for the first time. He insisted on going with me when I informed him that my friend who usually went, was going to be out of town and I was nervous about going alone. And when we arrived together at Eduardo's house, Eduardo came out in shock to see me with a man. A man that Eduardo did not know, or even know I had been seeing, and a man who was not scared to stare right back at Eduardo as he did, as he tried to intimidate the guy I was seeing.

When Eduardo came to the car with my daughter, he tried to say that I needed to let him know who was around my daughter and where I was living. I told him that the courts have on file where I was living and that it was none of his business who I was with, that I was my daughter's mother, and I would not ever put her in harm's way like I had done when I was with him. Eduardo claimed that he somehow knew I was not living in my apartment, and I stopped him, telling him I did indeed still live there, but the only way he would know I had not been there was if he had been there looking for me. At that moment, I thought this guy was going to second guess a relationship with me, seeing firsthand the craziness I had to deal with, knowing Eduardo had been to my apartment complex even after I had put a trespassing order on him.

Eduardo then said that I needed to give him this new guy's address, that he had a right to know where my daughter would be when she was with me. With that, my boyfriend stopped Eduardo, and explained to him, without raising or changing the coolness of his voice, that he had read our orders, and nowhere on there did it state I had to tell him about who I was dating, or even where the person I was dating lived since I had my apartment which I stayed at on the days I had my daughter. This simple confrontation infuriated Eduardo, and as we left, he stood there, watching and glaring.

After picking up my daughter, we went back to my apartment where he had parked his truck, and he asked me if I would like to bring my daughter to his house. That Eduardo made him feel uneasy in the fact he did not feel that I was safe being at my apartment. He also mentioned that his roommate was home and had his kids for the weekend, and if I wanted to, we could stay the weekend with all of them. I sat there and thought about his invitation, I went back and forth on the pros and cons in my head but realized he was right. Eduardo had said that he somehow knew I was not home on the days when I did not have my daughter, which meant he had been there or had someone else watching me. And I realized that Eduardo also had no idea where my boyfriend lived, which made me feel safe in knowing, so I took him up on his invitation.

We went into my apartment and packed some things to take with us to his house, and as we did that, he said that maybe I should leave my car there, and we all ride in his truck. I saw the idea as a good one, so if Eduardo came or had someone else come to see if I was at my apartment, they could see that my car was there. And with that, I spent the first weekend with my daughter, at my boyfriend's house.

The weekend was a fun one, where all the kids played together, his roommate's daughter colored, played with dolls, and dress up with my daughter. We had a cookout, had a Disney movie night followed by a sing-a-long that everyone joined in with, as the kids sang and danced around the house. And where I enjoyed the time, not worrying about Eduardo, but feeling like I was safe, and exactly where I needed to be. With this man and my daughter, spending time, and enjoying that time together. In fact, after that weekend, my daughter and I began to enjoy all our time there with him at his house. Where I did not worry about Eduardo showing up, and my daughter had a blast, even during the times when his roommate's kids were not there.

The time with the boyfriend was bittersweet; not only for the memories we were making with my daughter but also as a way to try and forget about the anxiety I had about the upcoming court date. The court date came just days before Christmas holiday but was one that I wanted to get done with, and finally move on from. Due to the custody issue, the lawyers insisted we try a mediation, which I agreed to but knew Eduardo would not agree to anything since I was not giving him what he wanted, and he was furious knowing I was dating someone.

When I showed up for the mediation, it was apparent Eduardo was not going to be fair on anything, only agreeing to the terms he put down and not even trying to meet me in the middle. Eduardo refused to even consider what my lawyer and I offered, and with that, the lawyers decided to set up depositions for court. As we began the depositions, Eduardo sat there with a smug look on his face, acting as if he was the shit and he was determined to take my daughter from me. Eduardo was asked questions on the stalking, abuse I endured, and the stealing from both myself and my family, to which he admitted to all of it, but admitted to every bit of it all with that same smug look on his face the entire time. Giving a little laugh when some questions were asked, glaring at me while he had a smile on his face that made both myself and my lawyer very uneasy.

After the depositions were over, my lawyer was sure we had this custody case, that I would win, and get everything I asked for. Showing we had evidence, and the fact that he had admitted to the abuse, stalking, and stealing of my information in the depositions. So, when we went to court a few days later, I went into that room, not thinking I needed anything else but myself present. To my surprise, Eduardo had many people there, which included the God Mother, his cousins, his brother, and a few of the sitters we had used. I asked my lawyer if she knew, which she said she did but did not think there was anything anyone could say that would make me lose this case. As we began, Eduardo's lawyer started by saying that I was unstable, that I did not have time for my daughter, due to school and work, and that I was a single mom. I sat there, thinking that there was no way anything he said would go against me because we had those depositions where he did not deny any of his crazy and wrongdoings.

When my lawyer stood up, she handed the judge the depositions, then asked me to go to the stand, where she began to go over some of the questions we had asked. Eduardo's lawyer stood up, and contested it, interrupting my lawyer with every question she asked me, which just seemed to upset the judge. His lawyer then came to me, and asked me about the medications I had taken, asked me why I went against the doctor's orders and stopped taking them, which happened nearly 3 years prior. The lawyer went on and asked me about the hours I worked at the hospital, and how I expected to keep my sanity and watch over my daughter with my plans to go back to school that Spring. Showing the judge copies of my work schedule and my school schedule, then pointed out that Eduardo was remarried, and that he and his new wife had plenty of time, patience, and love to give my daughter, which a single mom just cannot provide.

Following that scene, where I was in shock at what Eduardo's lawyer had said, his lawyer then asked the God Mother to the stand. Where she said I did not know what I was doing as a new mom, that I had taken my daughter to the doctor she worked for, and they had to admit my daughter. Saying I had waited too long to have her seen, and Eduardo was the one who suggested going to see the doctor, and if we had not, my daughter may have died. As if I had not taken my daughter to the other pediatrician before going to the office she had worked at.

The God Mother went on and said she had witnessed my unstable mind, where I told her about abuse, an affair, and begged for help, but that Eduardo explained to her as he did others, showing them the medication, I had been prescribed, saying that I was not right in the head. She told the lawyer Eduardo said to her and others, that I begged him to stay, upset he was seeing his now-wife, but I somehow would not get it through my head and Eduardo stayed around, worried for my daughter's safety.

My lawyer tried to ask the God Mother questions, but Eduardo's lawyer stopped her saying unless she had proof right there in the courtroom of our claims against his, it was not amicable, which the judge agreed to. Eduardo then stood up and asked if he could address the court with his concerns about me kidnapping my daughter. Stating I had gone against the temporary orders, to which my lawyer contested, then asked the judge if they would keep the stipulation on me, to where I could not move over 100 miles of where Eduardo lived. Stating if I did move out of that boundary, I would lose all rights to my daughter. And without ever reading the depositions or listening to my claims, the judge said he had come to a decision and was granting full custody to Eduardo, giving me visitation that his lawyer would draw up for me, along with the distance stipulation, forcing me to live within 100 miles of Eduardo or give up all rights to my daughter if I chose to move out of the boundary.

I was floored. I mean, shock does not even describe what I felt. I felt as if my heart had been ripped out of my chest, and all I wanted to do was embrace my baby girl and protect her, but I could not. She was being given to a monster, the monster who tormented me. And as we walked out of the courtroom with both myself and my lawyer not knowing what to say, Eduardo walked by and laughed at me then shook his lawyer's hand, exclaiming Eduardo won to everyone in the stands.

My lawyer tried to talk to me, but I could not talk to her, she had promised to protect my daughter and we lost. I was told I had nothing to worry about, but now the fears I tried to ignore that I was assured would not happen, happened. I was ordered to hand my daughter over to Eduardo later that day, and with that, I left and went to my boyfriend's house. He was there, watching my daughter with his roommate and the roommate's kids.

When I walked in, they could see I was distraught, and I went right over to pick up my daughter, hold her, and never wanted to let her go. I cried rocking her, and the roommate came to me and said that maybe I should go to the other room to talk to my boyfriend, that he would watch my daughter while we talked. I got in the room, and collapsed on the bed, crying uncontrollably. My boyfriend tried to hold me, console me, as I told him what happened.

As I began to calm down a bit telling him about what happened in court, my phone rang. It was Eduardo. I answered thinking that he was going to tell me where to meet him for the exchange of our daughter, but no, I was wrong. I put the phone on speaker and the roommate walked in, in shock at what we were all hearing this man tell me on the other line. Eduardo told me I got what he warned me would happen, that had I just done what he said and listened to him, things would have been better for me. But he warned me, and now it has happened just as he said it would. Claiming for being sorry, but I needed to learn this hard lesson, just like every beating he gave me, everything he ever did to me, were all hard lessons I needed to learn in order to grow and be a better wife and mother. And that, until he feels I have learned my lesson and made the right choice to be his again, I would be forced to suffer because that was all part of his plan to make me be a better woman for him.

Listening to Eduardo's voice made me cringe, I wanted to throw up at the idea that somehow, I felt I might have to submit to him once again, in order for me to keep my daughter safe. As he continued to gloat on the other line, my boyfriend left the room. He went to load the gun he had in a safe and was determined to get rid of Eduardo, sickened by what Eduardo was saying on the phone with the tone of having won. Reminding me of beatings, rapes, and harassment I had been subjected to, and saying they were all done to teach me lessons in order for me to understand I was not to ever disobey him. Having to see me with such sadness, and fear on my face to what Eduardo was saying, my boyfriend was infuriated, and could not stand by listening or watching any more of the sick and twisted things Eduardo was spewing on the other line. The roommate jumped up and tried to stop him, but my boyfriend was determined and did not want my daughter or myself to have to endure any more of the sick and twisted things Eduardo was sure to continue putting us through.

I hung up the phone with Eduardo, I did not want to hear any more of his way of thinking to where the judge sided with such a monster, not even considering any evidence that we had, with the depositions of him admitting to beating me, forcing me to submit, stalking me and everyone around me, stealing my identity, and trying to make me feel like I was crazy. Which was all part of Eduardo's twisted game, that the courts sided with him on. I right away called my boyfriend and had to beg him to not do what he was planning on doing, and to come back, that I needed him there with me. A few minutes later, he came back in and held me, then when he saw my daughter, he had her join our embrace, as he held the both of us, promising that he was not going to allow Eduardo to harm us ever again.

Within an hour, I received a phone call from my lawyer, informing me that she had the orders at her office for me to pick up. When I arrived, she informed me that I would have to drive to Eduardo's lawyer's office after leaving hers, to hand my daughter over to Eduardo. But his lawyer went by the laws in place for families, and even though Eduardo only wanted to give me the minimum amount of visitation time, I was given every Thursday and every other weekend with my daughter, along with holidays and a month each summer. I know she was trying to show me I got more than what he had proposed, but it was not enough. I could not be there to protect her from Eduardo and I did not want to talk to my lawyer about it either. He had won. Before leaving she stopped me and said that we can contest the decision, that we can gather the evidence we lacked this time, and fight this. I told her that I wanted to but wanted to first enjoy the holiday that was coming with my daughter and focus on her for the moment.

From there, my boyfriend drove me and my daughter to Eduardo's lawyer's office, where Eduardo was standing outside waiting for us. He tried to say my boyfriend could not be around my daughter when my boyfriend stopped him. He told Eduardo that he may have won this battle, but he has not won the war. With that, Eduardo laughed and said that it was over, he won, and that my boyfriend should just leave now because he was going to make things hard for us. Promising that he was going to make my boyfriend regret having ever met me. As Eduardo said this, his wife came out and took my daughter from me. My boyfriend embraced me as I collapsed in his arms and walked me to his truck. We drove away in silence, as I cried in spurts, thinking that I was living in a nightmare.

In the days following, I just focused on work and the upcoming weekend which went into the holiday break that I would have with my daughter.

The few days leading up to the time went by fast, and before we knew it, we were getting ready for Christmas. I was excited because that year, I had my daughter for most of the time, and I had taken off work for the entire time as well. The thing was, I wanted to also spend Christmas with my boyfriend, a man I had fallen head of heels for, and wanted to spend every moment with. He had stayed by my side, supporting me through the crying and sleepless nights that followed the day in court. I knew he did not have any family in the area, and that his roommate would be spending the holiday with his kids at his family's house. So, I asked him if he would like to join me at my parent's house for the holiday. He said he would but was not sure what my family would say about me bringing a guy home for the holidays since he knew that the last time I brought a guy home, it did not turn out so well.

I told him I would talk to my parents, and let them know, and that they did know I was seeing him since we talked nearly daily on the phone. And they also knew that I was falling in love with him, to where they, like everyone else, cautioned me knowing all Eduardo had put me through.

After I told my parents I had invited my boyfriend to join us for the holidays, they did not object and had been curious, so they said that it would give them a chance to meet this guy I raved about. And with that, he took off the time from work, we packed our bags, picked up my daughter from Eduard's house, and rode in his truck down to my parent's house for the holidays.

As we headed out, I received a call from my lawyer, who was just informing me that Eduardo had called his lawyer to try and stop me from going to visit family out of state. Where he was trying to enforce the 100-mile limit the courts put on me, where it had to be explained to him that I could take a vacation, that I notified the courts as per the orders that I was going out of state for the holidays. She said that after he was stopped with that, he tried to have me stopped from taking my daughter with my boyfriend. Eduardo got mad when he was told that unless my boyfriend was a proven criminal or a danger, there was nothing he could do about it. But if Eduardo tried anything, to just ignore him and write everything down. I thanked her for letting me know and was not going to allow Eduardo to ruin the time I had with my daughter.

When we arrived, my parents and sister came to meet us at the truck, to give myself and my daughter lots of hugs and kisses, as well as introduce themselves to my boyfriend. They noticed how he was a lot different from Eduardo, and even though they saw this difference, they still watched him and studied him carefully, which he did not seem to mind knowing the reason why they were cautious. The next day, some of my friends had called and wanted to meet up. They had planned an evening of starting at the saloon down the street from my parent's house, which would end up at a bar in the town below the mountain my family lived on, for music and dancing. They were all also eager to meet this new guy I was seeing. I found this as a wonderful way to introduce him to some of my friends and decided that before that evening, I would introduce him to some of my other friends, the ones who were more of the vocal type. The ones who disapproved of Eduardo when we had come for the festival, and who also offered to be there for me if I ever needed it. The protective ones.

I knew that this meeting would be a great test, one my boyfriend was aware of as well. I had explained why they were protective and how they are even more so after everything Eduardo had put me and my daughter through. So, when we drove up, I was not surprised to see the eyes staring at and judging this man who they did not know, who was with me. But as he went to introduce himself, the tension began to quickly disappear, to where I had some of my friends pull me aside and tell me that they approved, but as always to just be careful. Then at one point, he went into another room with several of the guys, which included the big brother of the group, leaving me wondering what was going on. As they all left the room, there were smiles on their faces, which left me even more curious as to what was going on, wanting to know what happened in that room, but no one would tell me.

The afternoon was a good one. After meeting up at my friend's house, some of us went to the park that was the community park to take my daughter and some of their kids to play. We all talked, and it seemed as if there was a secret, they all knew, but that I was unaware of. I must admit, I was somewhat annoyed in knowing they all knew something that I did not. And that did not end there either.

When it came time to go to meet up with my other friends at the lounge, I had gotten up to use the restroom. As I walked back to the table where everyone seemed to be talking, they all went silent, and just smiled at me. And this just seemed to continue throughout the night, where everyone knew a secret, I was being left out of. But I did not let it bother me and had a really enjoyable time catching up with friends I had not seen in years, laughing, and enjoying all the company.

The following day was Christmas Eve, where we had friends from the town my parents lived in, coming, and going to enjoy food and drinks. I noticed that my boyfriend had gone outside as my dad did to smoke a cigarette with my dad on the porch. The two seemed to be in a serious conversation but did not seem to get heated either. But again, no one said anything to me on to what was going on. That was until the next morning when we all got up to see what Santa had brought my daughter and exchange gifts.

We had completed the gift exchanges and were watching my daughter as she played with some of her toys. That is when my boyfriend insisted there was a gift that was missing, one I must have overlooked. So, as I began looking around the tree, my daughter joined me wanting to also find this missing gift. After searching and not finding anything, we turned around to my boyfriend, on one knee, holding a box with a ring inside of it. That is when my entire world shifted when he told me how he knew this was happening so fast, but he had never met anyone like me before nor had a connection with anyone like he had with me before. Saying that until me, he did not believe in love at first sight, but he wanted to know if I would do him the pleasure, of spending the rest of my life with him, as a family with my daughter, and if I would be his wife.

I began to shake, as tears ran down my face. The tears were those of joy, happiness which I was feeling throughout my entire body that was unlike any other I had ever felt before. And as this happened, I shook my head yes, gave him a huge kiss, and told him, yes! When I did this, he placed the ring on my finger and I looked up at my family, who all had tears in their eyes, running to hug me and congratulate me.

Within minutes of the proposal, my parent's phone began to ring. It was a friend after friend wishing me a Merry Christmas and congratulating me on the engagement, all knowing that he would be proposing to me, after he asked some, including my dad, for permission and told them what time he would be doing this. Letting me know that he pulled the one group of guys, my protectors, and brothers aside, asking them for permission to marry me. Telling my other group of friends at the dinner that he was going to ask, and my parents let me know that he asked them for permission to marry me as well. To where, he even asked my daughter if he could marry her mommy, to which she said yes to just as long as he married her too.

I was once again on cloud 9, feeling like a princess that my now fiancé, had placed on a pedestal. Ensuring that everyone who I cared about knew, making the day one that was not only extra special, but the most amazing Christmas I have ever had before and since. As the day went on, we had many visitors, all of who came to congratulate us and wish us all a very Merry Christmas.

The vacation went by way too fast after that, where I felt as if I was in a dream the entire time, waiting for the ball to drop. And I was not too far off either. When we got back, I had to meet up with Eduardo, so he could have his time with my daughter. I did not tell Eduardo about the engagement, but within an hour of dropping my daughter off with him, he called me. Eduardo was furious. He told me that I was making a huge mistake and when I asked him how he found out, he said when he took my daughter to his parent's house for a party, my daughter told everyone that she and her mommy were getting married. She said that her mommy got a very pretty ring, and she was mad because she did not get a ring, but she was going to get married to my fiancé as well.

I laughed at Eduardo because I knew that now that I was getting married, he could not stop me or force me to be with him, and my fiancé was not going to allow "him" to mess with me ever again.

A New Approach

After the holidays, my fiancé and I decided that we wanted to get a house together but would need to save up for both that and the upcoming wedding I began planning. With that, my now fiancé knew he could make a lot more money by going on the road and warned me that the time would make it so we were not together as much as we both wanted, but at the same time, we could save money for our future with this. I was torn on the decision, but I also knew he was right, and we both wanted to begin our lives together by planning things out now. He also told me we were not going to give up on my daughter, which I agreed to, and we were going to work at getting a compelling case, so we could go back to court and win.

I knew this was what we needed to do, but I also did not want to stay in my apartment any longer. I had sadness from my daughter's room being empty for extended periods, and he saw this. That is when my fiancé asked me to move into his house because his roommate was going to move to be closer to his kids as well. I found this as a great way to get away and hide from Eduardo. Where I kept my apartment, so the courts had it on file, but where I was never there. This also drove Eduardo nuts, because Eduardo knew I was not ever there, and he began following me.

I noticed the following when I was headed to a dress shop to look at wedding gowns. I had seen his vehicle behind me but paid it no attention, not until Eduardo followed me to this dress shop and parked in the empty lot across the street from the shop. I called my fiancé and told him, and he prompted me to call the cops and my lawyer. When I did that, the police showed up, and Eduardo claimed that he did not know I was there at first, then slipped and said that he wanted to see where I was staying. The police explained that what he was doing was stalking and was against the law, but only gave him a warning, letting him go.

My lawyer informed me what had happened after she requested to speak with the officers. She told me to be careful, and that we would note the incident.

Then about a week later, I was at my doctor being treated for strep throat, and I received a call from a CPS worker. This worker was calling to tell me that they had my daughter in their custody, explaining that she was at a center for children who have been sexually molested. This was because apparently after my weekend with my daughter, Eduardo claimed that my daughter went to his house grabbing her privates saying that my fiancé had touched her privates. And after an examination, the doctors noticed that her vagina was red and had been messed with.

I felt sick, I told the CPS worker that no one had touched her and that my fiancé was a truck driver. That during my weekend with my daughter, my fiancé was not even in the same state. Which Eduardo was unaware of since he tried to claim that both myself and my fiancé had dropped my daughter off earlier that day. But I explained I was driving my fiancé's truck since Eduardo would follow me when he saw my car. The worker then asked for the information from the company that my fiancé worked for, to verify my claim, she then said that she would get back to me, but I was not allowed to see my daughter until they could find out what was going on.

I started shaking, I called my lawyer, who told me to go to her office. She had called the center that had my daughter after I got off the phone, and was on the phone with CPS as I walked in. They had verified that my fiancé was not in the state and on the other side of the country when this alleged molestation took place, but my daughter had evidence of being violated on her. She also assured me they had removed Eduardo and his wife from the center because he was talking for my daughter, telling her to say things, which was strange. And due to the situation, they wanted to talk to my daughter without either one of us being there.

As we sat there waiting for the CPS workers to call back, my fiancé called me. He had received a call from his boss and wanted to know what was going on. I explained to him what I knew, and as I did this, the CPS worker called. They said after Eduardo and the stepmom left, my daughter said that the stepmom had pinched her vagina over and over again and that my daughter, who was just 2 years old almost 3, said that her daddy told her to say that her other daddy had touched her "te-te" as we had called it. They then explained that my fiancé would have to make a statement to the courts, that because of the severity of the allegation, which had evidence to support the claim at the time, it had already been noted and put in the system, and he would need to have his name cleared.

Within minutes, my fiancé's boss called, and informed us that he had told them what was going on, and they knew him for many years, knowing he would never harm a child. They said they were making arrangements to have him head back to where we were, giving him a load that would reroute him from his current route, which would have him there by the next evening if he drove straight through. Explaining that he was going to go so that he could do a lie detector test and a psycho-sexual analysis which the CPS workers had asked if he would be willing to undertake to help get his name cleared of these allegations. And by the next evening, my fiancé had arrived in town.

I picked him up at the yard where he dropped his truck off to unload, and we prepared for the next day to head to the courthouse. When we got there, the CPS workers along with a police officer, took my fiancé into another room. They explained that the courts were asking both him and my daughter's dad to undergo these tests, but my daughter's dad was refusing to do them. They continued and told me after asking again, that my fiancé had agreed to undergo the lie detector test along with a psycho-sexual analysis, which again, Eduardo was refusing to undergo.

My lawyer showed up and explained to me about the tests they were doing, that unless my fiancé did these, he would have an accusation of child molestation on his records for life, but this would clear him of the accusations. She continued and said that she had talked to Eduardo's lawyer, and she learned that he is no longer being represented, and owes money to the lawyer. But that the people from CPS had let her know that they advised Eduardo to take the same tests, but they could not make him do it, and knowing this, he flat out refused the testing. I looked at my lawyer and asked her if this meant I was getting my daughter back and if I would be able to keep her safe from this monster? She explained that I might, but CPS would have to do an investigation on both of us, and it could take months.

My fiancé did all the tests, which cleared his name from the molestation allegations, and we cooperated completely with everything CPS asked us to do. Where they wanted to set up home visits once a week to meet with me at my house and they would do the same at Eduardo's house. They explained that they were not going to be charging Eduardo or his wife with anything at the time, and until their investigation was done, we would have to continue to follow the orders from the courts. When we asked how long they would be doing this investigation, they said it could take time, months even.

I was livid, as was my fiancé, and lawyer. We could not understand how they were going to allow Eduardo to have my daughter after violating her, coaching her to say such horrible things, and making false accusations to where my 2-year-old baby was taken to a center where she was examined.

As the time went on, I continued to plan for the wedding we were going to have that summer and decided that with everything going on, and after the courts went in his favor, I would not go back to school. I felt I did not have a choice, since they used me going to school and working against me in court, and I was not going to allow them to have anything to use against me. I also went in to plead guilty to the charges of harassment for those phone messages, for which I was just given a fine as the judge ended up dropping the charges to a misdemeanor. And a few weeks after the initial allegations, the CPS worker who had been visiting me said Eduardo claimed I was mentally unstable and was again using the medications I had taken after I had my daughter, and the fact that I plead guilty to the harassment charges, against me. She asked me if I would be willing to go through a psychological evaluation, explaining she had already talked to my lawyer, and that it would help me in court when we go back. I of course agreed to this, and within days of doing it, they let me know that they had no worries about me but were making Eduardo undergo the same tests. Which raised some concerns over Eduardo's results.

When the CPS worker told me about the concerns on his part, I felt like I finally had something, something to prove I was not crazy like he told everyone and even the judge, and that he was the one who was crazy. She told me they were going to be making him, along with the wife and all the kids, go through therapy. Telling me during the visits, Eduardo pulled out videos of him taping my daughter, where he was coaching her in the videos to say things about me and my fiancé, trying to use the videos as evidence to have my daughter taken from me. She said there was more that had to do with Eduardo's wife's kids they were worried about as well, but they could not tell me what it was.

The idea of having to continue an investigation bothered me, not so much for the home visits that I continued to cooperate with weekly, but for the fact that he was coaching my daughter to say horrible things, and there was also something else going on with those other kids. The investigation continued for months. I got used to the visits, and during those I did share the marks on my daughter, showing that regardless of what CPS was doing, my daughter came back to me with welts on her that looked like belt marks. They agreed and took photos of the marks, but when they would go to Eduardo with the evidence, he would turn it all around and claim that I must have done it to my daughter. Every single time, Eduardo turned things around, changing my allegations and trying to turn everything I said around on me, making it sound like I was the one doing everything. This is why CPS said they were taking so long in doing the investigation, all while I had to hand my daughter over to Eduardo, as she cried and begged not to go with Eduardo, calling him and his wife monsters.

As this continued, I realized that I had not had a period in a few months. At first, I thought it could have been because after the holidays, I changed my birth control, and it was followed by the stress of planning a wedding and dealing with CPS, but I had to be sure. So, as I was at the store picking up a pregnancy test, my fiancé called as he did every day to see how my day was going. I told him I would let him know shortly, but that I needed to check out and go back to the house. He seemed to be confused, which he had a right to be, but I did not want to say anything until I knew for sure.

So, as we stayed on the phone, I went home and peed on the stick. That is when I saw it, a positive that came a lot quicker than what the package had said, and with that, I let him know my day was great and that I just found out I was pregnant. He was ecstatic, and we laughed about how I had been on the phone buying a test but did not want to tell him until I was certain. Then it occurred to me, that I could not remember when I had had a period last.

The following day, I made an appointment with my doctor. When I arrived at her office, I explained that I could not remember when I had a period last. She first confirmed the pregnancy with a urine sample and then said we could check and see by doing an ultrasound. As we did this, she informed me she was moving and that she would refer me to a new doctor. And that is when I saw it, a baby with a strong heartbeat on the screen, and after measuring this little angel, we estimated I was already 13-weeks along.

I left her office with the new doctor's information and signed the papers for my records to be transferred to his office. I then called my fiancé and congratulated him on us being pregnant. I was ecstatic, I mean, I had never been so happy to find out I was pregnant, but I was. I was marrying the man I loved, and we both discussed wanting kids, but now we were going to start having more kids sooner than expected. I had gotten pictures from the ultrasound we had done in the office, so when I went to pick up my daughter, I gave her a card with a photo of the baby inside, telling her that she was going to be a big sister. Just like myself and my fiancé, my baby girl was excited, she said she wanted a friend so bad, and "her baby" as she referred to it, was going to be her best friend.

After finding out I was pregnant, I knew that I needed to try to not stress out like I had been doing on the things Eduardo did. Shortly after, my fiancé and I had found a house that was a large one and began moving in together, to start the rest of our lives as a family. With that, I had to notify the courts of the address, to where within a few days, Eduardo showed up, just sitting outside the house taking photos of it.

But I was not going to let it bother me. I knew Eduardo also knew that I was pregnant because the CPS worker told me when she was at his house, my daughter told her that her mommy was having "her baby" that was going to be her friend. And when my daughter said this, Eduardo apparently looked very mad and stomped out of the room.

I did not care what Eduardo did or said anymore. I was not going to allow Eduardo to have any sort of control or sway over me. I was moving on, and he was not going to stop me. But when I told my fiancé about Eduardo parking outside our new house and taking photos, it made him feel uneasy. He then contacted his old roommate whose brother ran a local funeral home at a cemetery and had offered my fiancé a job at, being a grief counselor. He said he wanted to be there with us, and not miss any more of the pregnancy, as well as be there to keep us safe from Eduardo. I was incredibly happy at this choice, and within the week, he had turned in his truck and was going in for training to get his certifications to work as a family grief counselor.

This change also allowed the CPS worker who came by weekly, to get to know my fiancé better, which once she did, she said they were closing the case on us. That everything Eduardo had said about us was all a lie, and they were sorry for wasting our time with the visits. But she explained that they were continuing to investigate Eduardo and when I was ready to go back to court, they would stand up for me and my daughter on our behalf.

That news was something I needed to hear, something I think everyone who was on our side needed to hear, and within minutes my lawyer called asking if I had heard. I told her the CPS worker had come to our house to tell us, and that we were ready to go back to court as soon as we could get in.

I felt justified, even if we had not been back to the courts, I felt justified in everything. But at the same time, I was mad at the judge, for allowing this monster to do as much as he had, that if the judge had read the depositions or even listened to what I had to say, none of this would have happened. And I went online, and began looking up articles on the judge, seeing he was accused of being corrupt and had taken bribes in custody cases, including a bribe he was accused of taking from the lawyer Eduardo had hired, in a previous case.

There was article after article, with information on corruption from this judge, the same judge who gave the monster custody. I was livid, and after sitting there reading everything, I decided to draft a story on my MySpace, calling the judge out. The article I wrote gained traction, I had numerous commenters, who had dealt with this judge and who had witnessed this corruption. Made me feel like I had a leg up on everything, that was until we went to court.

We were able to go to court soon after CPS closed their investigation on me, and as we waited outside the courtroom, I saw the CPS worker talk to my lawyer and then leave. Apparently, Eduardo had printed off the article I wrote on the judge, which was the same judge we were about to go and see, and he had given the CPS workers along with my lawyer copies of what I had written. And was going to hand that over to the judge as well. My lawyer looked at me and said that CPS will not go in the courtroom with that, that they had to deal with this judge daily. She also said that if I walked into the courtroom now, I would lose, and I would not get another chance to get my daughter back through the courts, this was it. So, I agreed with her and decided to hold off on going back to the courts.

I felt defeated once again and knew I had to regroup and continue to go by the orders. When I got home, I deleted the post I had put up and told my fiancé what happened in court. We then decided to let CPS continue their investigation against Eduardo, in hopes that they would decide to help us to keep my daughter safe.

Time continued to go on, the days turned into weeks, and I was beginning to show. I had gone to have my wedding dress altered where they put a panel in that would stretch as my belly grew. Soon after, we had gone to the doctor to find out that we were having a baby boy, which was overly exciting news for everyone. Then after another couple of months, we received a call from CPS, they requested a meeting with us, which would include several CPS supervisors, a mediator, along with Eduardo, and his wife. I called my lawyer, and she went on to get copies of the investigation from CPS, so I could have an idea of what we would be going into. When I got to her office, she had a highlighter for me and asked me to follow along. She explained that all the blacked-out items had to do with the step kids, that there was a lot against Eduardo there, but I was not allowed to see it. She then wished me luck, hugged me, and told me to call her when we got done.

The next day I had been to my doctor for a routine check on the baby, and they showed he was doing well, growing, and thriving. After the appointment, we got a call from the CPS worker who said that they had the date for the meeting set for that Friday, which we said would work for us.

When Friday came, we were excited and ready to hopefully get my daughter away from the monster. My fiancé made copies of the depositions, the copies from CPS that my lawyer gave me, and copies of the papers that cleared us of any abuse, just in case we needed them we wanted to be prepared.

As we arrived, we noticed Eduardo was already there, sitting at a table with that smug look on his face, and his wife was sitting next to him. My fiancé and I sat on the other side of the table when the CPS workers began. They went over their findings when it came to my daughter, stating that they were closing the case. I right away asked why? Why they were not going after Eduardo for touching her vagina, coaching her, the welts and bruises, or anything else they found on him? They then explained that there were no laws on coaching your kids on what to say, that it was true that he recorded these coaching sessions but that they could not do anything about it. They also said that if we read the papers, the wife claimed that my daughter must have had a diaper rash and that Eduardo overreacted and was sure my fiancé had done something to my daughter. But that they could not prove anything, because everything we presented, he would then counteract. They also let us know that he was ordered to continue therapy, as was the rest of the family.

The wife then tried to say that I was not truthful either, trying to say Eduardo was a bad man, which is when I asked her if she had read the depositions from the court. She said she had not, so I handed her a copy, explaining that he admitted to everything, the abuse and more. Eduardo tried to take the papers from his wife saying that she did not care about that. His wife just looked at me, with the same look of fear that I once knew.

Eduardo then asked the CPS workers if this meant that they were not going to do anything to him and if the case was closed, to which they said it was true, he was not in trouble when it came to my daughter, and they had closed their case. That is when he began to laugh, Eduardo said yes, he did it all, he had his wife pinch my daughter on her vagina on purpose, he told her to say the things she did, he coached her, and that he had made everything, all of it up. Eduardo did it not knowing that my fiancé was a truck driver and not around and said that he did it because he did not want me getting married. And there was nothing I or anyone else could do because the case was now closed.

I was beyond livid, I felt sick, and angry and wanted to strangle Eduardo. My fiancé had to hold me, as Eduardo got up, told his wife to go, and left. We all sat there, as I stared out the window, feeling more pissed than I had been at anyone in an awfully long time. The CPS workers all had looks of shock on their faces, they could not believe what had just happened. They then each came to me, the workers, investigators, and supervisors, and apologized to me for everything. For not listening to me, or helping me and my daughter, but there was nothing they could do, not even with everyone in that room knowing that he confessed to pinching my daughter's vagina and coaching her, causing months and months of a mess that was all because Eduardo did not want me to get married. Hearing he confessed to making it all up, every bit of the allegations against me and my fiancé.

As the shock began to wear off, I was still livid, but we had to leave to pick up my daughter from Eduardo which was the start of my summer with her. That weekend, I tried to move past the anger I felt, but I couldn't. I could not believe Eduardo had the balls to say what he did, knowing that no matter what, there was nothing anyone could do to him. That Eduardo had once again won, which he gloated about with the smug look on his face when we went to get my daughter. I was in disbelief, thinking back on everything Eduardo had done, thinking how a person like him gets away with everything he has done. Things that were vile, morbid, and beyond sickening.

I found I had a hard time sleeping that weekend, I could not stop going over everything. I was stressing out about the fact my daughter was not going to be protected as I had hoped CPS would do. That Eduardo somehow knew what he was doing and knew how to get away with it and we were still playing his game, where he was using my daughter as a pawn in it all. I went over the fact I had a wedding coming up, and I would be preparing for a bridal shower in just a week. I knew that I would need to make sure I had everything ready as we prepared to go to my hometown to get married. Vowing to myself that regardless of what had happened, I was not going to allow Eduardo to win anymore and I would find a way to beat him at his own game.

Come Sunday evening, I began to feel sick and went to bed early that night. By Monday morning, the sick feeling was still there, and I realized I had not felt our son move since the night before. I decided to take a shower, hoping that the water running down my belly would wake him up, but it did not. So, as I got out and got dressed, I informed my fiancé of what was going on and called my doctor. The doctor asked me to come in, saying he had an opening that morning, so, I kissed my fiancé goodbye as he left for work, I got my daughter ready and headed to my doctor's office.

When I walked in, the nurse was able to take us back right away, asking me to lay on the table, and lift my shirt so that they could use the doppler to check on my baby's heart rate. As the nurse did this, I looked over at my daughter who was playing with some blocks. The nurse tried numerous times but was not finding a heartbeat. She then explained this can happen if say the baby had turned and was in a position that made it harder to find a heartbeat but to be safe, we were going to do an ultrasound in the room down the hall.

I got up from the table, went for my daughter's hand, and we followed the nurse down the hall, where I got on the ultrasound table, and she again instructed me to lift my shirt as she began the scan. As she did this, I can remember looking up at the screen, not seeing nor hearing a second heartbeat, only being able to hear my own, which got louder and louder in my head as I tried to focus on the screen. All the while my daughter asked what we were looking at, what was on the screen?

That is when I looked at her face, the nurse had this look of dread on her face, and with that, I looked over to the screen to see that my baby, my son, was not moving. There was no blood flow in the placenta. The nurse got up and said for me to stay put, that she was going to get the doctor, then looked to my daughter and asked if she wanted to go out to the nurse's station to color.

I lay there, staring at the screen. The screen that had the image of my son was still on it. I could not see or hear anything else, not even when the doctor came in and began the same scan as the nurse had just done. That was until I realized that his scan came up with the same dreaded result. I looked at the doctor, and he asked me if they could call my fiancé. I told him yes, to which he went on and explained that my son, had passed away, and there was nothing we could do.

My heart dropped, and I felt my world shift, with more sadness than I can ever remember feeling at any point before or since. As I felt this sadness take over me, the doctor said he was going to be sending me to the hospital, since I was at 24 weeks along, they would need to induce me, and I would need to deliver my son. With those words, I let out a scream, I could not hold it in any longer, and I cried harder than ever before. I wanted to wake up, I had been through so many horrors and felt that all of it, everything had to be a bad dream, I could not handle another nightmare. Thinking things were starting to get better for me, I had an amazing man at my side, we were getting married, and starting a family, and this was not supposed to happen like this. But it was, and as I cried, my doctor hugged me as another nurse came in to offer her support as well.

Within minutes, the nurse was able to get a hold of my fiancé. He had been in a meeting at his work but had been alerted of the situation. The nurse asked me if I wanted to wait there for him or meet him at the hospital, and with that, I looked over at my daughter who was at the other side of the office, coloring and telling some of the other nurses about her dolls. I then answered the nurse and said that I would meet my fiancé at the hospital, and that I would be okay to drive across the street to the hospital. As I said this, I got up, wiped off my belly from the jelly that had been used to do the scans, and went for my daughter's hand. The doctor came up behind me, put his hand on my shoulder, and told me he would meet me at the hospital, and that the staff there was being alerted now so they would be waiting for me.

As I walked out of the office and into the waiting room, I saw the expressions of the people there, the ones who heard my scream, saw my face as I walked out, and some who even had tears. Feeling like they were all there knowing I was a walking tomb. Where they had healthy babies in their bellies which they embraced as they saw me and saw that the fear that moms might find during pregnancy, had become my reality. I tried to get out of there quickly, to avoid making any sort of eye contact with anyone, I got my daughter in the car, then drove across the street to the hospital.

When I arrived on the labor and delivery floor, my friend was there. My fiancé had called her to tell her that they were admitting me, and she came to embrace me. The nurses at the station had already set a room up for me, one that had a white wreath on the door, a symbol to notify others that we would not be delivering a live baby, but that we would be delivering an angel. As I walked into the room, my friend asked my daughter to go to the lobby with her, while she bought her some cookies and got her a juice. I was then asked to change into a gown, and within minutes, they were starting a series of IVs on me. One that had Pitocin, one that was a saline drip, and one that was a pain killer, which kept me from feeling the pains of the labor that was about to take place.

Shortly after being set up, my daughter and friend came back to the room, where the nurses put on cartoons for my daughter. Following this, my fiancé, his boss, his boss's wife, and his old roommate all showed up. My fiancé came in and held me, allowing me to cry and let it all out. I looked over his shoulder to watch as the boss's wife and old roommate walked my daughter out of the room. The boss came to us and explained that they would be taking my daughter to stay the night with them, and their kids would be there to play with her as well. My friend then asked me if I wanted her to stay, to which I promptly answered that I would like her to, and my fiancé followed by saying that he too would like her to stay as well. The old roommate came in and asked if we needed anything, and as he did, my doctor walked in. We told the roommate that we were good, but that he was also urged to stay with us as well, to which he left to grab some food in the cafeteria, invited my friend along so that they could prepare for the long day we all had ahead of us.

When the doctor came in and our friends left, he sat on the bed and looked at both myself and my fiancé, then began to explain what the process was. He told us that it could take time, but once the baby was delivered, they would allow us to spend time with him. He continued and explained that we would then have to decide what to do with our son's body after that. If we wanted a funeral, then now was the time to make those arrangements. While he said this, the boss had been in the lobby, already making arrangements for us, which my fiancé let the doctor know. After telling us that part, the doctor continued to tell us how the delivery would go, that I was given strong pain killers, so I would not have to be in pain at any part of the delivery, making it somewhat easier in this very sad situation. Then before getting up to leave the room, he said that he would be back later in the day, to check on me, and would also be there to deliver when the time came, but if it happened sooner, he was just across the street and would come right over to be there for us.

With that, the doctor left the room. My fiancé's boss peaked in and asked my fiancé to go to the hall. His boss explained that once the baby was delivered, to have the funeral home notified, they were preparing the casket for us, and the transport arrangements had already been made. He then said he had to get back to the office, gave me his home number along with his wife's cell number, and said to call if we needed anything and that my daughter would be okay at their house. We both thanked him, as he gave us hugs and left. Leaving my fiancé and myself, alone in the room, waiting for the delivery of a baby who we loved, one we had discussed his future over as we daydreamed about him at night when he would kick.

The time seemed to be irrelevant to me. I remember our friends coming back up after eating and sitting on the sofa that was in the room. We then had many friends from the hospital I worked with come in, drop off flowers and offer their condolences. My fiancé had called my family, notified them of what was going on, and had also called his family letting them know as well. And as the time just kept moving, even though I felt as though I was frozen, not there during it all, I began to feel the urge to want to push.

As this happened, my doctor came in, checked me, and informed everyone that it was time. I was not ready for this, my friend stood behind my bed as the pushing began, the roommate went to the lobby to wait until it was over, and my fiancé, stayed by my side, holding me as I pushed. The delivery process was different than before, I had a bed that was not broken down, the room was quieter, no excitement was felt, no nurses waiting to weigh and wrap my baby up and the air seemed to have a heavy sadness hovering over us the entire time. Then as I went for that final push, I looked down, to see this perfect, tiny baby boy between my legs. The doctor wrapped him up, cut the cord, and continued to assist with the delivery of the placenta, as my fiancé, friend, and I all stared at this baby boy. He appeared to be sleeping, a tiny, precious, sleeping angel, who looked perfect, leaving me to question the doctor on to how or why this happened.

The doctor explained that these things can happen, without any warning or reason that they can find, and after he said this, he gave both my fiancé and me hugs, as he and my friend left the room. Leaving us to sit there, as we held, kissed, and cried over our lifeless baby boy.

The days that followed seemed like a blur. I had only visitors who came to offer their condolences, as I heard babies in other rooms crying, families celebrating new life, and only whispers as others walked past our door, seeing the white wreath. Respecting what it represented and feeling sadness for us, knowing that we were in that room, mourning the loss of a baby. When the time came to leave, I was wanting to get back to my daughter but had the dread of leaving that hospital, knowing there was no baby to bring home with me, to hold at night. I felt empty.

We got in the elevator, me holding flowers that did not fit on the cart we had been given to take out to our car, which was filled with flowers and cards. However, as we went to press the floor number to take us to the parking lot level, an older couple ran to get in the elevator with us. They were also coming off of the labor and delivery floor, and when they saw us, they congratulated us, assuming the flowers and cards were to celebrate a new baby. My fiancé could see me trying hard to hold back the tears and answered the couple by thanking them and holding my hand as his thumb gently rubbed my wrist. A comfort, showing me, that he was there for me, that we were in this together.

When we got home, my daughter arrived shortly after, excited to embrace me, which I needed so much. We then got a phone call. The call was my mom, informing me that my grandmother, the one who lived on the outskirts of town, a lady who I wished I had gotten to know better, had died the day after we lost our son, and we would be having a double funeral that coming Saturday, for both our son and my grandmother. As she said this, all I could think was, why had no one told me? I may have not known my grandma well, but I had spent time with her and did not expect to lose her the day after losing my son. However, my family saw that I had a lot I was dealing with and did not want to add more burden to the pain I was already feeling emotionally of losing our son.

Within a few days, we had family come in from all over. My fiancé had been up at his work, making the final funeral arrangements for our son. Having the programs printed out, getting the flowers for the coffin, and ensuring that there was nothing left for me to have to do. I stayed at the house, just taking in every moment I had with my daughter, trying to not think about the dreaded time ahead. Being grateful for her.

Then came the day, the day I will never forget. I remember getting up to get ready, standing in my closet, staring at everything in there. I stood there, thinking about what parents wear to their child's funeral. I mean, is there such an outfit? How have others done this? How have they continued with their lives? How have they gone on to bury their babies and then walk away, leaving them in a hole in the ground?

The thoughts continued, even after we left the house. And as we drove up to the cemetery, I could see a tent set up with tables, chairs, familiar faces of our families and our friends, standing and talking, as I looked over to see all the tiny graves. Where there were rattles, toys, balloons on top of headstones, and small statues of children playing in the middle of it all, realizing that this was happening. I sat there, not wanting to get out, not wanting to go to the table where I could see the tiny coffin sitting on top of it.

When we drove up to the tent, everyone turned around to see us. The pastor came to walk me to the front row and sit me in a chair, as he motioned for others to take a seat as well. My daughter held my hand the entire time until we sat down, and she seemed to be staring at the table. She let go of my hand, ran to the table where the tiny coffin was, and looked underneath it. She then ran around to the other side, as if playing a game of hide and go seek with someone who was not there, when she yelled, "I found you!".

As she did this, everyone gasped, and my daughter ran back over to me, with excitement on her face telling me that her brother was there. He was there with us. I agreed with her as I could feel the tears run down my face, she then reached over to dry a tear from my face and told me to not cry. That everything was going to be okay, because she was a big sister to an angel now, and that I was a mommy to a real-life angel. Assuring me her baby brother was going to be okay, and he told her as much.

The look in her eyes was not of sorrow, but that of joy, of innocence, where others agreed with her that her baby brother was there with us all and that he was indeed an angel. As she said this, the song we had chosen for the funeral began to play, bringing tears to everyone's, including the pastor's eyes. The song was called "Precious Child" by Karen Taylor Good, a song that even to this day, brings tears to my eyes, reminding me of that incredibly sad and emotional moment in my life.

I found that with that, I had to find a way to make this little girl's life, one that was better, one where she was not subjected to or witnessed the abuse her dad caused. I realized that even with Eduardo not being right there, he somehow still had control over me in a way. I allowed him to anger me, to upset me, and even though we had lost this time around, I had nothing but time and had to find a way to make things right for my daughter. Knowing that she as well as myself, deserved happiness, regardless of all the bad, we could move forward, and I would make sure of it.

Winning the War

A few weeks after burying both our baby boy and my grandma, my fiancé and I along with my daughter, friends, and both of our families, went to my hometown, where we got married. We knew we wanted to be together and even though we had experienced some rocky roads, we knew we wanted to continue the journey of life together.

After getting married, we went on with our lives together, as a family. My now-husband vowed to protect both myself and my daughter, and when the time came for the exchanges, he decided that he would deal with Eduardo, not allowing Eduardo to say or do anything to me. This novel approach angered Eduardo a lot, and he voiced this anger and tried to have my husband trespassed from his house, to try and force me to have to meet with him when we had the exchanges for custody of my daughter. And when Eduardo's tactics did not work, he just got more and more angry, revealing himself to many, which made the following of his moves, a bit easier for us to anticipate.

Within a few months, my husband and I found ourselves pregnant again, but in a pregnancy that was a fragile one. This is because once we hit the second trimester, I began to have issues with my heart, which concerned the doctor. He ordered partial bed rest, and my husband and I decided it was best for me to quit working, which in hand would allow me to take care of myself and the unborn baby, along with my daughter. So, when we went back to court, I would be a stay-at-home mom, and no longer a mom who had no time as was once said about me.

During this, Eduardo did continue with his shenanigans, stalking us, trying to cause fights during exchanges, and just being the awful person, he was. We learned from our neighbor and daughter that Eduardo would park in the empty lot across the street taking photos of us, where our daughter said that she and her daddy took lots of photos of mommy, pointing to the lot. And the neighbor had mentioned the truck Eduardo came in to pick up my daughter in, was the same truck that she saw on numerous occasions across the street in the same lot my daughter had mentioned. So, we chose to ignore Eduardo, regardless of what he attempted to do or say to us. Which just seemed to make him unravel little by little.

But then we found that within a few weeks of being on bed rest, we had more concerns being found when it came to our unborn baby. Where during a scan, it was found that our baby had abnormalities, leaving the heart on the right side of the chest, and what appeared to be tiny tumors taking up the space where the lungs were.

This concern made it to where I was ordered full bedrest, and where I had a whole lineup of specialists following my pregnancy. Where I was having to fly out of town for testing every few weeks, to a specialized facility, which could help the doctors monitor the baby I was carrying a little better. During this time, my husband had gotten a better job offer, that was a few towns over but still within the 100-mile radius that Eduardo had put in place on our custody orders. So, he took it, and within a few weeks, we had found a house closer to his new work and moved.

The move was one that we were glad to have made. It gave us peace of mind, knowing that Eduardo would not be coming around, stalking us as often as he had due to us being a good drive away from him. But he did try to make things hard, which was not too surprising. These minor inconveniences included instances where Eduardo would have my daughter at a sitter, insisting that wherever she was, we had to wait until it was not a second too soon to pick up my daughter. Being on the phone with the sitters, insisting they remain on the phone until it was the time on the dot. Even if we had to go somewhere, we had to wait until it was the exact time as per the orders. Which we just went along with, not protesting, and not giving Eduardo the pleasure in the tiny bit of control he had, knowing that we would be back in court and things would change. So, we went along with it, because the move was allowing us to focus on my pregnancy, enjoy our time with my daughter when we had our visitation, and continue to move forward.

This way of things was working for a while there, that was until I went into early labor. I was at the same gestation as I had been with our son that we lost, so the idea was horrifying for me. We had been at home, enjoying a movie, when the labor had started. I wanted it to be false labor pains, drank water, and put my feet up, but they were consistent, and after talking to the on-call doctor, we went to the little local hospital that was in the town we were living in. That is when things began to get real. When I arrived, the doctors had been waiting for me, so they could check me, and when they did, they noticed I was dilating, and the contractions were real.

The doctors got a hold of my doctor, who notified them to have me transported back to the town that we had moved from and to the hospital there. My husband offered to drive me since the doctors were going to have to call an ambulance to come and get me, which could take time. They agreed to let my husband take me, and with that, we drove to the hospital, the same one we had delivered our stillborn son at, less than a year prior.

When we arrived, I was rushed to the L&D floor, where my doctor was waiting for me. They right away began to start IVs, put monitors on me, and gave me some shots to try to stop the labor. The shots made me sick to my stomach, and want to get up and run, where I felt my heart racing, but at the same time, were working by slowing down the contractions.

After 48 hours of being on monitors and being given a shot of steroids for the baby to assist in developing the lungs, and another that made me feel sick every 12 hours, the doctor noted that I was still having regular contractions, but they were no longer strong enough to make me dilate. He then told my husband and me, that due to the stage in pregnancy, he did not feel safe in letting me go back home to the town that was about a 45 minute or greater drive from the hospital and wanted to either keep me on bed rest at the hospital or have me stay at the local Ronald McDonald House until it was safe to deliver.

He said that at the longest duration, I would be there for at most 4 months, to ride out the last 16 weeks of my pregnancy. Explaining that if I did go back home, if I happened to go back into labor, the hospital there where we lived was not equipped to handle the delicate nature of not just a premature delivery, but also of my unborn son's diagnosis. He went on to explain that even at the hospital we were at, they did have a team who would be prepared to care for my baby at any stage, but that they would also be able to have him transported to a specialty hospital right away if needed, compared to the delay that could take place if I delivered elsewhere.

After considering everything, my husband and I agreed it was best for me to stay in the town, and the doctor made arrangements for me to stay at the Ronald McDonald House for the duration of my pregnancy. We then knew that my husband would have to go back home and drive back and forth on his time off to be with me. Once we arrived at the Ronald McDonald House, we were informed that since I was in a fragile state, I needed to have someone stay with me during the time I was there.

With that, my husband left to pack my bags for me, and I made phone calls, making the arrangements needed with various friends who agreed to take turns staying with me when my husband had to work. The doctor also noted, that due to the ongoing contractions, which he described as me having an irritable uterus, along with the ongoing heart issues that he was monitoring, I was not allowed to drive until after I delivered, and he was able to clear me.

After everything we were told and were trying to figure out, I did try to reach out to Eduardo to discuss making the exchanges all at the Ronald McDonald House, since I was being confined to the bed there, only to leave to see my doctor. But I found it to be no surprise that Eduardo would have no sympathy or try to work with us on the pickups and drop-offs of my daughter. So, we found friends in the area who were more than willing to help us with what needed to be done. All who knew of the heartache we felt when we lost our other son less than a year prior, and who was there to help us make sure we had a successful pregnancy and delivered a baby who might have been diagnosed in-utero, but one that we were all determined to give a fighting chance at thriving for.

As the time went by, I noticed the ongoing contractions, which were at times ones that caused a bit of pain, but for the most part, just made my uterus tighten up. I saw my doctor weekly, where I had regular headaches that started up, which he explained had to do with the heart issues I was having. I also saw my daughter regularly while there, where we continued the scheduled visitations without a hitch, thanks to all our friends who offered their help.

At around 34 weeks, the contractions started to get strong again, where I was once again given the shot that had stopped them before. But this time, instead of just a couple of shots, I was ordered to be at the hospital once a day, due to the contractions starting right back up after each 24-hour time period in between getting the shots. With the time on delivery getting closer, my friends decided to host a baby shower at the Ronald McDonald House, knowing I could be having the baby soon. Then came the day, the day the doctor said that even though we still had another 4 weeks to go, due to my health, we would need to deliver.

My husband and I were both excited and scared. We were excited to finally hold our son, but scared for what his outcome would be, due to all the information we were given on his condition, and because he would be coming a month early. We were taken to have the baby measured the day before the delivery day when we were told that since our baby was going to be premature, he was going to be exceedingly small. With that, my husband along with many of our friends, headed out to pick up preemie clothes and diapers, since all we had were items for a newborn. We called my mom, who right away drove the 8 hours to be there with us, and we were informed that the doctor decided to hold off on the daily shot I was getting. He said that in the morning the next day, I was to be admitted so they could begin an induction but would also see if I would go into labor naturally due to the shots being stopped.

By the next morning, my mom had arrived and went to stay at the Ronald McDonald House with us, knowing we might have to stay there even longer after the delivery, depending on how our son did after birth. Whether or not he would be airlifted to a facility that could offer the care he might be needing.

Once my mom had dropped her things off, we all went up to the hospital. As we did this, I noticed the contractions had started back up again. The doctor was there, along with the neonatal team and a group of specialists who had followed me during my pregnancy, checking on the baby regularly to prepare for when he arrived. The nurses right away began to set up the monitors, which showed the contractions were coming back. The doctor talked to us, checked me then said that I was already dilated to a 5, the point in dilation where I could get the epidural if I chose to, which I did not hesitate in saying I wanted.

He then went to leave the room, saying he would be back later in the day to check on me. As the doctor left, the nurse came in to assist with the epidural. When they sat me up to prep me, my water broke, the contractions got extraordinarily strong, and I yelled that I could feel the baby coming. The nurse was confused, knowing the doctor had just checked me, and I was only at a 5, thinking it was not possible I dilated that fast, but as she had me lay back down to check me, she had realized that I was right, I was fully dilated and ready to deliver. They had to call off the epidural team due to what was happening.

The nurse ran to pull the emergency lever and helped my husband get gowned up, and then my husband went to get into place, seeing that I was getting ready to deliver our son and the doctor had just left the room. Luckily, the doctor had not gotten far and was at the nurse's station when he saw the emergency light go off where the nurse told the other staff on the speaker, I was ready to deliver.

With that, the doctor along with the neonatal team and another team of specialists all came running to my room. As they did this, the doctor saw my husband in a position to assist with the delivery, and instead of having my husband move, the doctor stood behind my husband as he instructed him what to do. From the delivery of the head to catching our son as he came out screaming, my husband delivered our son from start to finish, leaving all the specialists in the room speechless as to what they just witnessed. And to everyone's surprise, aside from the fact that our son screamed a healthy scream that was not at all what was expected, he was a lot bigger than anticipated, coming out at 6 lbs. 13 oz, which was not the preemie everyone had prepared for.

Later in the day, we found that my son was not as sick as the doctors had thought he was, even being a premature baby, where he was cleared to go home before I was after having a series of testing done on him. Leaving my husband and me with a feeling of joy, knowing all the uncertainties we had known prior to having him, were mostly gone, and allowing us to relax and enjoy having a newborn in the home. It was explained our son would be different in many ways due to the issues with the lungs, but they would monitor him closely for the next year or so, then set him up for a series of surgeries to remove the tumors but explaining that it all depended on if the tumors grew.

With that, we began our journey into raising 2 kids and having our family together for the most part. As time went on, we did deal with a lot of issues the so-called tumors caused, which made it to where we could not expose our son to others when someone was sick. Where we spent many days and nights in the children's hospital. Along with the doctors and the many tests they did over the next year and a half, we learned that the tumors were extra lobes of bad lung tissue which harbored bacteria, and when he got sick, he did not get a normal cold or type of sick, but sick to where he would end up in the hospital. Having the extra lobes just being cesspools of bacteria that did not allow infections to go away easily.

During this time, we had felt the repercussions of the recession, where my husband's posh job working in the oil fields as a truck driver, was lost. Where the town we had moved to, was all but shut down due to many in the town also having thrived off the oil field jobs that the area offered. Due to this, we ended up cutting our losses, and moving back to the town Eduardo lived in, near the hospital, which worked out for our son's health and made seeing the specialists easier to get to as well. But with that, we also noticed Eduardo began the stalking again. Taking the photos of our home, friends who came to visit. And even when we had our son in the hospital, at times being in the Pediatric ICU due to episodes of pneumonia which was harbored in the bad lung tissue and would flare up if someone had a cold, Eduardo did not offer us any sort of slack when it came to the exchanges, always determined we stuck to the orders to-a-t, no more no less.

Then came another summer break where I got my daughter for an entire month, one that went by faster than we wanted but one we enjoyed all the same, where we celebrated our son's 2nd birthday. And unexpectedly, we all found ourselves in a state of shock, I mean, we could not believe it when Eduardo called and notified me that he was giving us extra time. In fact, he had not given us a date when we would have to bring my daughter back to him, which was more than okay with us. Allowing us to focus on my son, during his many hospital stays for the surgeries he had to remove the bad tissues, where we had his "sissy" as he called her, at his side.

When the fall semester for the local schools was getting closer, we realized Eduardo had not called to make any arrangements, and my daughter needed to go to school. So instead of calling him, due to the fact he had not contacted us for anything during this time, we enrolled my daughter at the school that was near our house. Allowing me to not only prepare my daughter for her first day of school but also be the one to take her, pick her up and enjoy her as she lit up every day, telling me everything she learned. She would also share what she learned with her baby brother, and during all of this, Eduardo never once called for anything, it was crickets on his end.

Time continued to go by, without hearing or seeing Eduardo. We did hear from Eduardo's family during this time, where his mother, sister, and her family, along with some of his cousins, came by to visit my daughter but did not talk about what was going on with Eduardo. Which was fine with us. We knew the family cared for my daughter, and that she loved them as well, so we allowed them to visit and check in on her anytime they wanted.

Then as we got into the month of October, we realized it had been a little over 5 months since Eduardo had last seen my daughter, and at this time, my daughter got the Swine Flu. The time was a scary one for us. The hospitals were overcrowded due to the epidemic, which we were able to work around since we had friends who were nurses. We had to not only have round-the-clock care for my daughter, but at the same time, with the extra help, we were able to keep our son clear and disinfect everything constantly. Due to the doctor's warning us that if he got the flu, it could be deadly for him.

Our friends were amazing and offered their time to assist us where there were always two of us taking care of the kids all day and night, during the hardest time of the flu when the fever would not break. Taking turns with us, staying up with my daughter, putting her in baths, giving her breathing treatments, and monitoring her until we got past the danger zone which had lasted for about 5 days. From there, we still had a lot to deal with, as we helped my daughter gain her strength back. We had Eduardo's family come to assist as well, where even the wife came with lots of jello and frozen pops.

That is when we learned why Eduardo was not coming around or even calling, even after being informed his daughter had the swine flu. It was because the wife had left Eduardo at the time I went to get my summer visitation, and since then, he had focused on obsessing over her. Not even trying to check in on his daughter who lived within a 5-minute drive from his house.

The wife explained she had left Eduardo to be with another man, and that Eduardo drove her away after she got sick and tired of his obsession with me, along with some other disturbing things she did not get into at the time. Explaining for one, Eduardo had photos of me on as well as inside the bedside table, in the bedroom they shared. Another issue was the way Eduardo treated me, where he gloated about having custody of my daughter, trying to tell others I was an unfit mother, found by the courts, showing his paperwork like it was a trophy. Gloating and celebrating each time when he would get the child support from me, Eduardo would have parties on my behalf. Letting everyone know the parties every couple of weeks, were made possible by me, making it a joke, and not spending any of the money I paid him on my daughter.

She explained Eduardo would have my daughter wear hand-me-downs from not only her kids, but from clothing that he would get at the local church, where they had free, previously worn clothes for kids. Where when I sent new clothes that I would buy her, Eduardo would take them back to the stores and get himself something instead. And

Eduardo treated her kids horribly, causing issues with them both mentally and emotionally, and she had enough of it all. She then said when we wanted to go back to court, we had her support, because Eduardo was not fit to take care of his or anyone else's child.

We had a cousin of Eduardo's, who my daughter had considered being an uncle and would call him that, who came by often to visit my daughter. He had a child about the same age, and when he had learned that Eduardo was not coming around, had not been there when my daughter had swine flu, or even called to check on her, he was pretty upset.

The cousin could not believe any person could be so neglectful when it came to their child, and after everything Eduardo had put us through, it made him even madder, now knowing that it was like I had said to everyone. It was all a game for Eduardo. And since he did not have a wife or anyone else there to take care of his own kid, he would not even try to see her. The cousin asked if he brought Eduardo by and if we would allow him to see her. I said we would, and with that, the cousin left our house, and we learned that he forced Eduardo to leave his house and go with him to see his daughter.

The visit was a short one, but before leaving, Eduardo promised my daughter he would see her again, setting up a date with her later that week. When the day came of this date Eduardo had set up, my daughter sat staring out the window, waiting for Eduardo to show up. But he did not, and later that day Eduardo called to say he ended up having to work but would see her that weekend. Which, again, when the weekend came and went, my daughter was the one who was let down, as she waited all weekend by the window, for her dad to take her out and spend time with her.

This seemed to go on for weeks, where Eduardo would make promises to see my daughter, only to let her down over and over again. Where when Eduardo called, I did not tell my daughter he was saying he would be there, so I could protect her from the heartache she felt in being let down by her dad.

Then came the holidays, which we were extremely excited about, but waited to see if Eduardo was going to insist on seeing my daughter during his court-ordered time. When he did not call, we decided to go ahead with our court-ordered time and spent the holidays back in my hometown with my family.

My family and friends were excited to see us, knowing we had a hard fall due to my daughter getting swine flu. But we enjoyed the time, celebrating the holidays with family and friends whom we loved.

When we got back, to everyone's surprise, Eduardo showed up to take my daughter for his holiday time with her. We were all confused, but since we still had court orders in place, we had to allow Eduardo to take her. During the time he had her, he called to inform us that Eduardo would be going to take her back, going back to following the court orders, and come after the break, she would be switching schools. Apparently, Eduardo and his wife were back together and happier than ever according to him, so things were going to go back to the way they were. Or at least that is what he thought.

After we had the surprise of Eduardo showing up to get my daughter as per the court orders, after months of him not calling or coming around, we knew we had to get back in the courtroom and do so quickly. We had the majority of our finances going towards house bills, medical bills, and the child support I had to continue to pay Eduardo, even though he was not seeing my daughter. So instead of going to hire my lawyer, which many in my family offered to assist with, we chose to take another approach. We began talking to our family who had knowledge of the law, knowing that we had Eduardo on abandonment since he had not attempted to take her back or even contact her for over 6 months, we decided to take on the courts on our own.

During the holiday break, I spent several days at the courthouse, in the library, making copies of the paperwork we would need to go in front of the judge. Reading the laws and filing the papers as I found them and learned the order in which I needed to file them. By the time the break was over, I had filed for a modification of orders and had a court date set. The thing was, the court date was a few weeks away, which worried us since Eduardo said he had planned on moving my daughter to the school near him, taking her out of the school she had been to the entire semester prior which was near my house.

I found I was able to talk to the wife, who still stood by me, and had convinced Eduardo they should not move my daughter until after the school year was over because it was going to be too hard to do at the time. Eduardo agreed since, at the time, he would do and say anything the wife wanted, including allowing the wife to keep a photo of the man she had left "him" for in a collage of photos they had displayed in their living room.

This novel approach, and even friendship with the wife, was exactly what we needed, so when we had our day in court, we knew we would win. And until then, we got statements from neighbors, friends, school staff, and even the wife, on the abandonment, along with the fact Eduardo was incapable of caring for his daughter. A sentiment that he had voiced the concern to the wife and cousin, who both agreed to provide us with statements of such when we went to court. All, without Eduardo having knowledge of why and what we were going to court for, other than what he had been served with, thinking that we wanted to modify the child support. He was led to believe this by many, including his wife, where the papers stated "Modification of Orders" but told him, it was just for child support since the initial child support order was for quite a bit since I was working when the orders were put into place, and I had not worked in about 2 years, leaving my husband paying the child support.

Everyone involved knew that this blindsided approach was the only way we would win. Knowing in order to play Eduardo's game against him, we had to play it his way, and do so without giving him any knowledge of what was really going on. As the days kept on getting closer and closer to our court date, we noticed changes in others as well. Where we had some from Eduardo's family call or come up to us in public to apologize to me for taking his side. When everyone finally saw the truth behind all the deception Eduardo had displayed, they had all believed for years, and they felt guilt. Learning Eduardo was found to be the one with mental issues by CPS, and I had in fact, been cleared of any mental issues. Seeing for themselves, when it came to my daughter, my husband and I were the only ones in the fight, who truly had her best interest at heart. That everything Eduardo had done to her and everyone else involved, was all to get at me, all a sick and twisted game he was going to lose very soon.

Then came the day we had been waiting for, the day to go back to court. I woke up with a variety of emotions coming over me. From the feeling of being scared that somehow, the judge would go in his favor, knowing this was the one and only chance I would be given to change the orders. I also did feel a bit of guilt, knowing that in order to have a chance, we had to deceive Eduardo, but also knowing he did that and worse to me, all for his own pleasure of hurting both myself and my daughter in the process. Which followed with the feeling of excitement, after I read repeatedly, the proposal I had created to give to the judge and made the copies, to hand to Eduardo when we arrived. Showing Eduardo what we were really going to be there for. Looking over the statements and reports from CPS, which they gave me to use in the courtroom if needed. And looking at all the statements, from neighbors, friends, his family, and friends, along with the school and even our pediatrician. All of which I was assured and knew, would all help me in making my case to have the orders changed. As we left for court, we had to drop my daughter off at school, hoping to have good news to share with her when we picked her up later that day.

When we got to the court, my husband stood in the hallway with our son in his stroller, as Eduardo and I went in front of the judge. Once we got to the judge's podium, the judge asked me for the paperwork, wanting to ensure I had done everything correctly for the modification. As I handed the judge the original copy, I also handed Eduardo a copy of the new orders I proposed, which I had extra copies of as well. That is when it happened, Eduardo threw a tantrum right there in front of the judge. Jumping up and down, screaming like a toddler who was not getting his way, making a scene, where the judge had a look of disbelief on his face to what we were all witnessing. Eduardo screamed that he never agreed to this, exclaiming he would not agree to any of it, demanding that the judge does not listen to me or what I had to say. After a few seconds of this, Eduardo was asked by the judge if he was done with his tantrum, and at this time, I handed the judge all of the signed statements of abandonment and his confession to the wife and cousin of being incapable of caring for my daughter on his own, along with the report that the CPS workers had put together for the judge.

With everything that was presented and the tantrum that took place in the courtroom, the judge looked at me, and without batting an eye, apologized for anything I had to deal with due to Eduardo's childish behavior. Then said he was granting me everything I asked for, without even reading over each page of my request. Which overturned the original orders, giving me full custody of my daughter, giving Eduardo, the same visitation I had been given originally, making him pay child support, and also lifting the orders that kept me within the 100-mile radius, allowing my husband and I to move anywhere we wanted to at any time, as long as we notified the courts within 30 days prior to leaving.

This judgment infuriated Eduardo, but as the judge passed the judgment, he had asked the bailiff to bring my husband in as he let us know his decision. Which made the scene even more so one that angered Eduardo, where my husband held my hand as the judge signed off on the paperwork we presented, then instructed we file right away at the clerk's office. Before finishing, the judge not only ordered child support and gave me everything I asked for but ordered Eduardo to be responsible for all court fees which the various filing fees to the fee of seeing the judge. Instructing me that when I make copies after having the clerk's office stamp everything, I have copies made to hand to Eduardo and make sure that he pays for all the copies and pays me back for the child support I had paid him during the 6 months Eduardo had abandoned my daughter as well.

My husband and I left that room feeling like the weight of the world had finally been lifted from our shoulders. Where Eduardo snickered at us while we waited for the clerk to stamp everything and make Eduardo pay the filing fees along with the copies, we had made which included one I had to take up to the judge's office. As we got done, we left Eduardo to pay all the fees, and went back up to the judge's office, to hand over the paperwork to the secretary.

When we did this, the secretary stopped us and explained that apparently, our victory was getting around the courthouse quickly. She said many were in shock because I was the first person in the history of that judge's time on the bench, which had been for many decades, to go in front of the judge, represent myself, and win. We then had others from the office come out to congratulate us, as the judge walked in, giving us a nod of approval for what we had just accomplished.

The others in the judge's office said when we had filed to go in front of the judge, that the judge had been told I was the one who spent hours in the courthouse library, ensuring I knew the laws, got the correct paperwork, and filed everything on my own. Which the judge found to be very impressive. That having a citizen who was not a representative of the courts, do as much research as I had done in their library, was unheard of, no one else had ever attempted or knew where to look. Giving me kudos for a job well done, and as I was getting these praises, my lawyer walked in, gave me a huge hug, and told me how proud she was. That when she learned what I had done, she wanted to make sure she saw me before leaving the courthouse to let me know that she was proud of what I had accomplished. She went on and said that Eduardo's old lawyer heard as well, and he was shocked to hear but at the same time offered kudos for a job well done.

As we left the courthouse, I had so much relief in knowing that it was done and over with, and now feeling of being both proud of myself and what I had just accomplished. When we got home, I called my family who was waiting for the call, and with every person who we talked to, we explained what happened, the praises and all. Everyone congratulated us on a job well done, and for the fact that now we can all breathe a bit easier knowing my daughter will be kept safer, being in our care for most of the time.

Later that day when we went to pick up my daughter, she was surprised to see us picking her up, and right away asked us if we saw the judge. We told her that we had and explained that she would be living with us from now on, only seeing her dad during visitation times.

This news made my daughter cry from relief and excitement, and she told me she was so happy. She had her own room at our house, while at her dad's she had to sleep on the couch and did not have her own space. Where she was not treated as well as she was at our house, and where she could be there with her brother. She was excited in knowing she would be staying at her school, where she made many friends, and knowing that she was able to stay with her mommy. Which was a sentiment she had exclaimed from the day Eduardo took us to court the first time.

As the time went on, we found shortly after our son's 3rd birthday, that the specialists who had followed him since my pregnancy, were ready to set him up for his series of final surgeries. Decided to do all of these, before the coming fall and winter, giving him a better chance for recovery. It was at this time when we had to be going in for numerous tests before setting up for surgery, that Eduardo was completing his summer month of visitation with my daughter.

Making the coming and going to the hospital and many doctor's offices, easier since we did not have to meet with Eduardo at any time during this. It was nice to have my daughter there during the surgeries, and his recovery process, and have my daughter be there with us as it should be. Which we all noticed made our son's affect a brighter one knowing that his "sissy" was there the entire time. My daughter also enjoyed this time and liked being able to help and keep her baby brother happy, even when he did not feel so well after the final surgery.

We also found as time went on, Eduardo would still try to do things to try and control situations. Where I was more civil with him when he asked to have extra time. Where one such occasion happened during my daughter's birthday, when he, his wife, and her kids were taking a cousin to Camp Pendleton and wanted my daughter to be there to say goodbye. In exchange, Eduardo was giving me his spring break that year, which would allow us to take a vacation with my daughter. I was sad to have to miss her birthday but agreed to the change in dates, leaving others warning me that he was not going to honor his part. Which, when it came to that spring break, they were all right.

Eduardo was to have my daughter the Thursday prior to the break, but instead, he left town with my daughter. Keeping her the entire week of the break, not answering his phone, and showing me as well as others, that Eduardo is not one you can try to be civil with. I was furious, and when Eduardo got back, he pulled out his orders which showed he was getting that spring break, claiming he had forgotten about our deal. Going on to claim that since they had gone on a road trip, he had bad cell phone service, but he had not done anything against the orders. I was sickened by this, he took advantage of my kindness, took my daughter for her birthday when I should have not allowed it, then went back on the deal we had made, claiming "he" forgot all about it, even though that trip to San Diego had only taken place a month prior.

These types of shenanigans continued for years, where Eduardo would put me on speaker for others to hear, claiming I would not give him any sort of slack. Setting up parties right before he had to bring my daughter back to me, then calling minutes before she was supposed to be home, asking for extra time. Put my daughter on the phone, making her cry, saying that I was mean, and she would be missing out on huge and fun parties. Or claiming a family member was visiting, and my daughter had not seen this person in a long time, asking for extra time, which he had a huge family, so this happened often.

Along with all of this, Eduardo had begun going to church regularly, portraying himself as a saint. The perfect husband, father, and family man to those who did not know him well. Guilting me into allowing my daughter to attend certain church events, saying if I did not, I was denying her and hurting her. The guilt went as far as where I agreed to change the Thursday visits to Wednesday when they had a night of fun at the church for the kids. But where he continued to use me and my civil manners towards him, bringing my daughter home later and later each time. To where others pointed out how Eduardo would make me wait until it was time to pick her up on the dot and freak out on me if I was a minute late in dropping her off when the tables were turned, and he had custody.

Eduardo continued to stalk us over the years, taking photos, and trying everything he could to make us look like the bad ones. I knew this was because, in order for Eduardo to ever get the orders changed, he had to prove I was somehow an unfit mother, which he could not since there was nothing to prove. He tried to get me to change the orders with threats, which I just ignored, to where Eduardo even furnished new orders at the courthouse, asking me to sign them, when he tried to have the child support changed, saying he could not afford to pay it. Regardless of my refusing to sign, he continued to be hard to deal with, no matter how nice we were to him, it was as if he was constantly thinking of ways to get to me.

That was until my husband and I had had enough. We had another son, where the pregnancy was hard on me, leaving me on strict orders of bed rest in the dark, but where we delivered a healthy baby boy. We were so tired of everything Eduardo did, that if a week had gone by where we did not hear from him or see him doing something, we worried, knowing that he was planning something big. He had cops come to our house out of the blue, for welfare checks on my daughter when I did not answer the phone to him, or when I refused to give him extra time.

Then, the wife's ex-husband died from an accidental gas leak in his house. Which everyone thought to be odd, since for one, the day this happened, Eduardo, who claimed to be all high and mighty in the church, said he was unwell that morning and did not attend services. And for two, we knew Eduardo had tried to prove the ex-husband unfit and tried to adopt his wife's kids but was unable to. And on that morning when we all learned of this accidental death, my husband and I had a feeling that Eduardo had something to do with it.

This unsettling feeling became more of a rational feeling when we all learned when the news was given to the wife and her kids after church, Eduardo showed no emotion and seemed to be somewhat happy. It is something that was never investigated nor questioned by others at the time, but a feeling that I still feel strongly about in thinking Eduardo had something to do with the death of this man. This feeling became more of one we questioned because, within a few weeks of losing their father, Eduardo had the nerve to go on Facebook and write a statement about how he now had to step up and be a dad to this now dead man's kids, as if it was a burden on him. Going on to demand that it was time the kids moved on and got over their grief, saying that he was sick and tired of everyone crying over this man who had only died weeks prior. Leaving us with the uneasy feeling of possibly thinking Eduardo had played a role in killing a man.

After this unfortunate event, and the several years of dealing with everything Eduardo threw our way, my husband and I decided we wanted to move, not just to another town, but to another state, far away from Eduardo. By this time, my daughter was fixing to be a preteen, was showing signs of developing into a young lady, and had been told by her dad that she was going to be signing papers soon since she would be old enough, to go in his custody. She told us every time she left Eduardo's house that he would be making her sign and it scared her. Reminding her of the countdown he had going for her to turn of legal age where she could decide which parent to live with and trying to force her to go in front of the judge. So, when we began discussing the move, we asked my daughter if she would be okay with such a thing, to which she exclaimed it was exactly what she wanted, that she would feel safer being far away from her dad as well.

During the time that we had begun looking at where we wanted to move to, the wife had graduated from college and left Eduardo one final time to marry another man. Which, when this happened, Eduardo became homeless, couch surfing and using his friends and family. He also missed some of his visits, claiming car troubles as an excuse. He quit working, which did not surprise us since we knew he could not care for his daughter as he had told others years back, but also showed he could not care for himself either.

As the months went on, my husband and I saved, and we found a place we wanted to move to, which was across the country, knowing we would need to find work and have money put away for the move. During this time, when Eduardo did get my daughter for visits, she came back feeling uncomfortable. Explaining that when he would have her, a young lady, she was forced to share a small bed or couch with him. That it was uncomfortable because they not only shared a bed to which she explained he would hold her a little too close for comfort, but each time she went with Eduardo, she did not know where they would be staying. With that, we got my daughter a cell phone, so she could call us or the authorities if she ever felt in danger.

These issues my daughter voiced, made the urgency for us to want to move, one we worked hard at making happen. When we found a house in the place we were going to move to, we secured the house right away, we notified the courts as per the orders we had, 2 months before we were leaving, which was a lot more time than what the orders stated, but we wanted him to be aware of our move. We started packing, had gotten our moving truck reserved, and paid off the car we had that only had a few more payments left on it, but wanted to have taken care of before leaving. Then a few days before our move, we received a certified letter from Eduardo in the mail. The papers inside were forged papers of the orders we had, the same ones he had tried to get me to sign numerous times after I had gotten custody of my daughter. The papers had my signature forged on them, where Eduardo claimed that they were legal regardless of if I had signed them, but after talking to the courts, we found that they were not legal. That we had not gone in front of a judge together to have a judge sign off on these papers, and there was nothing Eduardo could do us with these fake documents.

When Eduardo realized we were not falling for his fake document scheme, he then began calling the police. He called them numerous times as we packed, where we had police at our door every few hours. Making claims that my daughter was in harm's way, demanding welfare checks, and claiming we were criminals, to whereby the 7th or 8th visit, the officers who showed up, asked if I could leave early. Drive on ahead of my husband, take all my court papers with me, and not post anything on social media, or tell anyone other than family, of our journey. We knew we could do this, but it would be hard when it came to packing the truck. But the next morning as we picked up the moving truck, I packed my car up, and left a day early with the kids, ahead of my husband.

We found this was the best way to go about things, because apparently after we left, Eduardo had continued to call the authorities who instead of going to our house, called me to make sure we were safe on our journey and were notifying us of the constant calls from him. Then, as my husband along with some of our friends loaded up the moving truck, Eduardo along with other people, parked down the street from our house, yelling for my daughter. Taking photos of the moving process, and even came up to our house demanding to see my daughter.

Leading to one of our friend's wives, deciding while the men packed the truck, she would keep Eduardo and the people he was with, away from the house.

This friend was a biker, and his wife was his ole lady. A small but very mighty lady, who did not take crap from anyone. She kept the other women from getting past her, the women who were with Eduardo, who would walk towards our house, yelling for my daughter and taking photos. She even bucked up to Eduardo who tried to get close to the house, warning him that he did not want to proceed and to turn around. As the day went on and the final items were being placed in the truck, our friends and neighbors all wished my husband a safe journey, insisting if anything happened, to give them a call.

The move was a scary one, where I was warned by the authorities that if Eduardo were to find out where we were at as we traveled through various states to get across the country, he could try to have me arrested. Where authorities in other areas who were not aware of the current situation, could take my kids until they could prove my papers were accurate by having to contact the courts. Which could take time and cause a lot more heartache and trouble for everyone. Leading the miles, as we got closer to our destination, we would feel relief as we left those miles behind us and put more miles between us and Eduardo.

When we arrived in the new place, we felt so much relief in knowing we were safe and extremely far away from Eduardo. We moved into our new house right away and began to settle in when a detective from the town Eduardo lived in called me. This detective asked me many questions, to which I had thought he had been calling due to Eduardo making false claims and using those forged documents against me. But the detective did not say that I was wrong on why he was calling me either. I had sent copies of the false documents Eduardo had forged to this detective and after not hearing from the detective, I thought it was all over. That was until my daughter began having panic attacks, and we were shocked when she finally told us why. She said that her dad called regularly, which we did not object to, but said that he was going to be getting her back and had even threatened to have her kidnapped from school.

We began to monitor the calls after this, warned the school, and contacted the authorities about the threats, to which they said that they did not think he would act due to the distance we were from him. Assuring us that we were safe.

The holidays came and went, and a couple of months later, my daughter had a birthday. That year, Eduardo was still without a job and did not have money for a gift that Christmas, which I ended up buying on his behalf. So, when her birthday came up, I was surprised to get a call from Eduardo, asking for my address claiming he was going to send flowers to my daughter. I gave it to him, not thinking much about it at the time. A couple of weeks after my daughter's birthday, I had a business event that took me to another state for a few days. On my way back, I had a layover at an airport in Dallas, and it seemed our flight was being held up for some reason, but I paid the delay no attention at the time. That was until after I finally got back home, and I had been relaxing after the exhausting trip.

My husband's younger brother came to visit and help out while I was on the trip. I was exhausted, and that weekend, my husband, along with his brother had taken the kids for a hike in the mountains, leaving me home alone where I spent the day cleaning and just enjoying the alone time. As I sat back to listen to some music, a loud knock came on my door, when I went to answer it, I was surprised to see the police there.

The officers asked my name, which I answered, then asked me about my daughter, and how long we had lived in the house, all with a confused look on their faces as they looked at me and came in to see our home. A home that was lived in, with family and school photos on the walls, drawings on the fridge, kids' rooms which had been slept and played in, where toys and outdoor equipment were in the yards, and homework was left on the table. A house that was a very nicely kept house, inviting, and where one of the officers mentioned it was larger than they had expected.

They asked if we had weapons in the home, which I said we did but pointed to the safes we had where they could see that they were all secured. The officers then went on to explain that they were there to arrest me, which made me sick to my stomach. They explained saying they were there for a federal warrant, and I was to be expedited. I thought it was due to the false paperwork Eduardo had tried to use to stop me from moving with and asked if I could go to my little office to get a file for them. They followed me to the room I used as an office, where I grabbed my orders to show these officers, I had custody of my daughter. They looked at the orders and did not seem to care or see why I would bring out such papers to show them. They then allowed me to grab my ID and phone to call my husband and let him know that I was being taken to jail.

When I arrived at the jail, I looked at the warrant and noticed that the name was my maiden name and that the birthday was not my birthdate. I pointed this out to the jailers, who did not seem to care about that at the time. Instead, forced me to stay in jail until the following Monday when I could see a judge.

That weekend I was sick the entire time, throwing up, shaking from the anxiety of not knowing what was going on, where I was told I was going to be expedited, thinking Eduardo had convinced the courts that his paperwork was real. While I was in jail, Eduardo had called the local authorities numerous times, trying to have my daughter removed from our home and put in state custody, making claims she was in danger, only for the authorities to find a family who was scared and confused to what all was going on. Where my daughter talked to the authorities, showing no signs of being in danger, or being scared, but voicing the fear she had of her dad and what he was capable of.

Eduardo went on social media asking for prayers to get his daughter back from us, praying she will be taken into state custody soon, away from us who he claimed were horrible people. Come Monday morning, I went in front of the judge. I had a court-appointed lawyer who did not say anything to help me, and when I realized this, I spoke up. The judge asked me about what I did for work, and I explained that I was a mom blogger and a freelance social media manager who worked from home. The prosecution demanded a $250,000 bail on me, and when I looked at the papers, I saw that the judge who issued the warrant suggested a $5,000 bail that I pointed out, which the judge granted me.

When my husband bailed me out, we right away called my old lawyer and told her everything. Within the hour, she called and asked me to have a seat. She explained that Eduardo had sworn a statement saying my husband and I were dangerous criminals and drug dealers, saying my husband was not my husband but my boyfriend, and that I was also a prostitute. Where we were supposedly constantly moving, were on several drugs, had weapons we kept on our persons all the time, and where our kids were all in danger. That we avoided the authorities regularly by moving around all over the country all the time.

She said there was so much Eduardo had made claims on without any evidence, and the warrant against me was being thrown out, that they should have never allowed it to go as far as it had gone. We noticed as she read over the warrant and we followed along, that it had been stamped and signed on Christmas Eve, which we all found to be odd. Something we can't prove, but where we believe he somehow got into an office of authority or had a family member who had access and stamped that warrant himself, somehow getting it on the pile to be signed off on by the judge. Which would make sense on why the judge suggested a $5,000 bond on a federal warrant that was to have me extradited.

My lawyer pointed out that Eduardo not only made false statements, but he did try to file false paperwork on our custody file, which was found, and that the name and birthdate for me were wrong, not matching up to our custody orders. Which is what alerted the courts to the documents being false ones. And as I looked at the birthdate, I realized it happened to be that first date I had with him. When we celebrated my 21st birthday, 2 weeks after the actual day.

We were floored, but at the same time felt vindicated in knowing that nothing was going to happen to me and knowing what Eduardo had been up to. I then began to keep an eye on him, following Eduardo's social media where he posted numerous times a day. Asking for support, and prayers that he will get my daughter.

Then the day came that we were supposed to go to court, Eduardo had been informed of the fact we knew what he had done, and the case was thrown out. He followed this news by attempting to commit suicide, which Eduardo voiced all over his Facebook page, asking for forgiveness. I took screenshots of everything he had posted, where he picked up a prostitute, and felt guilty about that as well. Eduardo called a couple of weeks after all of the drama and tried to talk to my daughter, who then asked him questions that he refused to answer. And following that, it was crickets from him. We only heard from Eduardo on occasion. He forgot his daughter's birthdays, and the holidays, and would only call when Eduardo's family would find out that he did not call and make him call my daughter. Other than that, he contacted my daughter on his own accord, on 2 separate occasions, not by phone either, but by sending 2 text messages. On one occasion, it happened to be when one of his former stepdaughters, got married, and the second occasion was when she announced she and her husband were having a baby. The texts were uncalled for, and he tried to make my daughter feel guilty for not choosing to live with him.

The Closing Act

After the mess we had dealt with and tried hard to put behind us, we had been asked by many why we did not go after him for having falsely put me in jail, and nearly extradited. The thing was, where Eduardo lived, I was informed that I could take him to court and sue him in a civil court, which can take a lot of time. But after thinking it over, I realized it would be a waste of time. I mean, what would I be able to get from suing him? He has nothing, at the time it all happened, he was homeless, since that time, he had moved into his brother's garage. Where he wrecked his brother's truck and last I heard, had yet to pay for the damages. Leaving me to just allow karma to deal with Eduardo, as I watch it happen from afar, by simply watching what he has posted on social media.

When I finally was able to come to terms with the rapes and torture I had endured when I was with him, I found I was too late according to the state's statute of limitations on spousal rape. The time limit was 10 years, and after years of living in fear of the next thing, he would do, going over in my head if I did go to the authorities, the fact that he always seemed to turn things around on me no matter what it was he did, when I had decided that it was time Eduardo pay for everything he has done to me, it was too late. Too late for a lot of things he got away with, where anytime stalking or harassment on his part came up, I was always told it was a civil matter and the police were not going to do anything. Texas is one of those "gold ole boy" states, where women are expected to sit down, be quiet, and not speak out against any man. Where time and time again, when the police were called on him when I had evidence of the beatings on my body, where he would be parked outside my home, following me or others, Eduardo's word was always believed over mine. All because I had sought out help when I had my daughter, was depressed, and because I, a woman, had been on psychiatric medications at one time in my life. Because, if you fight back against your abuser, both would end up in jail if the abuser also chose to press charges. And I did fight back during the beatings. Leaving it to where my word meant nothing, where my voice was silenced not only by Eduardo but by the authorities who I thought were there to help and protect myself and my daughter. But in the big picture of it all, played a big part in him getting away with everything he did.

Around the time that we learned about the case being thrown out, the ex-wife had contacted me as well, letting me know how Eduardo had stalked her kids after she had left him. Where he was showing up at the schools, going to their games, causing panic attacks when they would see him. At this time, he got into college at one point, to be a teacher, and got a job as a substitute teacher in the district her kids were attending school, to be closer to her kids. Making her kids scared to go to school, until the schools found out about his past and terminated him, barring him from being able to teach in the district.

We also learned that apparently after we had dealt with CPS, and at the time when the wife had left him that first time, Eduardo had been found guilty of abuse, neglect, and accused of molestation of not only her children but my daughter. A finding I was never made aware of until then, years after the incidents had occurred. She went on to explain she went back to Eduardo out of fear and being coaxed to, and that is why she sided with me when we went back to court because she knew it was best for my daughter to be with me. But for several years, Eduardo continued to stalk her and her family and was a Sunday school teacher at the church they all used to attend, playing off to be this God-fearing Christian, which others seemed to believe him to be.

Along with letting me know about the findings from CPS and the stalking of her and her kids, she also wanted to let me know another thing that she felt was important. Letting me know that years back, they had found Eduardo's other daughter. The ex-wife and I both knew why the mom left and tried to stay far away from Eduardo, but when they found the daughter, she learned he had known his daughter's name all along. That her name was the same name as I had, which also happened to be the same name as a niece whom the ex-wife had been raising when she had married him. A fact that is a haunting one in knowing that he possibly went after me and the ex-wife, becoming obsessed with us, all because I and her niece, had the same name as his eldest daughter. A daughter who, even after Eduardo found her, wanted nothing to do with him and had since disappeared again.

More time passed, and it had been two years since the incident where I was put in jail when we got another call from my former lawyer. She said that she came across some interesting files that she thought I would like to see. The files were sent to us, and in them, we found that during the two years where we had not heard from Eduardo, he had been to the courthouse numerous times. Claiming that I was a drug addict and a drug dealer, even though we live in a state that has laws where marijuana is legal but continuing to try and press charges on me since it is not legal in Texas. Stalking us from afar, by following my husband's Facebook page, taking screenshots of where my husband was part of a local cannabis club, had talked about marijuana and its use for relieving pain and insomnia along with PTSD. Went in every few months with false claims and accusations, not ever giving up on coming after me, but at the same time, giving up on Eduardo's own daughter.

Along with this, as more information came about from the abuse of his former step-kids, things he did to his ex-wife and continued to do to her family as far as stalking, my worst nightmare of this entire situation came to fruition. My daughter came forward to her therapist, and we were made aware that her dad had been molesting her since she was little. With this news, so much more made sense. The urinary tract infections my daughter had regularly after visiting her dad before we moved, suddenly went away and have never come back in the years since we have moved and since she has seen her dad last. The night terrors my daughter has had, where she would have many sleepless nights but would not tell me why. The anxiety she got when she would talk to her dad, and the relief she felt when he quit calling a few years back. I felt as if, regardless of everything I did to try to protect her, I still failed her by telling Eduardo that I was pregnant in the first place. But even then, he still got away with it. Even with the report, my daughter's therapist made to the authorities in Texas, he got away with what he had done to everyone. I saw it as being, just the way it is, regardless of everything, any evidence brought forth, any witness information, he got away with everything.

Over the years, I noticed that at one point, Eduardo had found new prey, a noticeably young, single mom, who was the same age I was when he began stalking me, to whom he devoted all his time. Including having the local fire department deliver a ride-on fire truck for her son's birthday, after forgetting his own daughter's birthday just a week prior that year. I worried for this girl, but I found that I was relieved for her when she got away when she appeared to cut all ties with him before she became his next victim.

It all seemed to be okay until he found another, young, single mother, with 4 little girls. I never met the lady, never knew the details of the relationship, nor did she ever attempt to reach out to my daughter. But I always worried about those girls, knowing what he was capable of and what he had done to my daughter, her step-siblings, and God knows who else.

I stayed in touch with many of his family over the years through social media, knowing they are not the same as he is, and that they are also my daughter's family. I noticed Eduardo continued to go on social media several times a day, pretending to be a God-fearing Christian, proclaiming to be a "good guy" that is never given a chance. Sharing posts on how it is hard to be a good man, but that women always overlook him due to his so-called shyness, which I know is because they all see and know Eduardo for the monster he truly is. That the real good men, do not have to proclaim how good they are numerous times daily, and the ones who do, are the ones you need to avoid and run away from.

I look back at it all now and realize that every bit of the horror Eduardo put me, my daughter, and anyone else involved through, was all to get to me. Where I separated myself from dear friends, my friends from my hometown whom he told me on numerous occasions he would have their kids taken from them with just a phone call, and even some family who I did not want him going near, to protect them from the harassment he had put many I was close to through. All because, I refused to submit to him, and I refused to let Eduardo win, and because I was no longer his to control.

When the pandemic hit, all plans of visiting family or friends that year had been put on hold. My kids, just like other kids around the country, began a new way of learning from home. Everything had changed. I had graduated from a local college with a degree in business and was working on my bachelor's in business with an emphasis in marketing, ready to take on the next chapter in our lives. Where, even the idea of taking all virtual classes with virtual graduation, seemed to be the new norm. We were taking it as it came and trying our best to all stay sane from the constant fear and worry over the unknown and isolation everyone in the world was feeling.

In the following spring, as we were nearing the 1-year anniversary of the lockdown, and I was completing my final semester in school while continuing to work as a freelancer, my daughter had a mental breakdown. She had to be hospitalized due to a stress-induced psychosis. We learned that she had not slept or been okay since her birthday that year, when her dad, after 5 years of silence, reached out to say happy birthday to her. The call triggered her. She began talking to herself and had uncontrollable night terrors, which left her mind doing what it thought was best by avoiding sleep. We noticed the change in her appetite, her mannerisms, and her overall effect. She was not the same person. Her therapist had been trying to figure out what was going on when during a Zoom session, the therapist texted me and instructed me to begin the process to have my daughter institutionalized. Letting me know that my daughter is somewhere else mentally, and we needed to get her help ASAP.

The week my daughter spent in the institution brought up so much anger. I was angry in knowing that Eduardo had caused this. Regardless of boundaries, the hope he had moved on, knowing that my daughter had outed him for all he did to her, he was still there, lurking. Even if just in the distant shadows, he was still there.

When my daughter came home, I was determined to complete school, find a corporate position in marketing, and provide my family with a very steady income. Allowing us to get better insurance and also purchase a larger house in the country, where we could grow and not have to stress about the current situations going on in the world or even when it came to Eduardo.

Then, just as quickly as it all began, it all ended the day I got the call.

Covid-19 turned the world upside down, and over the course of the virus, we lost friends and family to the disease. Which included several people who were part of my story; the new kid in town, "Joker" from chapter 1, my parent's neighbor, the doctor who had talked to me that one Thanksgiving about Eduardo and his mental illness, and one of my protectors who succumbed to the loneliness Covid caused where reality was just too much for him to take any longer. However, the one person I thought I would never be rid of, the one who haunted my dreams and even the daily lives of myself and my daughter at times, died from Covid.

We received the call from the ex-wife of all people when she learned Eduardo had been hospitalized. She informed us about his condition and that the family had hope. But it was the idea that made me think that even Covid cannot take Eduardo out, that left me skeptical of the outcome. That was until a couple of weeks later. I had not heard from any of his family or friends, no updates on his status leading me to think that he was not going to recover until early one morning I got a call. The call was not even from his actual family, instead, it was from his brother's ex-wife. I had gotten an amazing job that allowed me to continue to work from home, in a remote position, and had been working the morning of the call. The moment she heard my voice answer the phone, she broke down crying, telling me that Eduardo was going to die. That the virus had caused total organ failure and that the doctors were shutting down the machines which were keeping him alive.

I cried. I got angry at myself for crying and cried even harder for that. It was my husband who said it was okay to cry. And when he said that I realized the tears and feelings were of relief. The anger, anxiety, hopelessness, everything, all came to the surface and for the first time in 19 years, were all released once and for all. The family asked that my daughter be there to say goodbye. And after talking to my daughter about the situation, her saying she wanted to be there, I booked my daughter a flight back to Texas, to say goodbye to our monster.

Eduardo died just a few hours, before my daughter's arrival, which I think was actually for the best for the sake of everyone involved. I do not know how my daughter would have handled it; seeing her dad dying, what all she had prepared to say on the flight there, and how the family would have perceived what she would have said.

I say this because the evening he died; my daughter went to her uncle's house to meet up with the family. And as they went on and on about what a great person Eduardo was, how great a dad he was, she stopped them all. She scolded them, asking them what they defined a great dad to be, and asking if an abuser, a pedophile, or a monster, was what they defined as a great parent.

The outburst caught everyone there off guard, to where her grandmother, disowned her on the spot. One of my daughter's cousins saw and heard it, she had also witnessed some of the abuse years ago, and she had my daughter stay with her for the night.

The next day, my daughter decided she wanted to be with her stepmom and step-siblings, finding that they felt safe while she was there. They all went over the memories, the good and the bad, but embraced one another, and gave each other the support that was needed at the time. The stepmom had learned about the family meeting at the funeral home the next day from a family member, and after some thought, my daughter decided that she needed to be there to assist with the funeral plans

My daughter arrived at the funeral home the next morning, to the surprise of her dad's family. She took my advice on being considerate of the fact that they were mourning his loss, the loss of a son, a brother, and a family member. She assisted in picking out floral arrangements, with the obituary, and even the services on what everyone would wear and choosing the urn his remains would be kept in.

After the funeral arrangements had been finalized, the family invited my daughter to join them for lunch.

At the moment, my daughter was excited, thinking this was a good thing, and I supported her decision.

When the family arrived at the restaurant, my daughter texted me, saying she was happy to be with everyone. But that soon changed.

I received a facetime call from my daughter. At the time, I thought maybe she wanted to share her meal and maybe an update with other family members who were there whom she had not seen in years. But I was wrong. My daughter called in a panic, crying, and wanting out of there ASAP. Apparently, during the meal, a cousin had called my daughter out for the things she had said a couple of nights prior about her dad. Exclaiming that she did not matter, and whatever Eduardo did to her did not matter anymore. Also making it clear to everyone in the restaurant that my daughter was not even considered family, that they had all written her off years prior, and they did not know why she was even there.

I contacted her stepmom who was home with all of her grandbabies at the time and had no way to get to my daughter, but who also felt the anxiety I was feeling, knowing how that family is. I did what I could, I called an Uber to pick up my daughter. She went back to her stepmom's house, and I made arrangements to have my daughter fly back home the next morning.

When my daughter finally made it back home, she was relieved, as was I, but she also informed me that since the afternoon at the restaurant, not one family member had called to check on her.

That following Monday was the viewing for her dad. We only knew about it because the pastor from the church reached out to tell me. He was also the one who sent us the link to watch the services, where, in those days, not one of her dad's side of the family reached out to even check on her. Which, we realized, was for the best.

We both have mourned the loss, but not as one would think. We mourned the loss of all Eduardo had taken from us, and we cried a sense of relief, knowing that we finally had closure. Real closure, in knowing, he can never hurt us or anyone else ever again.

I realize now, that had I not left years ago, I fear that I may have been killed, or brought more innocent children into the horror I had once lived and been put through, for many years of torture that I believe Eduardo had fantasized about putting me through. Whether he had some sick fantasy about his eldest daughter that he somehow felt he needed to play out on me, or if there was more to it, and my name along with the niece's name, all being the same as the daughter, was just a coincidence.

Where I look back at it all, as lessons, and where I not only understand but also stand up for victims, knowing that getting away from the abuser is just the beginning for most, especially when kids are involved. Finding, even though the sexual abuses started when I was just a kid myself, and those horrors were used against me for a brief time in my life, I survived, showing I can't be broken. But also knowing that as a victim, you have to stand up, not give up, and there is a light at the end of the dark tunnel. Whereas you begin to think that happiness is not possible, you might find that happiness comes when you least expect it.